"*Raw* is the only word I can find to describe this piece. A journey through what many experience but are not brave enough to reveal . . . the dreams, the disappointments, and the ultimate triumph are so vividly recalled it's as if Rick were sitting across the room speaking directly to you. A must-read for *anyone* who has ever wondered if their past truly defines their future."

CHARLIE TROTTER

"Rick candidly shares his life journey as a person and a chef. This book is a true testament to his love of the kitchen and determination to succeed."

EMERIL LAGASSE
Chef, restaurateur, television personality, and author

"Knowing where Rick came from, I'm even more impressed with what he has been able to accomplish. If you enjoy reading about food, restaurants, and the people who create them, you'll find *Scars of a Chef* an interesting read. And if you are committed to personal growth and understanding, I think you'll be touched by Rick's journey. As he begins a new chapter in his life, I can't wait to see what surprises Rick has in store for us."

RICHARD MELMAN
Founder and chairman, Lettuce Entertain You Enterprises, Inc.

"This book gives young chefs a peek into what it really takes, not only to be a great chef, but to be a great person."

MICHAEL SYMON
Chef and owner, Lola and Lolita restaurants, Cleveland
2009 James Beard Award, Best Chef: Great Lakes
Author, *Michael Symon's Live to Cook*

"*Scars of a Chef* looks deep into the soul of an iconic American chef. Rick Tramonto is both brutally honest and open in his tale of how he beat the odds in life and saved himself and his family. A beautiful testament to love."

JOHN BESH
Chef/owner, Besh Restaurant Group

"*Scars of a Chef* is a page turner—not just because it details Rick Tramonto's troubling times or glamorous moments but because of the deep honesty with which Rick shares all of his life with us. Rick is one of America's most talented chefs; passionate, dedicated, and committed to the highest level of culinary art. And like any great artist, Rick is a complicated person with all the scars to show for his pain and passions. As we see him rebound and triumph even as his life takes new turns, we, too, find hope to dream new dreams."

MICHAEL LOMONACO
Executive chef/partner, Porter House New York

SCARS
— OF A —
CHEF

RICK TRAMONTO
WITH LISA JACKSON

**TYNDALE®
MOMENTUM**

*An Imprint of
Tyndale House Publishers, Inc.*

Visit Tyndale online at www.tyndale.com.

Visit Tyndale Momentum online at www.tyndalemomentum.com

Tyndale Momentum and the Tyndale Momentum logo are registered trademarks of Tyndale House Publishers, Inc., Carol Stream, Illinois.

Scars of a Chef: The Searing Story of a Top Chef Marked Forever by the Grit and Grace of Life in the Kitchen

Designed by Dean H. Renninger

Published in association with the literary agency of Dystel & Goderich Literary Management, One Union Square West, Suite 904, New York, NY 10003.

Library of Congress Cataloging-in-Publication Data

Tramonto, Rick.

Scars of a chef : the searing story of a top chef marked forever by the grit and grace of life in the kitchen / Rick Tramonto with Lisa Jackson.

    p. cm.

ISBN 978-1-4143-3162-1 (hc)

1. Tramonto, Rick.   2. Cooks—United States—Biography.   3. Cooks—Religous life—United States.   4. Spiritual life—Christianity.   5. Christian life.   I. Jackson, Lisa.   II. Title.

TX649.T73A3 2011

641.5092—dc22

    [B]   2010047573

ISBN 978-1-4964-1192-1 (sc)

Printed in the United States of America

21 20 19 18 17 16 15

7   6   5   4   3   2   1

I dedicate this book to my heavenly Father, whom I have a great covenant with, and my Lord and Savior Jesus Christ, who always leads me down the right road and who brings me through every storm every time.

To my best friend and wife, Eileen Tramonto, who keeps me on track. Thanks for your friendship and love.

Finally, to my mom and dad, Frank and Gloria Tramonto, who have both gone home to be with the Lord. I love you and miss you and wish you could have been around to see and experience what God has blessed me with, and the success I've found on my journey.

CONTENTS

ACKNOWLEDGMENTS

Thanks to my friend and cowriter, Lisa Jackson, who inspired me to put forty-eight years into not quite three hundred pages. I could never have done this without you. You've been such a blessing to do this project with. Thank you. I love you.

Thanks to my supportive and loving family: Eileen Tramonto, Gio Tramonto, and Sean and Brian Pschirrer. Thanks to my dog, Luke, and my cat, Noah, for getting along and making Old Testament and New Testament relationships.

Thanks to my Chicago spiritual family, Pastors Gregory and Grace Dickow of Life Changers International Church, for their love, blessings, teachings, prayers, and for feeding me the Word of God. Also to my Louisiana spiritual family, Pastors Dino and DeLynn Rizzo of Healing Place Church for their love, blessings, and keeping me close to God during my time in New Orleans. I also want to thank Bishop T. D. Jakes, along with The Potter's House, for continuing to inspire and illustrate God's love and teachings to me.

Thanks to my loyal and longtime agent and friend, Jane Dystel; my editor, Kim Miller; and the great team at Tyndale House Publishers for their trust and faith in this book and me. A special thanks to Jan Long Harris.

I would also like to thank Reggie Anderson, who kept me healthy and strong during the writing of this book and who kept me "Reggi-fied!"

Thanks to Gale Gand, my culinary partner, for taking this journey with me.

Thanks to my supportive friends whom I rarely get to see but who I love to cook for. God bless you all and may the grace of God be with you.

—*Rick Tramonto*

FOREWORD
by CHEF JOHN D. FOLSE

It's been said that our palates are set at the table of our forefathers. They determined the foods we ate, the first tastes that passed our lips, and the dishes that were handed down as family traditions. The same can be said for our character, our personal style, and eventually our accomplishments. After all, the values we carry through life are also delivered to each of us at the family table. Rick Tramonto is certainly a great example of this philosophy, and so am I. I suppose this is where our commonality begins.

I remember precisely the day so many years ago when I took note of the man who was to become my partner in a restaurant company. I was eating at Tru, Rick's Chicago restaurant. He caught my attention immediately as I observed him gracefully maneuvering through the dining room. Oh, I had met him before, but this was the night I came to know him and understand his passion. His love of the restaurant, the food, and the guests was obvious.

The diners were starstruck; it was as though the great Talleyrand, Carême, or Escoffier were in their midst. I watched as Rick stopped long enough at each patron's table to adore and be adored. It was a restaurant moment that we in the business all long for. Eventually he made his way to my table. After he greeted each of us with a gentle handshake and an attentive eye, I knew the rest of the evening would be magical. The artistic details, first-class service, and overall ambiance of that initial visit remain imbedded in my mind today, although I experienced that same award-winning combination many times afterward.

Once Rick and I became friends—or I should say friendly acquaintances—our respect for each other grew. I began to learn about his journey from obscurity to the pinnacle of the culinary world. It wasn't an unusual story—many people have faced similar journeys out of adversity. Yet few have reached the ultimate destination as Rick has.

The grandson of Italian immigrants in the blue-collar town of Rochester, New York, Rick had few options when he was growing up. The lucky ones in his neighborhood could expect a life of factory work and the hope of a pension. Between running their own small bar and grill and working their factory shifts, Rick's parents worked eighteen hours a day. Rick was left to "make do" for himself. With no parental boundaries, Rick allowed his darker side to take control, and he began a downward spiral. When his father was sent to prison for embezzlement, Rick turned to sex, drugs, and rock 'n' roll, making them his new altar of worship. It's astounding that he made it through that time in his life.

Rick's inspiring story, told so honestly and humbly, unravels the mystery of how someone can rise from the depths of despair to brilliance. From the time he was a young kid walking into Wendy's to the day he planted his feet firmly in classical cooking at the Strathallan Hotel and Grill in Rochester, we see the steps Chef Tramonto took to leave the demons of his past behind. From his first experiences as an apprentice in New York and Europe to the day God entered his life, it's all here.

During his culinary journey, Rick has shared the table with the greatest chefs, culinarians, and restaurateurs in the world: masters like Alfred Portale of Gotham, Anton Mosimann of Mosimann's, and Rich Melman of Lettuce Entertain You, as well as culinary icons such as Pierre Gagnaire, Alain Chapel, Paul Bocuse, the Troisgros brothers, and Michel and Albert Roux. The influence of these contemporary giants combined with Rick's drive to pursue greatness attracted Bob Payton of Stapleford Park Country House Hotel in Leicestershire, England. Rick's success there helped launch him to the top of his profession.

I knew nothing of Rick's story when I first observed him, the man whom I proudly call friend and partner today, during my first visit to Tru. I knew nothing of the trials and triumphs he personally had faced when he called to help during Hurricane Katrina, Louisiana's darkest moment. I knew nothing of his past when I joined him at a table in Osteria di Tramonto, his beautiful venture in Wheeling, Illinois. Rick's past didn't matter to me when he called me in December 2009, asking to talk during a low point in his life. The man I had come to know over ten years had such class and quality that I suggested a partnership between us called Home on the Range. It's the first partnership I've ever pursued in the thirty-two-year history of my company. I think that says it all about the character of Rick Tramonto.

Now it's your turn to read the story of this ne'er-do-well from Rochester who went from juvenile delinquent to the pages of *Esquire* magazine, from a hamburger joint to *Top Chef Masters*, and perhaps most important, from raucousness to redemption.

INTRODUCTION:
A CHEF'S SCARS

People always ask about the tattoos.

I don't blame them for being curious. I've got twenty-four different tattoos now, running up and down both sides of my body, on my arms, my legs, my chest, my back; they're pretty hard to miss.

Not that I haven't already been marked by the profession. Take a look at my hands and arms and you'll see the cuts, calluses, burn marks—the scars—all symbols of a life that includes working with razor-sharp knives, red-hot cookware, and vats of boiling oil.

But my tattoos are more than just battle scars. Each one is an intentional representation of my commitment and devotion, both to my Creator and to my career. They reflect a thirty-year life journey, a great picture of where I've been and what God has taught me along the way.

Much like my physical scars, each one of my tattoos tells a story. This book is my attempt to flesh out those stories a bit more. Though my stories—like my scars and my tattoos—are unique to me, you just might recognize something from your own life here. And I hope you'll come away with the conviction that the same loving God who has filled my life with peace, promise, and purpose can do the same for you.

1
THE END
2008

Come to Me, all you who labor
and are heavy laden, and I will give you rest.
MATTHEW 11:28

I stood inside my home office with my back against the heavy wooden door. I closed my eyes and sighed.

What am I going to do now, God?

I was so tired; the stress of the past few months was definitely catching up with me. Yet in spite of the exhaustion and physical pain, there was still a part of me that felt like I should be doing something—anything. I just wasn't sure what.

Right now, my staff at Osteria di Tramonto were wiping down the grill for the final time, boxing up the glassware and the china, and taking down the black-and-white photographs from the walls. One of the managers had called me earlier as I sat in traffic to ask me what I wanted to do with those photos—shots that I had taken on my many trips to Italy over the years. Beautiful Italian grandmothers rolling out pasta, smiling boys devouring slices of crusty bread, Italian families carrying bags of fresh produce home from the market—culture and food seen through the lens of my own experience. We had hung hundreds of them all over the restaurant, and they looked so striking against the exposed brick on the walls.

What use would I have for them now?

"Auction them off, give them away. I don't care what you do with them," I had said. "Just get rid of them."

Those photos represented everything I had loved about Osteria di Tramonto. I had been a partner in several other restaurants, but none reflected my heritage, my roots, and my passion for cooking as much as this one. Some of my earliest and best memories center around my grandmother's kitchen, where I watched my mom and grandmother transform fresh meats, seasonal produce, and aromatic spices into hearty and comforting fare. Whenever one of them invited me to help, I eagerly set about rolling out dough or stirring tomatoes into a sauce. Sunday dinners, which sometimes lasted all afternoon, drew our large extended family together for simple but satisfying food, laughter, and spirited conversation. Osteria di Tramonto featured homey family-style Italian cooking reminiscent of those dinners. In fact, some of the items on our menu had been inspired by the recipe cards passed down to me.

For years, I had made frequent trips to Europe, gaining the "continuing education" that is essential for any chef. Yet while building the Osteria, I had been drawn back to Italy again and again. Whether waiting at dawn for returning fishermen down on the waterfront, eating bread and cheese from small bakeries, or examining the produce at market stalls, I delighted in rediscovering my Italian heritage. And everywhere I went, I snapped photos. Each one captured some aspect of the country I had come to love. Now those photos, which I had so carefully framed and arranged on the walls, simply reminded me of the grief I felt over the Osteria's closing.

Osteria di Tramonto had felt like home to me. In fact, I had spent more time there than in my own home during the past three years. My culinary partner, Gale Gand, and I had created the Osteria from the ground up. We selected the china and designed the interior. We developed the menu, hired and trained the staff, and searched high and low until we found the perfect wood-burning pizza oven for our exhibition kitchen.

I had spent every waking minute getting ready for our opening. But that was only the first step. When the doors opened at 5:00 p.m., October 12, 2006, the hardest work was still ahead. Once Osteria went live, we quickly moved from planning mode to action mode. Our steps quickened, and our worry increased. We talked about food costs, labor costs, overhead costs, marketing costs. We dealt with the restaurant critics as we tweaked the menu, pouring everything we had—and more—into getting this new baby to stand on its own two feet. All in the hope that after more than a year of seven-day work-weeks, we might eventually get a night off just to breathe.

And then we had to do it all again—in fact, we had to do it three times. Osteria had been part of a much larger project that included three other concept restaurants. As we worked with a large hotel conglomerate on Chicago's North Shore, our vision had been to create a Las Vegas–style hotel, where guests could enjoy a wide variety of offerings all in one location.

Opening four restaurants simultaneously had been a daunting task, even for partners who had been part of more than twenty openings in our careers. But I had hoped it would be the start of a new phase in my career, bringing me on par with other celebrity chefs in my industry who had built their own brands through multilocation restaurants, television programs, and national publications.

I knew the odds. The research says one in four restaurants never make it past the first year. Over three years, that number rises to three in five. Osteria di Tramonto's demise was nothing new in the restaurant world, especially in light of all the big businesses we had seen fail during the economic crash of 2008. But knowing that didn't make it any less painful.

I had been in the culinary industry for over twenty-five years, so I was used to the physical demands of standing on my feet from dawn until well after dusk. Years of standing on hard tile floors, lifting, and using my hands had resulted in double knee and numerous back surgeries, as well as a rotator cuff surgery. Treating minor burns and cuts was just a normal and expected hazard of the job. I didn't mind that I often had no time to eat—ironic, of course, when you're working with food all day— or that I smelled like fish or the grill, no matter how often I showered. Even on the days when I felt mentally drained and totally exhausted, I couldn't imagine ever wanting to do anything else. Until now.

I was spent, both emotionally and physically. This project had been like a marathon for me, one I wasn't sure my body was going to recover from. Fifteen-, sixteen-hour days, seven days a week, I had been at the restaurant, carrying boxes, stocking shelves, moving equipment—whatever it took, I did it. I had lived and breathed that place, often fueled only by adrenaline, double espressos, and ibuprofen.

Now as I sat down at my desk, last week's special menu caught my eye. I read over the list of entrées we had so carefully created: the Tramonto pizza topped with olives, arugula, and a fontina-mozzarella mix; a carpaccio of sea bass sprinkled with a tart, red grapefruit vinaigrette; and the bistecca alla fiorentina, a Tuscan-style porterhouse grilled over a wood-burning fire with aged balsamic vinegar and extra-virgin olive oil.

Doesn't get much better than that.

Why, God? Was all that work for nothing? Was all that time spent away from my family for nothing? Missing my kids' school events, my wife's birthday, my wedding anniversary—was it all for nothing?

The reality of Osteria's closing began to sink in as I slid to the floor and began to cry. What happened? Where did I go wrong? And how was I going to fill my time now?

Cooking was the only thing I knew. I'd been in the restaurant business since I was sixteen years old. I didn't know how to do anything else. I never even had a paper route.

I supposed I could spend more time focusing on Tru, the fine-dining restaurant Gale and I had opened in downtown Chicago nearly a decade ago. Or maybe I could write another cookbook. I looked around my office at the thousands of books that lined the walls, six of them with my own name on the front. Six hundred magazines were organized by category and issue date—every *Gourmet, Bon Appétit,* and *Food & Wine* printed in the past ten years. Culinary awards and recognitions filled in the empty spaces, a record of my accomplishments and successes.

It had been a good run. I had really made something of myself. I had worked with the best of the best; I had cooked for royalty, dignitaries, celebrities, and three U.S. presidents. I had been on more television programs than I could count and in more food magazines than I could stack on my shelf. I had written books and earned the highest culinary accolades. I had done it all—and done it well.

But now I wondered, *What if I've reached the end?*

BRUSCHETTA WITH OVEN-DRIED TOMATOES AND GORGONZOLA SPREAD

One element of the Osteria that I loved was the wood-burning oven. It cooled down slowly overnight, so I'd slide trays of sliced tomatoes into the oven soon after closing time. The next morning, I'd pull out perfectly dried tomatoes—the inspiration for this tasty bruschetta.

Garlic oil is one of the cooking staples I keep in my refrigerator at home, and it can be prepared the day before you make the bruschetta. — *SERVES 4*

Loaf of sourdough or baguette, cut into eight ½-inch slices
1 c. olive oil
1 clove of garlic, smashed
Extra-virgin olive oil, to drizzle
1 Tbs. flat-leaf parsley, chopped

For the oven-dried tomatoes
12 ripe medium Roma plum tomatoes
½ c. extra-virgin olive oil
1 Tbs. fresh thyme, minced
½ tsp. red chili flakes, crushed
6 garlic cloves, crushed
½ tsp. sugar
½ tsp. kosher salt
¼ tsp. ground black pepper

For the Gorgonzola spread
6 oz. Gorgonzola cheese or Gorgonzola dolce
2 to 4 Tbs. heavy cream
2 Tbs. basil, chopped
2 Tbs. large green onion, minced
Kosher salt, to taste
Ground black pepper, to taste

Combine and refrigerate for at least 24 hours.

TO PREPARE GARLIC OIL
Combine 1 c. olive oil and 1 smashed clove of garlic. Refrigerate for at least 24 hours.

TO PREPARE OVEN-DRIED TOMATOES (can be made one day in advance)
1. Preheat oven to 250°F.
2. In a pot of boiling water, blanch tomatoes. Drain, refresh in ice water, and drain again. Peel and core the tomatoes; cut them into quarters and remove seeds.
3. Line a baking tray with parchment paper and arrange the tomato quarters on the tray, cut side down. Drizzle generously with olive oil. Sprinkle with thyme, chili flakes, and garlic. In a small bowl, combine the sugar, salt, and pepper, and sprinkle the mixture evenly over the tomatoes.

4. Bake until tomatoes begin to shrivel, about 1 hour. When the tomatoes are cool enough to handle, transfer them to a container. Drizzle with more olive oil and cover. Refrigerate until needed.

TO MAKE GORGONZOLA SPREAD

1. In a small bowl, use a fork to mash Gorgonzola cheese with enough cream to make a spreadable consistency. Add basil, green onion, salt, and pepper to taste.
2. Refrigerate for at least 24 hours.

TO SERVE

1. Slice bread.
2. Lay on sheet tray. Brush liberally with garlic oil on both sides.
3. Grill both sides of bruschetta on pan grill or outdoor grill until crusty.
4. Top bruschetta with 1 Tbs. of Gorgonzola spread. Add 2 to 3 pieces of tomato and drizzle with oil from tomato marinade. Garnish with parsley.

PART I

THE EARLY YEARS

Early 1960s through the late 1970s

2

BLUE COLLAR

O LORD, you have examined my heart and
know everything about me. . . . Every day of my life
was recorded in your book. Every moment was
laid out before a single day had passed.
PSALM 139:1, 16, NLT

Though I have been cooking professionally since I was sixteen, my love and knowledge of all things food related actually goes back much further than that. My earliest—and best—memories include times spent in the kitchen with my mom and aunts and grandmothers. The women in our family were always getting together to cook and bake, especially on the weekends or during the holidays. And I was usually in there with them, sleeves rolled up and ready to help.

I can still remember sitting up on the counter in my Grandma Adeline's big Victorian kitchen, rolling out hearty, fist-sized meatballs while the women made the pasta and the sauce.

"Ricky, don't make the meatballs too big," Grandma would say in her heavily accented English.

As they worked, the women laughed and talked and joked, sharing the latest gossip or the events of the week. They spoke in Italian, so I didn't understand much of what they were saying, but I knew enough from their smiles and laughter that this was *their* time. As their excitement grew, their conversations got louder and their actions more animated. The time they spent in the kitchen together was just as nourishing to them as the food they were preparing.

As they worked the dough, carried cast-iron skillets, rolled out the pasta, and chopped vegetables, I watched and learned.

A little of this and a little of that. *Taste, taste, taste.* A little more of this and a little more of that. *Taste, taste, taste.* They were always seasoning and tasting as they went, sometimes lifting the wooden spoon to my lips so I could learn how things were "supposed to taste."

"Here, Ricky, taste this," someone would say, holding her hand under the spoon. "*This* is just right."

My grandmother never left a dish on the stove or pot in the sink, always cleaning as she went, and it was often my job to dry and put away the dishes once they were washed.

I especially loved to watch my Grandma Adeline. Though she was tiny and hunched over by osteoporosis, my grandmother was really quite strong and very funny. She lifted heavy stockpots with ease and never seemed to stop moving.

Born in Melfi, Italy, Adeline and her sister Teresa had come to the United States after a twelve-day journey at the bottom of an ocean liner. Their brother, Michael, was a tailor in Fashion Park, the top men's designer clothing district in Rochester, New York, and was eventually able to bring the entire family to the United States.

My mom's father, Vincenzo Gentile, also emigrated from Italy to Rochester. He and Adeline met at a local neighborhood party and were married shortly thereafter. Even after they were married, my grandma and her four sisters stayed very close, all living in the same neighborhood with adjoining backyards.

Rochester, New York, was a blue-collar, working-class community where family came first and food ran a close second. Eastman Kodak's corporate office was located right in the heart of the city, its nineteen-story tower rising up from State Street. Factories lined the outskirts of town—Kodak, DuPont, Genesee Beer—their smokestacks a symbol of steady pay, stable employment, and the promise of pensions.

Rochester was a strong union town. Unions meant protection for the little guy from "the man." If you got a factory job—and nearly everyone I knew did at one point or another—you figured you were pretty much set. Kids often went to work right out of high school and never looked back.

But life in Rochester was more than just factories and smokestacks. Craftsman-style bungalows and big Victorian homes with wraparound porches lined the streets, with lilac bushes and rose gardens filling out the landscape. The city's modest skyline really was gorgeous, especially when we drove over the Ford Street Bridge that crossed the Genesee River.

My Grandpa Vincenzo—Poppa to me—owned a barbershop just down the street from their house. I loved visiting the shop and listening to the men swap stories about the good old days. Like the women, the men had a great time just being together, telling fish stories, and reminiscing about their childhood triumphs. Smoke from their cigars swirled in the air as they waved their newspapers and complained about President Lyndon Johnson's policy in Vietnam or the latest happenings over at the local factory.

Occasionally, Poppa pulled out the leather-covered booster and placed it on top of one of his barber chairs so I could get a haircut, too. I wished he wouldn't cut my hair so short, but I had been taught to always show respect for my grandparents. I was also grateful that my grandpa always made sure my hair was cut, my socks didn't have holes, and my belly was full. At closing time, my dad, Poppa, and I walked back to my grandparents' house together, where a plentiful meal was always waiting for us.

Sometimes Grandma sent me to the fruit cellar for one of Poppa's prized homemade finocchiona or sopressata salami or a jar of green beans. Although the cellar was cold and musty, and all my cousins were afraid to go down there, I never minded. I loved being surrounded by the food: jars of pickles, tomatoes, and peaches lined the shelves; salami and other meats hung from the ceiling; and blocks of cheese and big jugs of red wine and root beer stood along the walls. Poppa made the root beer himself in the basement, and I sometimes stood down there a little longer than necessary, just to inhale the scent of that home brew.

It seemed to me that our family was always eating, and if we weren't eating, we were getting ready to eat. My mom cooked every day—big, homemade meals, even though I was an only child and on weeknights it was just the three of us at home. On the weekends, she made even more since we always had family members coming in and out. Though Mom had a temper, the one time I could count on her being happy was when she was in the kitchen.

After a meal, the adults usually moved to plastic-covered sofas in the living room to watch *The Lawrence Welk Show* on the huge, old Zenith in the corner. The conversations—half in Italian, half in English—were often loud and always passionate, as they told stories of the old country or discussed the goings-on within the family or neighborhood. While the adults talked, my cousins and I played soccer outside in the street.

I was the youngest of the bunch and the apple of everyone's eye: "Little Ricky." After several failed attempts at having children, my parents had eventually had me—my mom was nearly forty when I was born. I was considered something of a miracle. Though I had no siblings, I never felt alone within my big Italian extended family.

We lived in a small fourplex on Dewey Avenue in the Tenth Ward neighborhood, with a single stairwell that divided us from our neighbors. Our unit consisted of a dining room, living room, and a kitchen, with a long narrow hallway leading to a bathroom at the very end. Our bedrooms were off of the hallway, and when I was home, I liked to close all the doors and set my plastic bowling pins up in front of the bathroom door. I spent hours "bowling" down that long hallway, pretending I was one of the pros I sometimes saw on TV.

My parents owned a small bar and grill on Edgemere Drive, the Topper Inn, and it seemed to me that they were always working. My mom worked in the kitchen, while my dad worked the front of the house, bartending, seating customers, and managing the waitstaff. In addition, they both worked the swing shift at DuPont in order to make ends meet. Sometimes my mom might cook at the restaurant until eleven o'clock or so, and then go straight to her midnight shift at DuPont.

Consequently, I didn't see them very much. When my parents were at work, I was usually shuffled from one side of the family to the other. This was fine with me. When they weren't together, I didn't have to worry about my mom getting angry or my parents getting into a fight. Also, I loved being with my grandparents, aunts, uncles, and cousins.

My dad's family lived on the other side of town. My dad came from the quintessential blue-collar Italian-American family. Real, earthy, and very rough around the edges, the Tramontos were a hardworking bunch.

My Grandpa Mike had come to the United States from Naples when he was twelve. After moving from Boston to New York, he met and married my Grandma Liz, and they eventually had three children: Raymond, Frank (my dad), and Paul. Grandpa Mike worked at Rochester Gas and Electric for pretty much his whole life, and he embodied Rochester's working-class values to me. He taught me to always work hard, no matter what. With his raspy voice and big Cadillac, he reminded me a little of the cool Italian gangsters I saw in the old black-and-white movies my dad and I sometimes watched.

Even though my parents worked a lot, they were always home on Sundays, which were really long. Sundays started with breakfast bright and early before we headed to eight o'clock Mass at Sacred Heart Church, the huge Roman Catholic Church a few blocks from our house.

While my folks visited and drank coffee with the other parishioners, I took religious instruction classes, taught by extremely strict nuns. I quickly developed a very healthy fear of the nuns after watching them discipline some of the rowdier boys in the class—and, yes, they did use rulers to maintain order. I knew I would be smart to stay on their good side.

After our class, the nuns walked us through the courtyard to meet up with our parents so we could go to Mass. I was always a little awestruck by the formality of Sacred Heart. Stained glass windows encircled the church—starting from right to left, each window depicted one of the fourteen Stations of the Cross. The images showing Jesus' journey and death always made me sad for some reason. *How could this possibly be a good thing?* I wondered.

Stone pillars with ornate carvings rose up along the walls, and the smell of incense and candles greeted us as we slid into the old wooden pew, folded down the little kneeler, and began to pray quietly. I was never sure what I was supposed to be praying, so I just waited until my dad was finished and then crossed myself when he did, first touching my forehead and chest and then the tips of both shoulders. I liked to finish up with a loud "ah-men."

When I was older, I began to attend catechism classes in preparation for my first Communion. I learned a lot about the Bible—the stories of Adam and Eve, Jonah in the belly of the whale, and Moses and the Ten Commandments. We learned who Mary was, and where Jesus was born—but God always seemed too big and too far away to have any real connection to me.

I especially liked Sundays because going to church meant there was always an "after." After church, we made the rounds, once again visiting my grandparents, my aunts and uncles, and tons of cousins. Sundays meant fun, fun, fun and food, food, food.

If we were visiting my dad's side of the family, I knew my mom would be staying home that week—she always seemed to have issues with his parents. But even so, we were sure to have a good time eating, laughing, and catching up with everyone. At each house, there would be coffee, cookies, an antipasto tray, or my favorite: calamari pie. Hugs and kisses all around—especially for "Little Ricky"—and then my dad would send me off to play downstairs.

"Go on now," he would say. "The grown-ups need to talk." Often, I would hide at the bottom of the stairs, waiting for the extra tray of cookies to be brought out. The conversations were sometimes somewhat confusing, but I knew they always had something to do with family members getting in trouble, owing money, or being thrown in jail. The talk of unions and gambling didn't make much sense to me at the time.

By the time Dad and I got home after hours of eating and talking and more eating, Mom would start making our own dinner, and with the onslaught of our own company, we'd prepare to start the whole process again. I guess that would explain why our whole family was so overweight—and why I was well on my way to joining them.

MOM'S VEAL PARMESAN

Baseball and hot dogs may go together in many people's minds; football and veal Parmesan go together in mine. I can remember eating it on many Sunday afternoons while watching football on TV. In fact, this recipe was one of the tried-and-true classics in our home. A staple of my mom Gloria's cooking repertoire, it was one of the first recipes I learned to cook on my own. If you like, you can substitute chicken for the veal. It also makes a killer sandwich. — *SERVES 4*

3 lbs. veal top round, sliced and pounded into four 12-oz. cutlets
2 c. all-purpose flour, seasoned with 1 tsp. kosher salt and 1 tsp. cracked pepper
3 eggs
½ c. milk
1 c. seasoned bread crumbs
1 c. grated Parmesan cheese
4 Tbs. olive oil
3 Tbs. whole butter
4 c. pomodoro (or marinara) sauce
4 oz. provolone cheese, sliced
2 Tbs. chopped parsley
2 Tbs. basil, julienned

1. Preheat oven to 400°F.
2. Cover cutlets lightly with flour mixture; pat off the excess.
3. Beat together eggs and milk to make egg wash. Dip the cutlets in the egg wash and let excess drip off.
4. Mix the bread crumbs and Parmesan cheese. Coat the cutlets in the mixture, again patting off the excess.
5. Heat 2 large sauté pans to medium-high heat. Add half of the olive oil and half of the whole butter to each pan.
6. Once the butter has melted, place the cutlets in the pans and brown them on both sides.
7. When the cutlets are golden brown and nearly cooked through (about 8 minutes), drain the excess grease from the pans. Add the pomodoro sauce, splitting it evenly between the two pans.
8. Place the provolone slices on top of the veal cutlets and place pans in the oven for 2 to 3 minutes until the cheese melts.
9. Remove pans from the oven and place each cutlet on a plate. Sprinkle with chopped parsley and basil, and spoon any extra sauce on top. Serve piping hot.

3

NIGHTMARES

A soft answer turns away wrath,
but a harsh word stirs up anger.

PROVERBS 15:1

Even though I was only seven years old, I knew a little bit about fear and the sick feeling it can cause in the pit of your stomach. Sometimes the fear was triggered by something as simple as a car door slamming or the sound of a dish hitting the floor. Other times it was a look on my mother's face or the tone of her voice when she asked my dad a question.

My parents didn't fight and try to kill each other every day. It was more like they argued every day, fought every week, and tried to kill each other every few months. When things at our house were good, they were really good—those were the times when I saw what real love and marriage and family were supposed to be. But when things at our house were bad, they were really, really bad: during those times, I saw only anger, violence, and pain. There was never a middle.

Although coarse language was fairly common in our family, the verbal abuse really escalated when my parents were fighting. Then their words took on an evil edge of venom and vengeance.

By the time I was in grade school, I was pretty much always walking on eggshells, afraid of when the next fight might start. I was constantly on alert for signs of anger or frustration that might lead to another violent episode. The sound of a cupboard door slamming made me freeze in my tracks and hold my breath. I never knew if it was a false alarm or the start of the next "big one."

I loved my mom, but I was pretty sure she was the one who started most of the arguments. She had a really mean side to her, and she always seemed so angry. She might be washing dishes or cleaning up the kitchen, and she would be talking to herself, slamming doors, and banging stuff around. Sometimes it seemed that she intentionally picked the fights with my dad. I never could understand why she did it. Now looking back, I realize that she probably suffered from some kind of mental illness—maybe psychosis or bipolar disorder. How unfortunate that people just didn't understand those kinds of things back then. As a child, it just seemed to me that my mom was really mad all the time.

One Sunday, my mom was getting ready for Sunday dinner, and she was clearly upset. Moving about the kitchen, she slammed the heavy stockpot onto the stove and muttered under her breath, "Doesn't matter what I do, it's never enough. Who's going to pay for this place? How are we going to pay for all this stuff?"

As she continued to rant, my dad tried to figure out what she was upset about.

"Come on, Gloria," he said, turning her by the shoulder. "What are you slamming things around for? What's the problem?"

She would have none of that. Pushing him away, my mom continued her tirade against my dad's inability to provide, his mother, her mother, other women, and anything else she could think to use against him. Frustrated and angry now, Dad yelled back, his voice rising to her level. I hated the names he called her and the words that they used against each other.

"You whore," he shouted. "You are lucky I put up with your crap. Anyone else would have killed you by now."

My mom's face grew red with anger, and she reached for her cup of still steaming coffee. Without a second thought, she threw the hot coffee at my dad, causing him to howl in pain. He retaliated with a hard, open-palmed slap. What had started as verbal abuse quickly escalated to a pushing and shoving free-for-all. I tried to get in between them, yelling for them to stop.

"Just get a divorce and stop fighting!" I screamed. "Please move into different houses!" I continued to beg and plead with them, but it was as if I wasn't even there.

I jumped onto my dad's back, wrapping my arms around his neck and trying to pull him away from my mother as the fight moved into the living room. But my seven-year-old body was no match for his three-hundred-pound frame.

He gave her one hard shove, causing my mom to lose her balance and fall. My mom landed square in the middle of our large glass coffee table, shattering it into a thousand little pieces. She lay there in the middle of it, bleeding, crying, and continuing to scream at my father. She was going to finish making her point if it was the last thing she did.

Dad lifted her out of the glass shards, careful to avoid the jagged edges of the broken table. We grabbed towels to hold over her cuts and quickly drove to the hospital, where my mom received a dozen stitches. Dad hovered over her, bringing her water and watching to be sure she wasn't in any pain.

In the days that followed, my parents were especially polite to one another. Of course, I knew the peace would not last. Fighting was too much a part of their makeup.

When the fighting got really intense, I always felt so trapped. But there was really no place for me to go to get away from it all. If things got too intense, I often went into my room and sat in the back of my closet, where I couldn't hear them fighting anymore. Other times, I went and hid under the stairs, where I pretended it was all just a movie. I told myself that the screaming and drama going on upstairs was nothing more than a program on TV.

Sometimes my Uncle Paul or Uncle Rudy stopped by to take me home with them for the weekend—especially on the nights when the cops were there, which happened a lot. Nearby neighbors would call the police when the noise level got too high, and then the cops would show up. Usually they just sat with my mom until she calmed down, though sometimes they had to physically separate my parents when the fighting was especially bad. I was always very glad to go with my uncles. As much as I missed my folks, I hated being around when they were fighting.

When I got a little older, I started staying with a babysitter, Alice, after school. Sometimes I stayed with her until seven or eight o'clock at night when my dad got off work. She lived in a big old Victorian home within walking distance of the school. A tall, gray-haired German woman in her early sixties, Alice was a widow with four kids of her own: two sons in college and two daughters in high school. She provided for her family by babysitting. Her house was always filled with multiple pets and kids from the neighborhood.

I loved Alice. Though she was a tough disciplinarian—she didn't take any flack from any of us—she truly cared for us. My parents never checked on my homework or asked me about my day. Alice did. I had never seen an A in my life. I always struggled in school—a straight C, D, and F student—but Alice spent a lot of time helping me work through my assignments. The only time I managed to pull a B—in gym class—Alice made a big deal out of it, baking me a special dessert and gushing over my achievement.

Every day when we walked in the door from school, Alice had a snack waiting for us: apples, cookies, milk. We all gathered around her big wooden table to eat our snacks and do our homework. Once homework was finished, we were free to play outside or watch television. Alice made dinner while we climbed the cherry tree in the backyard or watched our favorite programs: *Hogan's Heroes, Batman, Gilligan's Island, Petticoat Junction.* Rather than pasta and salamis and sauces, Alice's meals consisted of sausage and sauerkraut, Wiener schnitzel, meatloaf and mashed potatoes, pot roast, baked chicken, hearty salads, and homemade crescent rolls.

And dessert. Alice believed a meal was not complete unless you had dessert. I agreed. She also felt very strongly about families sitting down together around the table, so we always ate together as a group. Even on Fridays, when she let us bring our food into the living room on TV trays, we still ate together. For me, this was different, too.

After dinner, all of us kids—Alice's daughters *and* those she babysat—were expected to help with the dishes and clean up the kitchen. We were each assigned a task—washing, drying, and putting away the dishes; wiping the table; taking out the garbage; sweeping the floor. It never really felt like work to me. It was just expected of us.

Dad usually came to pick me up around seven, sometimes later. On the ride home, I could feel my stomach tightening up, not knowing if things would be good or bad when we got there. One night around eight o'clock my mom walked in the back door with a broom in her hand. She was clearly upset, shrieking and screaming as she swung the broom at anything that happened to be in her path. She walked toward my dad, sending a lamp crashing to the floor as she went. Dad didn't say a word. He simply grabbed me by the arm and walked me to the car.

"Lock the doors, Ricky," he said, moving the shifter into reverse. Mom came running out of the house and down the driveway, broom held high in the air. Before we could get out of the driveway, the broom came smashing down on my dad's side of the windshield, causing jagged cracks to spread rapidly from one side to the other.

Dad didn't wait. With a quick glance over his right shoulder, he stepped on the gas and pulled out into the street. Throwing the car into drive, he sped away from the house, leaving Mom standing in the driveway, the broom still in her hand.

We drove to the Howard Johnson on Ridge Road, where we immediately got into bed and went to sleep. Over the next couple of days, we watched TV together and ate in the hotel restaurant. I didn't have to go to school, so it was kind of like an adventure for me. Dad didn't mention the fight or how long we might be staying. And I never asked.

When we finally returned home later that week, everyone acted as if nothing had happened, though Mom was especially quiet. Something about this fight was different. Maybe my parents were just worn out, or maybe they were embarrassed that things had gotten out of hand. Whatever the reason, I was just happy for a little peace and quiet in our house, though I never did find out what that fight was about.

I was an eyewitness to many of my parents' arguments, but I never once saw them make up. I never heard one of them say "I'm sorry." They always just picked up and acted as if nothing had happened.

Even though I hated all the fighting, I never questioned their love for each other or for me. Though I knew there was danger in our home, I never felt endangered, nor did I worry that they would turn their anger toward me.

In fact, I didn't even realize that the rest of the world didn't see this as normal. I thought everyone lived like we did.

ESCAROLE SOUP WITH MEATBALLS

Sometimes served as the first course, sometimes as a meal in itself, escarole soup with meatballs was another staple in my home as I was growing up. It makes a perfect winter or holiday starter or appetizer. This soup freezes well, so you can make it in bigger batches. I also use it to make a brothy-style pasta. — *SERVES 4*

½ lb. ground veal or lean ground beef
⅓ c. Parmigiano-Reggiano or other Parmesan cheese, grated
2 Tbs. flat-leaf parsley, chopped
2 Tbs. bread crumbs
1 medium egg, beaten
Ground black pepper, to taste
4 Tbs. extra-virgin olive oil
1 c. onion, chopped
2 tsp. garlic, minced
4 c. packed escarole, rinsed and dried, chopped
2 c. chicken stock
Kosher salt and pepper, to taste

1. In a bowl add the veal, 2 Tbs. Parmesan, parsley, bread crumbs, egg, and freshly ground pepper to taste. Form the mixture into 12 walnut-size balls. (The mixture will be soft.)
2. In a large, heavy saucepan heat 1 Tbs. of the oil over moderately high heat until it is hot but not smoking. Sauté the meatballs, turning them, for 3 minutes or until they are just firm to the touch and browned lightly. Transfer the meatballs to a plate using a slotted spoon.
3. Add 2 Tbs. oil and the onion to the saucepan and cook the mixture over moderately low heat until the onion is translucent. Add the garlic and cook, stirring occasionally, for 2 minutes.
4. Add the escarole to the saucepan and cover. Cook the mixture over low heat, stirring occasionally, for 3 to 4 minutes, or until the escarole is wilted.
5. Add the chicken stock and meatballs, along with salt and pepper to taste. Bring the mixture to a boil and simmer for 5 minutes.
6. Serve the escarole soup sprinkled with the rest of the Parmesan cheese and drizzled with 1 Tbs. extra-virgin olive oil.

4
DEATH

Let not your heart be troubled;
you believe in God, believe also in Me.

JOHN 14:1

For Italians, every event is a reason to cook, but the really big events—weddings, baptisms, funerals, holidays—give us a reason to *really* cook.

I was eight years old when my Poppa, Vincenzo Gentile, died. I had never known anyone who died, so when the phone rang early that Saturday morning, I was completely unprepared for the frenzy that was about to take place within our family.

From the living room where I was watching cartoons, I could hear my dad talking on the phone. As he talked, his voice became louder and more animated. He was speaking a mixture of Italian and English, and I could tell he was upset about something, but I couldn't quite make out what he was saying.

After a few minutes, I crept into the kitchen. Dad was standing over my mom, who was sitting at the table, her face buried in her hands. She was crying, the large Virgin Mary pendant that hung around her neck rising and falling with her sobs.

Dad looked up and saw me standing in the doorway.

"Get dressed, Ricky," he said. "We have to go over to Grandma's house. Poppa's dead."

What? I couldn't process the words. *Poppa dead? As in, gone forever?* I couldn't imagine Poppa dead. Who would cut my hair?

We arrived at Poppa's house on Driving Park Avenue and let ourselves inside without knocking. Aunt Violet was already there, sitting on the sofa next to my grandmother. Grandma Adeline was clearly distraught, her eyes red from crying and her hanky twisted tightly in her hands. She held out her hands to me and my dad, clinging to us without saying a word.

Clearly, Grandma Adeline was too upset to make any decisions, so Dad stepped up.

"Don't worry about anything, Adeline," he said. "Eddy and I will take care of all the arrangements. You just stay here and rest." We went into Poppa's bedroom, where my dad pulled a dark suit and dress shirt from the closet; then he moved to the dresser for socks, underwear, and a handkerchief. As I looked around the bedroom at my grandpa's things— a handful of coins and a package of gum on the dresser, a pair of shoes on the floor against the wall, and the bed where he had slept just the night before—I still couldn't believe he was gone. I half expected him to come through the door and holler at us for going through his closet.

"Come on, Ricky," my dad said briskly. "We have to meet Uncle Eddy at the funeral home, and we've got a lot to do today."

We drove to the DiPonzio Funeral Home on Spencerport Road, where a well-dressed man met us at the door, greeting my dad like they were old friends. Apparently the DiPonzios had already buried dozens of people in our family—Tramontos and Gentiles alike.

"So sorry for your loss, Chick," Mr. DiPonzio said to my dad, calling him by his nickname. Mr. DiPonzio held the door open so we could slip through. We followed him down the hallway to a small office, where Uncle Eddy was waiting for us. Mr. DiPonzio pointed to a couple of leather-bound chairs and invited us to sit.

"We'll try to make this as easy as possible for you," Mr. DiPonzio said, pulling out a yellow legal pad for notes. "First, we need to talk about caskets. You have several options to choose from. Take a look and let me know if you like anything here." He pushed a black binder across the desk toward us, and Eddy began to thumb through the pages.

I had never seen a casket before. Some of them were really fancy, with gold carvings along the sides and plush satin cushions on the inside. Others were simpler—not good enough for my grandpa, if you asked me.

After looking at the book and talking about prices for a bit, Mr. DiPonzio led us down into a basement room where we could see what he had in stock. The basement was damp and cool, and I was more than a little freaked out by the number of caskets that surrounded us—a dozen or more in all sizes and colors. Along a far wall was a display case of candleholders, vases, photo frames, and statuettes. It seemed surreal—almost like a movie set.

"That one looks good," said Eddy, pointing to a silver-gray casket that wasn't too plain, but not too fancy either. Happy to get out of this room, I ran back up the stairs ahead of the men. I didn't like this place; it was too quiet and it smelled funny.

I fidgeted and squirmed, shifting my weight from one foot to the other as my dad finalized the details with Uncle Eddy and Mr. DiPonzio. I was getting bored and I really couldn't follow what they were saying.

By the time we got back to Grandma's house, the women were already in the kitchen, slicing and stirring, rolling and kneading, and making space in the refrigerators and on the countertops for the trays of food that neighbors were bringing in one after another.

My mom and grandma sat in the living room with a plate of fig cookies between them, talking quietly and dabbing at their tears with their handkerchiefs. I wished I could do something to make them feel better, but I was feeling pretty sad myself.

I was glad when it was finally time to go home. I was so worn out from all the day's events that I fell asleep on the short ride home and Dad had to carry me into the house from the car. I was vaguely aware of him putting me into my pajamas, and then before I knew it, we were getting up to do it all again.

Mom dressed all in black for the first viewing. She wore dark sunglasses even though we were still inside, and she was unusually quiet. I didn't like seeing her like this; she was usually so loud and over-the-top. Even when she was screaming at me, at least we knew what she was thinking and feeling. Now it was like she had just shut down—she just sat in the chair, staring into the distance and not saying a word. When it was time to leave, she stood and walked toward the car, almost in slow motion. I knew how close she was to my grandpa, but I found her silence to be really unsettling. Was she going to snap?

As we pulled up to the funeral home, I saw Mr. DiPonzio waiting for us again. He opened my mother's door and then led us through the front foyer to a large room just down the hall. My grandma was already there, sitting in the front row with Uncle Eddy and Aunt Vi on either side of her. Mom went straight over to where they were sitting and wrapped her large arms around my Aunt Vi—clinging to her and rocking back and forth as they cried together.

Flowers and plants filled every corner of the room; I wrinkled my nose at their heavy, sickeningly sweet scent. The silver casket lined with soft, white satin was sitting center stage at the front of the room. Poppa was lying inside.

After talking to my Uncle Eddy for a few minutes, my dad grabbed my hand and walked me up to the front, past the bank of memorial candles flickering against the wall. Poppa was dressed in the three-piece suit we had picked out the day before, and someone had placed his Rosary between his hands. I wasn't used to seeing him so dressed up. Poppa had always worn just white short-sleeved shirts when he worked at the barbershop.

"Why is he all powdery?" I asked, standing on my tiptoes to look at him. He looked like a wax figure, not at all like my Poppa.

"Shh, not now Ricky," he said. "Go sit with your cousins and be a good boy."

I was happy to get out of that room and away from all the sadness. My cousins were all hanging out in a little room off to the side of the bigger room. And clearly, they were having a lot more fun than the adults were. We spent most of the morning playing cards and goofing around. Occasionally one of the moms would pop her head in and remind us to lower our voices—which we did for a little while, until we forgot and got rowdy again.

We stayed at the funeral home all morning, as the whole family gathered to greet the visitors and well-wishers who poured in. It seemed like the entire neighborhood was there, some of them waiting in line for more than an hour to talk to Grandma and pray over Poppa. As the local barber, he had been a friend to everyone.

Finally, it was time to head back to Grandma's house for lunch. Some of the neighborhood women were already there, serving up a spread to feed the army that was our family. The table overflowed with hot, steaming platters of food that made my mouth water: Italian sausages cooked with peppers and onions, homemade spaghetti and meatballs, chicken cutlets drizzled with lemon and olive oil. Food was everywhere: trays of cheese and crackers were strategically placed in every room, along with elaborate displays of Italian pastries, cookies, cannoli, and éclairs.

Unlike the somber environment of the funeral home, the atmosphere at Grandma's was much lighter. Though we were missing Grandpa, with everyone talking and laughing and telling stories, it almost felt more like a family reunion or a party than a funeral. We found comfort in the food and being together as a family. Everyone—including me—seemed happy to take a break from the grieving process. Before long, the noise level in the room began to rise as the sound of laughter overcame the sadness and pain.

But then, just when the party seemed to be getting started, someone announced that it was time to go back to the funeral home.

"Why do we have to go back again?" I asked as my dad knelt to straighten my shirt and adjust my little clip-on tie.

"This is the way we do it in our family," he said. "We show our respect for the dead by having a wake. We will do this for two more days after today, every morning and every afternoon. Then we will have a funeral service at the church, and after that, we will all go to the cemetery where we will put roses on Grandpa's casket. Okay?"

Even though I would have rather stayed and played with some of the neighbor kids in Grandma's backyard, I knew I had no choice but to follow my dad down to the car.

The pattern of grieving and eating went on for three days, sometimes lasting well into the night. I couldn't believe my grandparents knew this many people, or that we could eat this much food. But somehow we did.

On the final day, the family was led to the front for one last good-bye before the casket was closed. I watched my mom slowly move toward Poppa's casket. She stood there for what seemed like hours, not moving or talking. Finally, I went up and took her hand. It was soft and limp, as if she were sleeping and didn't even know I was there. I pulled on her arm and led her to the back of the room, tears burning my eyes as they rolled down my cheeks.

We stood together in the back, while my dad took his turn saying good-bye. He stood over Poppa's body, and when he turned his head, I could see that he was crying too. I couldn't believe it. I had never seen my dad cry before. He leaned over the casket, his shoulders shaking in grief. As much as I knew I should, I couldn't tear my eyes from the sight of my dad draped over Poppa, wailing in grief.

Finally, two of my uncles gently pulled him away and directed him toward us. Together, we walked to our car, which someone had pulled up out front for us. No one spoke much on the way home that night. Mom still wore her dark glasses, and Dad seemed lost in his own thoughts. It had been a very long, exhausting three days. I was glad it was over.

On the fourth day, it was finally time for the funeral Mass. Sacred Heart was packed and the service was a lot like a regular Mass, except much more sad. Outside, a line of black limousines stretched down the road in front of the church, and even though my grandma, mom, and aunts all wore black veils over their faces, none were able to hide their sorrow when the pallbearers lifted Poppa's casket off the pedestal at the front of the church and rolled it out to the hearse. Once it was over, we all moved down the aisle to the steps of the church where a limo was waiting to take us to Holy Sepulchre Cemetery on Lake Avenue. On the way to the gravesite, I looked up at my dad, who was staring out of the window.

"What are we going to do at the cemetery?" I asked.

"We'll listen to the priest say a few more words, then we'll drop flowers down on Poppa's casket, and then it will be done," he said. "It's good for you to learn how to do these things, Ricky. We all have to deal with death. But remember, that's not him in that casket. We're just carrying his body with us and doing all these things because we loved him so much."

When we arrived at the cemetery, I watched closely as the casket was lowered into the ground. My mom wailed loudly next to me, clinging to my aunts, who were also sobbing. *If Poppa isn't really in there, why is everyone so upset?* I wondered. This made absolutely no sense to me.

Once the silver box reached the bottom of the grave, my dad reached for my hand and led me toward the gaping hole. He knelt down and scooped up a bit of the gravelly soil; I did the same. Somberly, the priest continued his spiel: "Ashes to ashes, dust to dust. . . ."

And then it started to rain. My father stood and tossed his handful of cool dirt down onto the silver casket, and again I copied his actions.

"Good-bye, Vincenzo," he whispered, a sob catching in his throat as he spoke. The sight of my father crying was terrifying to me. Years later, I would be asked to serve as a pallbearer for other family members, and every time I lifted a casket, I couldn't help but remember the image of my dad crying over Poppa in the rain.

ITALIAN SAUSAGE WITH ROASTED PEPPERS AND ONIONS

I based this classic recipe of an antipasto, or first course, on my memories of similar dishes prepared by my mother, grandmother, and aunts. The key to this dish is great Italian sausage—so seek out a quality sweet or hot Italian sausage at your supermarket or butcher. If you are adventurous, you can even make your own sausage! — *SERVES 4*

1 lb. (4 links) sweet or hot Italian sausage
¼ c. olive oil
1 large onion, sliced
1 green bell pepper, seeded and sliced into 2-inch strips
1 red bell pepper, seeded and sliced into 2-inch strips
1 yellow bell pepper, seeded and sliced into 2-inch strips
1 tsp. red chili flakes
3 cloves garlic, chopped
¾ c. chicken stock
1 Tbs. butter
2 Tbs. basil (chopped)
Kosher salt, to taste
Cracked black pepper, to taste
2 Tbs. Parmigiano-Reggiano, grated

1. Preheat oven to 400°F.
2. Place the sausage on an oiled sheet tray and bake until 75 percent cooked, turning occasionally (10 to 15 minutes).
3. While the sausage is roasting, heat the olive oil and sauté the onion, peppers, chili flakes, and garlic in a heavy-bottomed sauté pan for 4 to 6 minutes, or until peppers start to wilt.
4. Remove the sausage and cut into 1½- to 2-inch pieces. Add sausage to the pan with onion and peppers; stir. Add chicken stock.
5. Place sauté pan in oven for 5 to 7 minutes. Remove pan from oven and swirl in butter, chopped basil, salt, and pepper.
6. Spoon mixture onto plates and garnish with grated Parmigiano-Reggiano.

5

GARAGE BAND

Do not be deceived, God is not mocked;
for whatever a man sows, that he will also reap.

GALATIANS 6:7

The summer I turned twelve, we moved to a new house on Ridgeway Avenue. The house was so much bigger than our little apartment on Dewey; I couldn't believe it was really ours. As the movers carried the furniture into the house, I ran from room to room and front to back—upstairs, downstairs, outside, inside. We had so much space!

Though I never would have said it out loud, I wondered how we could possibly afford such a cool house. I knew my parents had sold the Topper and Dad had just gotten a new job as the treasurer of the Hotel and Restaurant Workers Union. I had heard him talking about the good benefits that the union jobs paid—maybe this new position meant a lot more money too. Whatever the reason, the house seemed to make everyone in the family happy. And after all the sadness of the last few years, we needed a little happiness.

My dad was excited to finally have a garage where he could park his car and keep his tools; Mom couldn't wait to host a Sunday dinner and cook in her new kitchen; and I was really looking forward to swimming in our very own inground pool, playing cards with my dad in our screened-in gazebo, and hanging out in the basement. Our basement was the coolest thing I had ever seen. It was partially finished, with carpet on the floor and wood paneling on the walls. I was already picturing the sleepovers I could have with my friends, and how great a pool table would look over in the corner. There was a full bar and a kitchen in the back, with a refrigerator and a freezer just waiting to be filled with drinks and snacks.

This was going to be a great house, I was sure of it. The neighbors were mostly Italian like us, and everyone seemed happy to add us to the "family." We lived close to Number 40 School for eighth- through twelfth-graders, which is where I would go in the fall. After exploring a bit, I was excited to see that we were also within walking distance of a great park, a big baseball field, and a bowling alley. Down at the school, a bunch of kids were playing football. As I wandered over toward the group, one of the kids out on the field hollered to me, "Hey, you wanna jump in? You'd even up the team."

Somewhat overweight, I had never been very athletic, but I certainly didn't want to pass up an opportunity to hang with the kids from my new neighborhood. I managed to hold my own in the game, and when we were done playing, a couple of the kids hung around to introduce themselves.

"My name's Marco," said a tall, athletic kid. "And that there is Paulie. Where did you come from?"

I told them we had just moved from Dewey Avenue in the Tenth Ward neighborhood, and pointed down toward the house.

"Hey! I live on this street too," said Marco. "You live in the house with the pool and diving board? That's a great place! Come on, let's go back to my house and grab a soda. I'll introduce you to my mom and my brothers and sisters."

And so began my friendship with Marco and Paulie.

Hanging with Marco and Paulie opened a whole new world for me, a world that was filled with brothers and sisters and crazy dogs and noise and activity. Marco was the youngest of nine, and his house was always buzzing. When I was there, I felt like I was just one of the family—his brothers pretty much took me in and protected me from any neighborhood kids who might give me a hard time.

Marco had the biggest heart, always treating me better than I deserved, really. I relied heavily on him to help me with my school-work. For whatever reason, I never could make sense of the homework or even understand what the questions were asking. But Marco was patient with me. He would read over my assignments, and then ask the questions in a way that made more sense to me. He knew how tough school was for me, and he just wanted to make sure I didn't get left behind.

It hadn't taken long for my mom to start entertaining in our new house. And it wasn't long before friends and family were stopping over for a dip in the pool, a Sunday meal, a card game, or an elaborate holiday celebration—and that was just fine by me. My mom was at her best when she was surrounded by people. She loved to cook and make people laugh. When she was in the kitchen, she was smiling, and when she was smiling and cooking, she wasn't screaming or talk-ing to herself.

Most mornings, my folks were home with me while I ate break-fast. Mom worked in the lunchroom at Number 40 School, and Dad worked at the Local 466 office downtown. When I came home in the afternoons, Mom was there waiting for me, but usually just long enough to make dinner before catching the bus for John Marshall High School, where she worked as a nighttime janitor.

Dad was working two jobs as well. After a long day at the union hall, he came home for a quick bite before heading down to the Hotel Americana where he tended bar. Most of the time, I stayed home alone, watching television or doing homework. Sometimes if he planned to be especially late, Dad would let me come and hang out at the Americana while he worked.

My dad definitely had that bartender personality, and he knew what it meant to go above and beyond for his customers. Watching him from my seat at the end of the bar, I saw the way he catered to the "guests," as he called them. He was always at the ready to light people's cigarettes or refill their drinks, usually before they even had to ask. He carefully watched the sweat on each glass, making sure to replace the cocktail napkin before a ring could form.

His customers called him "Chick," which seemed to me a perfect nickname for someone in that role. He even dressed the part: white dress shirt with gold cuff links, spit-polished shoes, and a black satin tie. With his slicked back hair and winning smile, he reminded me a little of Frank Sinatra or an old-school gangster played by James Cagney.

Everybody's best friend, my dad somehow seemed to know everyone who walked in the door. If they were people he worked with down at the union, he made sure to treat them especially well—offering complimentary drinks and Cuban cigars to the real bigwigs. Those hotshots always carried big wads of cash, wore lots of gold jewelry, and usually had a girl or two hanging on their arms. And they all had really cool names: Jimmy the Ox, Tony the Fat, and Al the Fence. They seemed to be nice enough, always laughing and joking around. But even so, there was something about them—something I couldn't necessarily put my finger on—that scared me just a little. Maybe it was the fact that most of them carried guns under their coats and weren't afraid to show them.

As I got older, I began to stay home on my own more and more. With no one there, I had plenty of time to get into trouble. And since I was the only one in my group whose parents both worked nights, my friends all started to congregate at my house.

Mom was thrilled that I had kids to keep me company, and she always left a lasagna or eggplant Parmesan in the oven so we would have plenty to eat. We spent a lot of time in the basement, watching TV, hanging out, and looking for trouble.

My dad was a heavy smoker, and he always had an ample supply of cigarettes lying around. He bought his Marlboros by the carton, so it was easy for me to take whole packs without him noticing. I liked the way they made me feel: independent and grown up. Soon I moved from stealing cigarettes to nabbing a couple of beers out of the downstairs fridge or digging into the two-door liquor cabinet. I suddenly found myself pursuing a whole new goal: getting wasted and staying wasted.

One afternoon when I was fourteen, Marco, Paulie, and I pooled our money so we could buy Queen's newest album, *News of the World*. We had been anticipating this release for months and couldn't wait to get it into the tape deck in Marco's little Pinto. As I pulled the cellophane wrapping off the bulky eight-track cartridge, Marco glanced over toward Paulie and me.

"You wanna get high?" he asked with a smile.

Did we want to get high? You bet we did!

"You got stuff?" I asked. Marco nodded toward the glove box, and when I opened it up, I found that he had already gathered everything we would need: a Baggie filled with marijuana, a lighter, and the rolling papers. We had all watched the older kids roll pot and load up bongs and pipes plenty of times, though none of us had ever done it ourselves. Marco pulled out one of the small sheets of thin paper, sprinkled a little of the leafy drug into the center of the sheet, and then rolled it up as if he'd been doing it for years. I did the same, trying not to spill any of the pot onto the floor as I did.

Finally, with joints in hand, we lit up, pushed the tape into the player, and proceeded to get high as the words of "We Will Rock You" pounded from the stereo speakers.

From that day forward, I was a pot smoker, spending all of my allowance and time collecting drug paraphernalia, pipes, and bongs. I loved the way drugs made me feel: free, fun, fearless. Smoking became an everyday activity; sometimes we smoked a lot and sometimes just a little, depending on how much money we had.

My house was usually the gathering place. We swam in the pool or watched TV in the basement. My dad welcomed my friends with open arms—regardless of the time of day or night.

"Come on over," he would say. "Let's go swimming!" Then he'd fire up the grill and turn on the stereo, laughing and joking with all the kids who had suddenly filled our backyard and pool.

Paulie and Marco were both jocks, and they played all the sports. Not me. I liked eating my grandma's pasta and pastries too much to give them up—even for my friends. Once I got to high school, they were both always busy with practices and games, so I started hanging out with another group of kids: the heads.

Like Marco and Paulie, the heads were all a couple of years older than I was. But even though they were all pretty tough in their black leather jackets and wallets hanging from chains off their belts, for whatever reason, I fit in with their group just fine. Maybe it was because as an only child I didn't have any younger siblings tagging along with me. Or maybe it was because they liked what I had to offer: an empty house, a loaded fridge, and a well-stocked liquor cabinet.

Pot—and the stronger hash I started using before long—were pretty accessible and affordable back then. For twenty bucks, we could get enough to last us at least a couple of days, so while Marco and Paulie worked out on the athletic field, I studied Drugs 101. I learned to clean the stuff, pick out the seeds, roll my own joints, and take care of my own drug paraphernalia. I drifted in and out of both groups of friends, managing to stay high more than I was sober, and my folks never had a clue.

Since my folks were almost never home, they were oblivious to my activities and interests; it made sense to store all of our drugs and para-phernalia at my house. Over time, we built up quite a stash above the ceiling tiles and behind the furnace in my basement. One night a bunch of us were watching TV, playing Pong, and getting high at my house. Our water bongs rested on the table in front of us.

Overhead, the click-clacking of my mom's footsteps moved toward the basement door. We all froze in place, listening to see where she would go next. At the sound of the door creaking open, I gathered up the bongs in one swipe and quickly shoved them into the freezer. I was back on the couch, feet up on the coffee table in front of me, before she turned the corner.

"Hi, Ma," I said.

"Hi, Ricky. You boys having fun down here?"

"Yeah, Ma. Just hanging out."

She went to the kitchen in the back of the basement and opened the refrigerator door. We held our breath, each of us willing her to stay away from the freezer.

And then . . . "Ricky? What are these things here in the freezer with water in them?"

We looked at each other, eyes wide. I said the first thing that came to my mind: "Oh nothing, Ma. We're just making ice."

"Oh, okay then." As she climbed back up the stairs and closed the door behind her, we each breathed an audible sigh of relief. We were safe.

Making ice?

We burst out laughing; I couldn't believe that she bought it. Looking back, I have to wonder why my parents never questioned me. Did they really not know what was going on? They seemed to be happy living in denial and acting as if we were the perfect family. Their lack of involvement just made it that much easier to bury myself in my drugs, which eventually included cocaine.

My other obsession back then was hard rock, and my friends and I made sure we saw every concert that came through Rochester: Aerosmith, Judas Priest, Cheap Trick, Van Halen, Black Sabbath, Foreigner—we saw them all. A lot of times, my dad would drive us down to Rochester War Memorial Stadium and then come back to pick us up after the concert was over. He loved my friends and thought this was a good way to bond with them. He never even seemed to notice that we were all wasted.

For me, music and drugs went hand in hand. In my bedroom at home, I set up a huge stereo with six speakers as big as refrigerators. I had papered the room with pages torn from *Circus* and *Creem* magazines, my favorite heavy metal rags. I spent many a night getting high in my room, as I looked into the faces and listened to the blaring music of my favorite bands: AC/DC, Judas Priest, Aerosmith, Rush, Led Zeppelin, Pink Floyd. It was my dream to one day play in a band and live that life myself.

At John Marshall High School, we were required to take a music class, so I signed up for bass guitar lessons. As I played, I imagined a time when my band and I would play on stage for a screaming crowd of fans. Before long, Marco and I decided to start our own band. He was a great drummer, so we pulled in a couple of other guys from school and started Star Struck, our first garage band.

Surprisingly, we were pretty good. We put together a song list and eventually started playing school dances and little gigs. One afternoon, my dad handed me a hundred dollar bill and told me to go buy some stuff for the band. Knowing that one hundred dollars wouldn't go very far, I bought fifty dollars' worth of pot instead. But as we were walking back to the garage, a thought struck me: maybe there was a way we could make the money we needed *and* still get high. We stole a balance scale from our science classroom and quickly divided up the marijuana into little nickel bags.

Setting some aside for ourselves, we headed down to the bleachers at Number 40 School, where kids were more than happy to pay our asking price for the little bags. Within an hour, we had doubled our money—pretty good economics. Once we had enough money, we made a beeline for the House of Guitars, which sold all kinds of instruments, equipment, and albums.

Our little band had lined up a couple of local gigs, and we were really excited. We needed a mobile keyboard like the one we used at the school, but even with our newfound source of income, we still couldn't afford to buy one. As we mulled over our options, the wheels started turning in my head. We needed a keyboard and the school had one. We could just steal it.

The next afternoon when we all went to class, each of us unlocked one window in whatever classroom we were in. That would give us plenty of options in case a janitor or teacher noticed one was open and locked it before leaving for the day.

That evening after dark, we carefully scaled a smokestack to the third-floor music room and climbed in through the open window. We found the keyboard we wanted and tied a sturdy rope around it. We carefully began lowering it down to a couple of the guys who were waiting on the ground.

On his way out the window, one of the guys slipped and fell to the roof on the first-floor level, breaking his leg. A couple of the guys went with him to the hospital, where our friend was put in a cast and told to stay off his feet. The rest of us hauled the keyboard back to my house and unloaded it in the basement. At some point during all the shuffling and commotion, the keyboard was damaged.

The next day, word of the robbery buzzed around the school. It didn't take long for some of the parents to put two and two together and figure out what we did. The police showed up at my house, found the keyboard, and within hours, we were all charged with robbery and suspended.

When I saw my dad later that night, I broke into tears, begging him to forgive me.

"It's going to be okay, Ricky," he said, patting my back. "We'll call Uncle Rudy. He'll know what to do." Uncle Rudy was an attorney, and he always handled all of our family legal matters. Later that week, he went with us to juvenile court where the school administrators announced their request to have all of us kicked out of school. Since the keyboard was found at my house, I took the most heat.

Rudy argued that since I had never really been in trouble before, I didn't deserve such a harsh sentence. The judge agreed, ordering my parents to pay for the broken keyboard and keep a closer eye on me. He gave me six months of community service, cleaning up garbage along the highway.

I was now on the troublemaker target list at John Marshall. Worse still, the hole in my life that I had been trying to fill since childhood was still raw and gaping. I felt hopeless and trapped—and it didn't matter what I did—no amount of food, drugs, or alcohol could stop the pain.

LEMON RICOTTA BREAKFAST BRUSCHETTA WITH BERRY MARMALADE

I love breakfast, perhaps because it brings back happy memories of the mornings when my mom, dad, and I would sit down together to eat before heading off to work or school. As a chef, I rarely get a chance to eat breakfast, though I love to take my kids out to breakfast after church or prepare a simple treat like the one below.

This bruschetta is particularly great to make in the spring or early summer when berries are ripe. At other times of the year, you can substitute orange or another type of marmalade. The simple sugar can be made ahead; the excess can be refrigerated for up to a few weeks. It's another great staple I like to have on hand to sweeten beverages or use as a glaze. — *SERVES 4*

For Lemon Ricotta Bruschetta
1 lemon
1 c. ricotta cheese
1 tsp. cracked black pepper
1 tsp. kosher salt
8 pieces baguette or Italian or sourdough bread, sliced ¾-inch thick

For Berry Marmalade
4 Tbs. simple sugar syrup (see step 1 below)
1 Tbs. lemon zest (from second lemon)
1 piece star anise
8 oz. mixed berries (strawberry, blueberry, blackberry)

1. To make simple sugar used in marmalade, combine 2 c. sugar and 2 c. water in a small saucepan over medium heat. Mix together until sugar dissolves. Raise the heat to bring to a boil; remove from heat. Set aside to cool.
2. To make lemon ricotta bruschetta, zest the lemon and throw zest in bowl with ricotta cheese. After mixing, squeeze juice from lemon into the bowl. Add salt and pepper.
3. Mix until all ingredients are incorporated.
4. To make the berry marmalade, combine simple syrup, lemon zest, and star anise in a nonreactive saucepan.
5. Bring to a boil, reduce heat, add berries, and simmer until berries have softened.
6. Remove and discard star anise; cool marmalade.
7. Preheat oven to broil setting.
8. Lay bread out on a baking sheet; lightly toast under broiler until golden brown.
9. Remove pieces of toast and spread liberally with lemon ricotta, followed with a generous spoonful of berry marmalade.

---- 6 ----

ROCK BOTTOM

*Better to have little, with godliness,
than to be rich and dishonest.*

PROVERBS 16:8, NLT

On an afternoon like any other, I was shocked to arrive home from school and find my dad sitting at the kitchen table. He was never home from work this early.

"Come on, Ricky, I need you to take a ride with me," he said, a somber look on his face.

Oh man, he must have found my stash. Or one of my teachers called about my skipping school. Or maybe he found the parking tickets I'd been hiding. I wasn't quite sure what I was going to get busted for, but I was sure I'd been found out for something. How was I going to get out of this one?

I climbed into the passenger seat of the car, and we headed up toward Number 40 School. Then we turned down behind Hollander Stadium and parked in a neighborhood cul-de-sac.

I couldn't imagine why he had driven me only a few blocks from home just to yell at me for doing drugs. Maybe he knew everything; maybe he was really mad and didn't want the neighbors to hear him screaming at me. Or perhaps he was finally going to smack me around and wanted to do it in private.

Keeping his hands on the wheel, my dad stared straight ahead for a long time before he started to speak.

"I need to confide in you something and you can't tell your mom—you can't tell anyone. This isn't a joke. I'm in some real trouble that I can't get out of."

As soon as I realized he didn't know about the drugs, I was instantly intrigued. Trouble? What kind of trouble could he be in? My dad was everybody's friend.

"I've been embezzling money from the union for a little over a year now," he said, still staring out the front of the car.

Embezzling? I didn't know what that meant, but before I had a chance to ask, he went on.

"Since I am in charge of the union's treasury, I've had access to a lot of money. I had every intention of putting it back, you know. I just have not had the opportunity to do so. And now, sometime in the next few days there is going to be an audit."

Audit. Another word I didn't know.

"What's an audit?" I asked.

"People will be coming in and going through our records and books to see if there is any money missing. Once they find it's not there, they'll be pointing the finger at me."

He went on to explain that in addition to embezzling the cash, he had gotten involved with racketeering and money laundering for some of the crime families in Rochester—the same guys I had seen hanging out at the Americana bar. Although I couldn't really follow all the logistics of what he was telling me, I did understand that the lifestyle we had been living on Ridgeway was probably a benefit of my dad's mob activity and embezzling. Now things were starting to come together for me. The new house, all the nice things we had, my dad's new Bonneville—he had paid for it all with stolen money.

"I'm going to leave for Mexico tomorrow morning," he said. "No one is going to be looking for me until well into next week. I'll have to stay down there for a while—at least until they have forgotten about me and the statute of limitations expires." That would be seven years.

I was sixteen, so I would be in my twenties when he came home—if he came home.

My mind raced as I tried to make sense of what he was saying. Could my dad really be involved with organized crime and embezzling? There had been a lot of news coverage about Mafia activity in and around Rochester in recent years, so I was very familiar with what was going on, but I still couldn't believe my dad was part of it.

I was angry and impressed all at the same time.

"What about Mom and me? Who's going to take care of us?" I asked.

"Once you finish high school, I will send for you," he said. "In the meantime, there's a suitcase in the trunk with ten thousand dollars in it. You need to hide it someplace safe and use the money to help your mom pay the bills. You're going to be the man of the house now, and I need you to step up and take care of your mom." For a moment, I felt disoriented. Could I just be tripping? Then reality set in and it all became very real.

We decided to hide the money inside the big CB radio unit I had in my room. Dad was already packed and planned to leave for the airport as soon as I left for school and Mom left for work the next day. I understood the plan but still didn't quite accept that it was really happening.

We pulled out of the cul-de-sac and drove home in silence. Mom had veal Parmesan waiting on the table, one of our favorite meals. Dad and I just sat down as if nothing was wrong. We made it through the meal in near silence, though I could feel my mom's eyes on me. I'm sure she was wondering what kind of trouble I was in now . . . if she only knew it wasn't me this time. Dad was watching me pretty closely too, probably waiting to see if I would say anything. I just kept my head down, eating quickly and escaping as soon as I could.

I headed to the basement and flipped on the television set, trying to get lost in somebody else's story. But even *Starsky and Hutch* couldn't hold my attention this time. I could hear my folks upstairs, laughing and joking as they cleaned up the supper dishes. It was rare for them both to have a night off together. I wondered if my dad had arranged that. Could he really be part of the Mafia? To me, he was still just the same old guy: fun-loving Frank.

Finally, I gave up on the television and just went to bed, pushing all thoughts of organized crime, racketeering, the feds, and money laundering out of my mind. Strangely enough, I didn't do any drugs that night. I wanted to have a clear head in the morning so I could be sure this wasn't just a flashback of a bad trip.

The next morning we all got up and had breakfast together, same as always. Dad kissed us good-bye, got in his car, and went to work, same as always. And Mom went about her business, preparing that night's dinner and getting ready to catch her bus for work, same as always. Had I dreamed the whole thing? Nothing was different today than any other day. I decided I had better just go to school.

But when I got there, I knew I would never be able to concentrate. Every time a door opened or a teacher called my name, I jumped. After first hour, I found Marco and Paulie and convinced them to skip with me. We headed down to our favorite greasy-spoon diner, the Pepper Mill, and then to a park. When I told them the unbelievable story about to unfold, they were speechless. Frank was more than just my dad; he was their friend, the one they affectionately called Mr. T. They couldn't believe it any more than I could.

We spent the rest of the day hanging out on Marco's big stone front porch, dangling our feet over the edge and keeping an eye on my house a few doors down.

Later in the day, my mom came home to put dinner in the oven and get ready for her second job. By now, I was starting to think maybe my dad had been wrong. Maybe he had been able to work things out down at the union hall.

Marco tapped me on the shoulder. "Hey, look," he said, pointing toward a black-and-white squad car that had just pulled into my driveway. It was followed by two dark cars with tinted windows.

"You think this is about your dad?" Paulie asked.

I didn't know. My dad had said that no one would come looking for him until next week. The cars just sat there without anyone getting out. *I'll bet this has nothing to do with my dad,* I thought, paranoia setting in. *Somebody busted me and now I'm in trouble.*

Finally, two uniformed officers climbed out of the squad car, turning to talk to the drivers of the other cars who were both wearing suits. As they walked toward the front of my house, I thought about all the drugs and paraphernalia I had hidden in my room and in the drop ceiling over the washer and dryer.

I figured I had two choices: I could run or I could go check it out. I decided since my mom was in the house by herself, I had better at least go see what was going on. When I walked in the front door, my mom was sitting on the couch talking to the two guys in suits. The others were rifling through drawers and closets.

"Hello, son, what's your name?" one of the detectives on the couch asked, gesturing for me to sit down. I took a seat in my dad's big recliner, trying to look tough and innocent at the same time. I was pretty sure I wasn't succeeding.

I quickly figured out that these guys weren't after me. The detective explained they had a search warrant to look through the house and my dad's things. They also had a federal warrant for his arrest. Apparently, what he had done could result in a lot of prison time if he was caught.

My mom was very confused and distraught.

"Your father would never do this," she said to me through her tears. "There's got to be a mistake. I can't believe this."

"Ma, you need to call Uncle Rudy. He'll know what to do."

When Rudy got to the house, he pulled one of the detectives aside and talked to him for a long time. The longer the officer and my uncle talked, the more withdrawn my mom became. Her face was blank and her eyes glazed over. She hugged a sofa pillow to her chest and rocked slightly back and forth.

I continued to sit stoically in my dad's big chair, saying nothing and wishing I could just go downstairs.

Finally, the detectives and police officers convened back in the living room. Rudy walked them to the front door and closed it behind them. When he came back into the living room, he pulled me aside: "They found your drug paraphernalia and took it," he said. "You need to get rid of anything else you have in the house now. Your folks have enough to worry about without you getting in trouble too."

I nodded, knowing that the detectives were cutting me some slack. Then he turned to my mom and told us what he knew about my dad.

"According to their allegations, Chick is going to be charged with embezzling, money laundering, and forgery. They say that the money is definitely missing and that Chick never showed up for work today. They're pretty sure he's armed. I think it's safe to assume that he's made it out of the country and he's going to be okay. You two just hang tight and don't let anyone else back into this house without contacting me first. Do you understand?"

We both nodded.

"I don't know what we'd have done without you," my mom said.

Rudy patted her on the shoulder.

"You can call me anytime, day or night. I mean it."

As soon as Rudy walked out the door, my mom began sobbing.

"How can this be happening? I just can't believe it. What are we going to do?" She turned to face me: "How could I not see this coming? Did you know anything about this?"

I told her Dad had told me about it the day before.

As I spoke, her expression changed from one of shocked sadness to fierce anger. "How could he do this to us?" she screamed, spittle flying and the veins in her neck bulging.

"He didn't do it *to* us; he did it *for* us," I said.

She glared at me, unleashing a stream of profanity. Then she shrieked, "How could he just kiss us good-bye this morning like nothing was wrong? How could he lie to us?"

"He didn't lie to us; he was protecting us. And anyway look at this stuff we have," I said, waving my hand around our home. "Where do you think all this came from?"

Her eyes narrowed into slits and moved wildly around the room, finally landing on a glass globe sitting on the bookshelf. Marching over, she picked it up and hurled it across the room, glass shattering everywhere as it smashed into the kitchen sink.

Unable to contain my own anger and panic any longer, I started to cry and shouted back at her. I had to get out of there. I ran down the stairs into the basement and pulled out a couple of ceiling tiles in the laundry room. After gathering up what was left of my drugs and drug paraphernalia into a box, I headed for Marco's house.

After I told the guys what had happened, I pushed the box toward Marco. "The cops didn't find this stuff," I told them. "You need to keep it here for a while. That was way too close for comfort."

We found a spot to hide the box, and then we spent the rest of the night drinking, getting wasted, and talking. Nothing like this had ever happened to any of us before. We didn't know whether to think it was cool or be scared to death.

The next day, Saturday, the story hit all the local papers. Our phone started ringing early and didn't stop all day long. Neither of us really wanted to talk about it to anyone, so we ended up turning the ringer off. I wondered where my dad was and what he was doing. Did he know how hard this was for us?

On Monday when I went back to school, everyone was asking me about it, even some of the toughest kids, whom I had never spoken to in my life. "I heard your dad was in the Mafia and he fled the country," they'd say, leaning against my locker or sitting down next to me in class. "That's so cool."

We had all seen the *Godfather* movies, and with the recent string of mob arrests so much in the news, I quickly became something of a celebrity tough guy. At first, I didn't mind it so much. I had always been kind of a loner among my peers, and it was nice to be noticed for something other than my bad reputation.

After about two weeks, my uncle Rudy called. Dad had been arrested at O'Hare Airport, of all places. Apparently, he had made it to Mexico without a hitch and was free and clear. He had gotten a hotel room in Mexico City, where he spent days agonizing over his crime and missing his family. He decided to return home and turn himself in. The feds had put warrants out for his arrest at all major airports, and when he was changing planes in Chicago, they grabbed him.

"Chickie is in the Cook County Lockup," Rudy told us. "He's going to be there for a few days before they transfer him back to Rochester for his trial."

Again, my emotions fluctuated between happiness that he was coming home to sadness that he had gotten caught to anger that he had put us in such a rotten situation. I was only sixteen. I just wanted to have fun and hang with my friends. I didn't want to deal with this kind of craziness and have to grow up so quickly.

When my dad returned to New York, Rudy picked us up and drove us down to the Monroe County Courthouse for the arraignment. Everything became suddenly real when I turned and saw my father entering the courtroom wearing an orange jail jumpsuit, his hands and feet cuffed.

He glanced over to where my mom and I were sitting. In his eyes I saw tears of sadness and shame. It was almost more than I could bear. Next to me, my mom sobbed silently, her whole body shaking with each breath.

As the judge read off the charges against my dad, the severity of his crime struck me for the first time: racketeering, embezzlement, forgery, possession of a concealed weapon. Any of these on their own was serious enough, but put them together and I knew he didn't stand a chance of escaping jail time.

After the arraignment, they led my dad away, back to his cell where he would await trial. We were allowed to visit with him briefly before heading home, though we had to talk to him on a telephone because we were separated from each other by a glass partition. When it was my turn, I didn't know what to say.

"I'm so sorry, Ricky," he said. "I know it's been hard. I should never have pulled you into this." It was obvious he wasn't just sorry he'd been busted; he was extremely remorseful, period.

"What happened? Rudy said you made it to Mexico."

"I did. I got there and got a hotel room in Mexico City. But it was awful. One night while I was eating dinner in my room and watching *The Flintstones* in Spanish, I just started to cry. I realized that I couldn't stay away from you and your mom for seven years. I couldn't leave you holding the bag. I had to come back and face the music and make things right."

"What's going to happen now?"

"We'll have to go to trial," he said. "I'll probably see some prison time. You need to understand that we are probably going to lose a lot—maybe everything."

I wasn't sure what that meant, but I nodded and tried to look reassuring.

Mom and I didn't have anything else to do but go home and wait for the trial. With each passing day, she became more and more messed up. I had never seen her like this before. She quit her daytime job as a lunch lady, and when I got home from school in the afternoon, I often found her sitting in the dark, crying and watching TV. Some days she just sat there mumbling to herself. Seeing her that way didn't make me feel any compassion, just anger, and I blew through the living room as fast as I could.

My aunts started bringing food in for us to eat when they realized she wasn't cooking or buying groceries. As they moved about the kitchen, I caught snatches of their conversation: ". . . nervous breakdown . . . need to get to a doctor . . . thought the Valium might help but it only makes her worse . . . thoughts of suicide." They never talked with my mom about any of this, though, or even suggested she talk with a counselor.

Personally, I wasn't doing any better than she. Now that my mom was completely oblivious to me, I was getting wasted and staying wasted all day, every day. As the excitement of my dad's arrest faded, kids at school began to make fun of me—and him. Driven by a desire to protect his reputation, I started getting into fights, often right in the middle of the hallway or in gym class. I was really angry all the time—with everybody and anybody.

My friends and family were worried about me.

"You gotta stop doing the drug thing," Marco told me one afternoon as he helped me clean up after another knock-down, drag-out fight behind the school. Marco and Paulie had slowed down on their drug use a lot. With only another year left before graduation, they were starting to get more serious about their futures. I, on the other hand, was going in the opposite direction.

One afternoon, I was walking home with Marco when a black Lincoln Town Car pulled up alongside us. Two guys sat up front and one rode in the back. The man in the passenger seat rolled down his window and called me over.

"Hey, Rick," he said. "We're friends of Frank. We need to talk to you. Get in; we'll give you a ride home."

Too high to think better of it, I climbed into the backseat. The car hadn't even pulled away from the curb when the man in the front turned and started to read me the riot act.

"You need to listen up and you need to listen good, you little punk," he said. "We're here for Frank. We're his extended family, and we take care of our own. That means you and your mom don't need to worry about anything, but you really need to step up, be a man, and stay out of trouble. We can't help you if the police are always watching you, trying to nail you for drugs. We can't take care of you then."

Now I recognized them! I had seen all three of these guys in the bar years earlier, talking with my dad over drinks. Jimmy and Tony and Al all must have been part of the same outfit as my dad.

Al continued the lecture. He rattled off all kinds of information about me: my juvenile record, my lousy grades, even the name of my drug dealer.

"If you want things to go well for Frank, you better stop with the drugs," he said. "Stop being so selfish. None of this reflects very well on him, you know. You're just making it harder for us."

As I stepped out of the car in front of my house, my legs were shaking. These guys were tough. I didn't want to see what they would do to someone who didn't follow their "suggestions."

With the trial coming up, I decided I'd better cut back on my wild activity. I tried to limit the hard drugs to weekend parties, and just stick with pot and beer. Unfortunately, without the drugs to act as a buffer, I found myself getting into even more fights than usual. And it wasn't long before school officials said "no more." I was permanently suspended from John Marshall and had to enroll at Charlotte High School, where I didn't know anyone.

On the morning of the trial, Rudy again drove us down to the Monroe County Courthouse. We sat directly behind the defendant's seat, and even though we were warned not to touch or even talk to anyone on the other side of the wooden partition, when my dad entered the courtroom, he reached down and put his hand on my head before taking his seat.

The trial lasted two days. My dad ended up taking a plea bargain, which reduced his sentence to only four years in the county jail— much better than the seven years in federal prison he'd been looking at. With good behavior, he'd be out even sooner.

Even so, when the judge handed down the official sentence, it still fell like a lead balloon in the courtroom. My dad was really going to jail, and he would be gone for a long time. My mom and aunts began to cry; my uncles sat in stony silence, not sure what to do next.

Since it felt like someone had died, we did what all good Italians do after a funeral: we went home and ate.

And then we tried to get on with our lives without my dad. It wasn't easy. The family tried to help out when they could, but my mom was really in bad shape. After a while, my aunts would simply slip into the house, put a casserole or chicken cutlets in the oven, and slip back out without saying a word. They never would have let us go hungry, but beyond that, they had no idea how to help us.

In the months to follow, Jimmy and Tony and Al kept pretty close tabs on my mom and me. Sometimes one of them would show up with a wad of cash or a bag of groceries. Other times, they'd bring us information about my dad's case or just check in to see if we were doing okay.

By now, it was pretty clear that school and I were never going to be a good fit. I'd only been at Charlotte for a couple of months, but already I was failing all of my classes and skipping school. When the principal found pot in my locker, I was suspended. Now I would have to attend Edison Tech, one of the worst schools in the district.

Everything felt so empty. What was the point of it all? I just wanted to live my life and hang with my friends. Worrying about my family, getting in trouble at school, trying to fly under the radar—I hadn't signed up for any of that.

On Christmas Eve, some of my family members and I headed down to the prison to visit my dad. I could tell that he was trying to be positive as he joked about how bad the food was and how he had hung our family photos on the wall of his cell using toothpaste. But the more he tried to act like everything was normal, the more apparent it was that nothing was normal anymore.

This was just so wrong. We shouldn't be here. We should all be home, eating meatballs and mostaccioli, opening gifts, and watching TV.

I glanced at the guard in the corner. He had such a smug look on his face, I just wanted to pummel him with my fists. I was getting madder by the minute, and my face began to burn with anger.

Finally, I just couldn't take it anymore. I shoved back my chair and stood to my feet. Everyone turned to look up at me. "I'm going home," I snapped. "I'll take the bus!"

I stormed out of the room, toward the set of double glass doors that led from the prison. As I struggled to get the door open, I kicked it with my combat boot. The glass shattered into a million pieces, shards exploding into the air with such force the whole room shook.

I walked out into the cold night air and a raging snowstorm, not waiting to see what would happen next. Actually, I didn't really want to know.

GENOA HAM AND OLIVE TAPENADE PANINI

During my teen years, I loved experimenting with sandwiches—whether submarine, club, or grilled. In fact, I went through a two-year phase of creating many different grilled cheese and pressed sandwiches, like this one. Now I enjoy working with my kids as they create their own varieties. — *SERVES 4*

For the olive tapenade
1 c. green Cerignola olives, chopped
2 roasted red peppers, peeled and diced
1 oz. capers, rinsed and smashed
2 each anchovy filets, drained and crushed
1 Tbs. red wine vinegar
3 oz. extra-virgin olive oil
1 tsp. fresh ground pepper
¼ oz. parsley, chopped
Kosher salt and freshly ground pepper, to taste

For panini
1 ciabatta or sourdough loaf
10 oz. smoked ham, sliced
8 oz. fontina cheese, sliced
6 oz. olive tapenade
4 Tbs. unsalted butter, softened

1. To prepare the tapenade, mix the olives, peppers, capers, anchovies, and vinegar together.
2. Add remaining ingredients and mix well; season to taste.
3. To prepare each sandwich, cut bread into eight ½-inch slices.
4. Add one-quarter of the ham slices, 2 fontina slices, and one-quarter of the tapenade mixture to a piece of bread.
5. Top with another slice of bread.
6. Spread 1 Tbs. soft butter on the outside of the sandwich and place on panini machine. Grill to perfection and serve.
7. Repeat steps 4 through 6 with remaining ingredients until all four sandwiches are made.

PART II

CULINARY HIGH SCHOOL

Late 1970s through early 1980s

7

WENDY'S

Let us not grow weary while doing good,
for in due season we shall reap if we do not lose heart.

GALATIANS 6:9

With my dad in jail, things at home seemed to be going from bad to worse to awful, and my attitude reflected it. Most of the time I stayed to myself, walking under a cloud of anger, resentment, and frustration, fueled by drugs and depression.

Things weren't any better for my mom. She sank into a depression that no one could break through. The doctor prescribed electric shock therapy and antidepressant medication, but they only pulled her further and further from reality. I often came home at night to find her sitting in the dark, crying and talking to herself with the TV playing in the background. The only time she really focused on anything was when Jim and Tammy Bakker, Oral Roberts, or Jimmy Swaggart were preaching. I couldn't figure out what she saw in these flamboyant televangelists.

"Why do you watch this crap, Ma? These guys are so bogus. All they want is your money." This kind of religion seemed so cultish, radical, and strange—nothing at all like the Catholic services I remembered at Sacred Heart.

"Don't you say that, Ricky," she said, never taking her eyes off the television screen. "Jimmy Swaggart has something special. He is a man of God. It wouldn't hurt you to listen to him once in a while."

If nothing else, at least my mom found some comfort in it. When the TV preachers were talking about the Bible rather than pitching for contributions, my mom sat up a little straighter. Even I took note. But not even Jimmy Swaggart or the *PTL Club* was enough to pull her out of her funk. It wasn't unusual for my mom and me to go two or three days without saying a word to one another—even when we passed on the stairs or sat across from each other while eating dinner.

I was really getting sick of going to school. Having been expelled from John Marshall and Charlotte, I was now near the end of the line: Edison Tech. Rather than offering a traditional academic program, Edison focused on teaching students some kind of trade to help them survive in the real world. I took a few carpentry and plumbing classes, as well as one called "Foods."

The school itself was really rough. The building was old and had not been maintained very well at all, as evidenced by the rats that often scurried into the corners of the stairwells as we passed from class to class. We sat in busted-up desks and worked with worn-out or outdated tools and equipment. Graffiti covered every square inch of wall space, and gang symbols carved into lockers clearly designated where we could go and where we could not. The district had recently started busing inner-city kids out to area schools like Edison, which created a highly volatile, very tense environment. Fights constantly broke out between the black kids and the white kids—mirroring the violence and race riots our city had just experienced. Even going to the bathroom was dangerous; you never knew who might jump you with a chain or a knife.

I figured I had only one choice: get through school as quickly as I could and with as little pain as possible. I needed to make Edison Tech work because I knew my only option after that was the School Without Walls, which I saw as more like a juvenile center than a school. I started to focus on the few classes that I kind of enjoyed, like woodworking with Mr. Fred. In order to earn a passing grade, we were each required to do a really big project showcasing our woodworking skills. I decided to make a three-drawer jewelry box of varnished oak with a nice flip top.

After two weeks of concentrated effort, I was actually very pleased with the way my box had turned out. I thought it might even be good enough to earn an A—something I had never done in any other class before.

The day it was due, I carefully wrapped the jewelry box in soft cloth and brought it to school, where I locked it in my locker until lathe class. But when I went to get it just before third period, I found myself staring at an empty shelf. Someone had broken into my locker and taken all my stuff, including my project.

I had no choice but to walk into lathe class empty-handed. I tried to explain that someone had taken my project, but of course the teacher had no reason to believe me. I had never shown any initiative in his class before—or any other class for that matter. Why would this time be any different? Frustrated and angry, I sat through that entire period watching other kids show off their projects and knowing I could expect a big fat zero in the grade book.

As I entered the cafeteria to eat lunch the next hour, I happened to glance over at a group of kids sitting in the corner of the room. There, right in the middle of their books and cafeteria trays, was my jewelry box! I walked over to the table, my own meal tray still in hand.

"Hey, that's my jewelry box," I said. "Give it back to me—now." Three of the guys at the table stood up, clearly itching for a fight.

"What are you talking about?" one of them said sarcastically. "That's my box. I made it myself, and I'm getting ready to turn it in next hour. What are you going to do about it?"

"Give it to me," I said again.

The kid held my box above his head, then dropped it on the floor.

This was too much. I couldn't take one more rotten thing happening in my life. Suddenly, all the resentment and frustration and emptiness I had been carrying with me for so long boiled to the surface. I started whaling on the kid with my tray, beating him on the side of the head, screaming and punching and kicking all at the same time. Before long everyone in the room was fighting and yelling. It was a full-blown riot, completely out of control. Kids were throwing food, schoolbooks, chairs, plastic trays—anything they could get their hands on. Someone pulled a knife and stabbed the kid standing next to him. Others settled for pencils, which made equally effective weapons.

Within minutes, school officials, security, and police were on the scene, and everyone in the room was put on suspension. I left in an ambulance with a huge gash over my eye, a fractured nose, and a cracked wrist; hunks of hair were missing from my scalp and blood was drying on my face.

An hour later, as I was getting ready to leave Park Ridge Hospital with ten stitches across my forehead, I noticed a black Lincoln Town Car parked outside. My dad's friends had already heard the news. One of them got out and met me at the door as I was leaving.

"I'm done," I screamed, my face turning red as the fury rose within me. "I'm not going back. I'm quitting school. It's over. I will go find a job, but I'm out of there."

They tried to calm me down, realizing this was no time for another lecture on staying out of trouble. "We'll talk to your dad and see what we can do," one of the guys said. "In the meantime, you need to stay home."

When I got home, my mom took one look at my face and started to sob.

"Again, Ricky?" she asked. "Why do you do these things? Is it not enough that your dad is in jail? Why do you keep getting into trouble?"

I told her what I had told my dad's cronies: I was done with school for good. I was going to get a job and work. Realizing that she wasn't going to change my mind, she finally agreed that if my dad okayed it, she would sign the papers allowing me to drop out of high school.

The next day, Paulie and Marco skipped school to join me on the 5:00 a.m. bus downtown to visit my dad. They knew I might need a little help telling him what was going on. Even though my dad's buddies kept him up to date with some news, I tried to keep our conversations fairly positive whenever I visited. I didn't think he'd have any idea how bad things really were for me in school.

My dad was on work release at the time, working for the Ragú sauce company. So we met him at the bus stop in front of McDonald's, where we knew he would be waiting to change buses to get to his factory job.

Taking one look at my swollen face, my dad immediately knew something was up. I took a deep breath and started at the beginning. I told him about the riot and the fighting, about all the racial problems at Edison Tech, how awful my grades were, and how frustrated school made me.

"Why are you holding me back? I think it's time for me to get a job and earn a living," I said. "I just can't do the school thing anymore."

He obviously wasn't thrilled with the news, but surprisingly, he understood. At this point, school officials wanted to send me to the School Without Walls.

"I think you should at least *try* that school," my dad said. "You commit to two weeks there and see what you think. In the meantime, I will make some calls to see if I can hook you up with a job."

I agreed to do it his way, even though I had no intention of making it work. Two days after my two weeks were up, I said good-bye to school forever, even though I knew that by quitting I had forfeited any chance to work for Kodak, which required applicants to have a high school diploma.

Thankfully, my dad had gotten me an interview at a new restaurant that had just opened in Rochester: Wendy's Old Fashioned Hamburgers. I had never heard of Wendy's before. The new Rochester franchise was located on Lake Avenue up in the Tenth Ward, not too far from where I used to live.

My interview was with a guy named Tom, a friend and coworker of my dad's from his bartending days at the Americana. I tried to look presentable for the appointment, but it was pretty tough to hide the bruises and cuts on my face.

Tom didn't seem to care. What I didn't realize was that my dad had already filled him in on the details of my situation.

"So, tell me about yourself, Rick," he said, gesturing for me to join him at the small Formica table in the spotless dining room. I sat down and told him my story, how I had never really done well in school but that I liked to cook at home with my mom and grandma. I loved to work, I told him, and was willing to do whatever it took to be successful in a job.

"Well, you're not quite old enough to work full-time," he said hesitantly, circling the "16" on my application. Clearly, I was not the perfect candidate, and this guy had no reason to hire me—except that he was friends with my dad and wanted to cut me a break.

I got the job.

I started the very next day, and for the first time in my life, I found something I was actually good at. The work didn't even really feel like work. Everything just came natural to me.

I punched in at six o'clock in the morning and immediately began slicing tomatoes, portioning meat patties, cutting up lettuce, and setting up stations. Something about the work fascinated me. I liked the order and structure: one sheet of butcher paper between each square hamburger patty, fifteen patties to a stack. Each pile of burgers went into a deep hotel pan, which held a total of eight stacks, or 120 patties. After I had filled a pan, I wrapped and labeled it before storing it in the cooler for that day's service.

After prepping and setting up all the stations, I usually worked the grill from 11:30 to 2:30. I offered to organize the coolers, scrub the floors, clean the bathrooms, and wash the Frosty machine—whatever I could do to stay at work and not have to go home. Other days, I might work the sandwich station, loading up each burger to order. Everything we prepared was fresh, not frozen or canned like other fast-food joints. The produce was fresh, and the meat was good quality. I was responsible for checking everything in, labeling it, organizing it, and putting it away. I was proud of the end result.

Because we were a new franchise in the Rochester area, the place was usually packed. Some days we did up to five hundred orders at lunch alone. But I loved it. I was relieved to be out from under the pressure of high school and thrilled at the chance to be away from all the negative things in my life. I picked up as many shifts as I could, in part to make extra cash, but also because I really wanted to learn all that I could about the job.

In the morning, I worked with a super pretty girl named Eileen Carroll. I had seen her around—she went to Charlotte High—but we'd never really talked until now. Like me, her family was rooted in Rochester. Her dad worked for DuPont, and Eileen assumed she'd get a job there after high school graduation.

All summer long, five days a week, we opened the restaurant together, and we quickly became friends. Standing at the prep sinks, we'd talk for hours about anything and everything: her boyfriend, our schools, my dad. She became a good friend to me—almost like one of the guys, someone I could really trust. Though I was attracted to her, I knew she would never date me, a druggie. Plus, lots of boys were interested in her.

Franchise owner Dick Fox often came in to see how things were going in his new store or to work a shift with us during the rush. Sometimes he was accompanied by Wendy's founder Dave Thomas. Both were very kind, always taking the time to show us something new or teach us a faster method for getting the food out.

I really liked Dave a lot, and working shoulder to shoulder with him at the grill gave us plenty of time to share stories. Dave hadn't finished high school either, but he did have his GED, and he constantly encouraged me to get mine as well.

"You don't necessarily need a diploma," he said, "but you at least need your GED."

"Yes, sir," I said. "Someday."

Most of my Wendy's coworkers partied, so I fit right in. Of course, I was the youngest in the group—nothing new for me—I had been hanging out with older people my whole life. But this crowd was on a whole different level. These guys were adults, not just a bunch of punk kids. They were serious about work and serious about their drugs, and I didn't want them to think I couldn't keep up, so when a manager invited me along to see the movie *The Wall* (based on Pink Floyd's album of the same name) and get high, I went along.

I did try to lay off the chemical drugs, however. I didn't want to be running the grill or the slicer while wasted on acid. I had learned the dangers of the job pretty early on when prepping tomatoes one afternoon. In order to create uniform tomato slices, we used an industrial slicer. For whatever reason, ours didn't have a guard on it, and on this particular day, my hands were wet and slippery.

As I pushed a large tomato between the blades, my hand slipped and my knuckles hit the slicing mechanism head-on. As the pain shot from my fingers to my hand and up my arm, I jerked back and looked down at my fingers. Four perfectly even little slices crossed my four knuckles. This wasn't so bad . . . but when I bent my fingers into a fist, bones and tendons popped out of each opening, causing the room to spin all around me and sending me to my knees.

Next thing I knew, I was in an ambulance en route to the local hospital where they immediately sent me up for surgery to repair the damaged tendons. I was off work for four weeks after the surgery, with nothing to do but go to physical therapy and get high.

I didn't know it at the time, but this would be the first of many job-related accidents I would have in the years to come. Fire, knives, slippery floors, grease burns—all were hazards of the trade I would choose to devote my life to.

For the next two years, I was nothing but a Wendy's workhorse. I spent nearly every waking moment in the kitchen and quickly earned enough cash to buy my first car: a 1978 V8 dark blue Chevy Camaro. It had a spoiler, big chrome wheels, and a crazy 300-watt stereo with six speakers and a subwoofer. It was loud, it was fast, and it was paid for.

By the time I turned eighteen, I felt pretty confident about the Wendy's drill. I had worked my way up from morning prep cook to evening line cook, and I knew I'd gone as far as I could there.

The managers trusted me with the codes to open the restaurant and check in the orders. I could take the inventory and make the prep lists—but I was never allowed to handle the money or work the registers. Only managers could do that, and I couldn't be a manager without a diploma.

Without a high school degree, my options seemed pretty limited. But there was no way I was going back to school at this point—that would feel like a huge step backward. I was fairly sure I could make a living off of this cooking thing. I just needed a plan, some time—and practice, practice, practice.

RICKY T. BURGER WITH ROASTED GARLIC AIOLI

I believe in giving burgers the respect they deserve. With this recipe, I tried *to* take the burger to another level by inserting compound butters into the meat so the patties can baste while grilling; *Gourmet* magazine once named this one of the best burgers in America. I'm sure my burger mentor Dave Thomas would be proud. — *SERVES 4*

    2 lb. ground beef (80/20 mix)
    Compound butter (recipe follows)
    Kosher salt and freshly ground pepper, to taste
    4 half-inch-thick Vidalia or other sweet onion slices
    1 Tbs. olive oil
    4 slices cheddar cheese
    Roasted garlic aioli (recipe follows)
    4 brioche burger buns, toasted
    4 romaine leaves
    4 slices beefsteak tomato

1. Prepare grill.
2. Cut four ¼-inch-thick slices of compound butter.
3. Form ground beef into 4 large meatballs and insert a butter slice into the center of each.
4. Flatten each ball into a patty about 1¼-inch thick, completely enclosing the butter.
5. Season the patties with salt and pepper.
6. Brush onion slices with olive oil and grill on a rack set 5 to 6 inches over glowing coals until softened, about 3 minutes on each side. Transfer to a plate and season with salt and pepper. Grill burger 6 minutes and turn over. Cut 4 thin slices of compound butter and top each burger with a slice of butter and a slice of cheese. Grill about 7 minutes more for medium rare. (Instead of using a grill, you can also cook the burgers in a large cast-iron skillet with a little oil over moderately high heat.)
7. Spread roasted garlic aioli on top halves of rolls. Serve burgers on rolls with grilled onion, romaine, and tomato.

For compound butter

    ½ lb. unsalted butter, softened
    1 large garlic clove, minced
    ¾ tsp. minced fresh tarragon
    ¾ tsp. minced fresh basil
    ¾ tsp. minced flat-leaf parsley
    ¼ tsp. fresh lemon juice
    Pinch of cayenne
    Kosher salt and freshly ground pepper, to taste

1. Stir together all the compound butter ingredients; then spoon the butter mixture onto plastic wrap in a 3-inch-long mound.

2. Fold plastic wrap over butter to enclose it; roll to form a log about 2½ inches in diameter.
3. Chill butter until firm, about 2 hours. Excess butter will freeze well for up to a month.

For the roasted garlic aioli (makes 1 cup)

1 head garlic, unpeeled; plus 1 small clove garlic, peeled and chopped
1 c. mayonnaise
1 Tbs. fresh lime juice
1 tsp. hot paprika
¼ tsp. cayenne
¼ tsp. ground cumin
Freshly ground pepper, to taste

1. Preheat oven to 400°F.
2. Wrap the head of garlic in foil and roast in the middle of oven until tender, about 45 minutes.
3. Squeeze the garlic from its papery casing; puree in blender with remaining ingredients.

Note: Aioli may be made 2 days ahead and refrigerated, covered.

8

SCOTCH 'N SIRLOIN

The wise are cautious and avoid danger;
fools plunge ahead with reckless confidence.

PROVERBS 14:16, NLT

Living at home with few expenses, I was able to sock away a good bit
of money. I was dealing drugs on the side, so cash was never really an
issue. My future, however, was another story.

Most of my friends had graduated from high school and were settling into regular full-time jobs—Marco had been hired on at Kodak
and Paulie went to work at Rochester Gas and Electric. None of us
had much time to spend with the band anymore. And we all knew we
weren't good enough to make the music thing work forever anyway. It
was time to get serious about cooking.

I started to shift my focus from being a rock star to doing this cooking thing for a living. And honestly, the thought kind of excited me.
Unlike doing construction or standing on an assembly line, cooking
didn't really seem stressful or boring. In my experience, making food
had always meant making people happy. If I could party on the side
and still get paid for doing my job, even better!

Wendy's had given me a good start by teaching me the basics of cooking burgers, making chili, and prepping in the kitchen. Beyond that, I
had an understanding and comfort in front of the stove that other people

just didn't seem to have. I was confident in my skills, and I was willing to work hard, just as I'd seen my mom and dad do all my life. I knew I had a lot to offer someone—even without a high school diploma.

One morning, an ad in the classified section caught my attention: the Scotch 'N Sirloin in Rochester was looking for kitchen help. I had eaten there on special occasions with my family and knew it served good quality food. This might just be the next step. I called and set up an interview for that afternoon.

When I walked in the back door later that week, I was immediately blown away. To my right was a glassed-in office and just past that was a full-blown butcher shop where three guys were standing at big wooden tables with thirty or forty pounds of prime rib in front of them. I watched as they butchered these huge hunks of meat; their knives slid through the meat like it was butter. I couldn't believe how accurate they were. I watched them sharpen their knives on their steels at lightning speed. Then they turned to the filet or sirloin on their table to begin slicing and portioning it. Every strike was as precise as a painter's brushstroke—accurate, fluid, and smooth. I must have stood there for twenty minutes, mesmerized.

A waitress led me to the office and introduced me to Jim Kurtz, the owner and general manager. A man of few words, Jim shook my hand and nodded for me to sit down. He asked me about my background and my experience.

Even though I had just met him, for some reason, I trusted this guy. I told him everything: about my past and about my dad. I told him I had been in trouble at school and what I had learned at Wendy's. "Look," I said, "I don't have a high school diploma, but I promise I will work hard and do a good job. I'll take as many hours as I can get and am willing to do anything if you'll just give me a chance."

Jim didn't say anything for a full minute. It seemed as if he were looking right through me and seeing himself at my age—a diamond in the rough.

"Come in this weekend," he said finally. "We'll do a working interview, or a *stage*, as we call it in the business," he said finally. "Let's see what you've got."

Then he started to open up. He told me he had served in Vietnam and seen some pretty rough things in his life. He shared how his passion for cooking had given him something to really focus on. His story inspired me. This guy was really rough around the edges, but he was a straight shooter and he had made something of himself. I liked him and trusted him. He was the real deal.

When I returned on Saturday, one of the guys pointed me to a locker room off the back of the kitchen and assigned me to a locker. *Well, that's a good sign,* I thought. He told me to find a chef coat in the rolling wardrobe just inside the locker room door and showed me how to tie the strings of my knee-length apron and hang two towels at my side. When I returned to the kitchen, he handed me a toque—a paper chef's hat that fit my big head perfectly.

"Come on," said Jim. "I'll show you around." The restaurant itself was huge, easily seating three hundred customers at once. The atmosphere had that old western steakhouse feel: rough hewn paneling on the walls and peanut shells littering the floor. Just off the dining room was a well-stocked double-tiered salad bar. As we toured the seating area, Jim introduced me to the bartenders: "This is Ricky." The head bartender nodded at me from behind the bar, a cigarette dangling from his mouth. I felt pretty comfortable with the guys back there; they reminded me of my dad.

In the dining room, everything was extremely clean, from the deep leather booths to the spotless tabletops. Hurrying to get ready for service, the waitstaff was bustling around the room, running a broom under the tables one last time and making sure all the condiments were set up as they should be.

"Let's go, let's go," one of the managers was yelling. "Pick it up, pick it up."

The focus and concentration of the cooks and waitstaff left me feeling excited and intimidated all at the same time.

In the kitchen, two hot lines mirrored one another—each made up of a full broiler station, a prime rib station, a sauté station, and a grill station. Two smaller stations stood between the lines.

"We call those the spud stations," Jim said. "That's where we do all of our sides: fries, baked potatoes, mashed potatoes, rice pilaf—every dish gets a side, so the spud station never slows down."

Behind the lines was the prep area and off to the side were the dishwashers, with both a dish pit and a pot pit. Jim made it very clear that we were never, *ever* to mix china and stainless.

I was so impressed. This was so much cooler than Wendy's.

Jim put me on the spud station, right in the middle of the action.

"Okay, kid," he said. "Let's see what you can do."

I wasn't too worried. I had made plenty of French fries at Wendy's, and I figured potatoes couldn't be that tough.

"Your main job is going to be just making sure we don't ever fall behind. You've got to time the cooking of the potatoes so you always have just enough ready," the line cook said after I joined him behind the line. The prep cooks had already scrubbed a huge number of the potatoes and wrapped each one in foil, lining them up on baking racks. Each rack of potatoes baked for an hour, so I knew I would need to time my quantities well. After that, it was simply a matter of following instructions. As the dining room started to fill up, the expediter called out the orders one right after another:

"I need four baked, one loaded, one no bacon, two butter only."

"I need two rice pilafs, three orders of fries, and two sautéed mushrooms."

"Give me two baked potatoes, one with sour cream only and one with sour cream and butter!"

We did six hundred and fifty covers that night, and somehow I managed to keep up pretty well. Even more importantly, I never ran out of potatoes. We went through about ten cases of French fries and about half as much rice pilaf. Although the work had a familiar feel to it, it was certainly much more labor-intensive than anything I had ever experienced at Wendy's.

This adrenaline rush was better than any drug I had ever used. The pressure, the stress, the high that came from keeping up with the organized chaos was amazing—and I loved it. I was hooked!

Jim was convinced too.

"Okay," he said. "Looks like you can handle this. Come back tomorrow and we'll fill out your paperwork and get you on the schedule ASAP."

I was so pumped to start working in the "real world," I could hardly wait for my two weeks to be up at Wendy's. On my first official day at the Scotch 'N Sirloin, I showed up at 8:00 in the morning, four hours before I was scheduled to be there. I couldn't help it—there was so much to learn and I wanted to learn it all *right now*!

Jim looked up in surprise from his butcher's table, where he was cutting sirloin with Doc and Ralph, the two other butchers.

"What are you doing here so early?" he asked. "You're not scheduled until noon."

"Don't worry," I assured him. "I won't punch in. I just want to learn. This is when all the butchering and prep is happening, and I wanted to see how it's all done."

"Well, by all means, be my guest," Jim said, smiling at me. "I know you're excited, but you're going to be here all day and all night. You need to pace yourself. It's a long race. Don't burn out early."

I spent the morning—and those that followed—watching the butchers as they stood around the stainless steel tables and wooden butcher blocks. I still couldn't believe how many different kinds of meat and seafood there were. I had never seen a whole fish before, and I didn't have the first clue about scaling and filleting. These guys made it seem easy and even fun. They told great stories about the Vietnam War and sports; it was obvious they had great camaraderie. As they talked, they moved their knives effortlessly through the muscle and sinew of a beautiful side of Black Angus, aged in a massive cooler and labeled chronologically. All the beef was aged for twenty-eight days before we used it.

By the end of my first week, I knew I really wanted this. The energy in the kitchen was addicting; and for whatever reason, I felt completely at home behind the line.

My official title at the Scotch was line cook, but everyone just called me the spud guy. We made everything from scratch: all the soups and stocks and dressings and sauces. All of our fries were hand cut and nothing came from a can or the freezer. Every day was an educational experience. I learned to butcher whole cuts of beef, pork loins, and whole chickens, as well as how to fillet salmon and cut down barrels of fresh swordfish and loins of tuna that came in the back door. I seasoned and marinated the whole prime rib before slow roasting it in huge roasting pans. And after it had been in the oven for three hours, I made stocks for the au jus from the root vegetables and pan drippings that had been under the meat.

After a full day prepping to set up the line—every container in its spot like little soldiers, labeled and organized—I moved to the line, occasionally stepping away from my spot at the spud station to help out other guys when they got in the weeds. At the end of the night, our stations looked like a train wreck.

I was working very long days, six days a week, and I was tired. But I was also excited. Before long, I realized that to be really valuable, I would need to be cross-trained so I could be put to work where I was needed most. I was getting a lot of experience, and I was getting it very quickly. Putting in extra hours, covering people's sick days and vacation days, I found that work could be just as addicting as drugs or alcohol.

I had a great vantage point from my spot on the potato line. Tony was usually up to his elbows making chicken French and veal piccata, and David ran the prime rib station like a well-oiled machine. We served a lot of prime, and David cut every slab to order: single cuts, double cuts, triple cuts, and even the "big man's cut." Sometimes on a busy weekend, we might go through six or eight prime ribs.

I really hoped that I could one day move to David's station and then eventually the sauté station. If all went well, I might even be able to work my way up to the broiler station and fill in for Doc or Ralph when they weren't there. I knew it would take time, but I was determined. For the first time in my life, my eyes were on a goal and I resolved to reach that goal—no matter what.

Over the coming weeks as I baked and dressed my potatoes, I kept a close eye on Doc as he worked the broiler station. He kept his station extremely well organized, with all the different meats labeled and separated by cut and weight. And by observing the way Doc did things, I began to pick up some of the subtle techniques and tricks of the trade.

At night, Ralph took over the broiler station. He really was a master at his craft, running the huge volume broilers and sometimes handling up to four hundred steaks a night. Ralph saw my interest and made it a point to talk to me about what he was doing. Somehow, he was able to keep track of all the orders, cuts, and temperatures and really make it all happen.

Both Ralph and Doc had an instinct about their work that really intrigued me. Those guys could throw down on the grill and the broiler like no one I had ever met before, but they never sacrificed quality or attention to detail in order to turn a ticket. These guys were passionate and humble about their work, but to me, they were rock stars.

I was actually in awe of just about everyone at the Scotch. They were all at least five to ten years older than me—once again, I was the baby of the bunch—and some of them had been in the industry longer than I had been alive. These guys were the real deal, and I knew I had better raise my game and pay attention because they were also great teachers. These were professional butchers and chefs who took their craft seriously. As a result, the Scotch 'N Sirloin was more than just another nice restaurant; it was Rochester's number-one steakhouse.

It took me about two years of working double shifts at the Scotch 'N Sirloin to fully understand all of the different stations, prep recipes, and kitchen procedures. As I listened to my coworkers discuss the merits of acid levels and tannins, I realized that I had learned more in that time than I had in ten years of school. This was my culinary high school. My classes included Food 101, Butchering 101, and Wine 101.

Since I was still living at home, it was easy for me to take on extra shifts. Just as I had done at Wendy's, I came in early and stayed late nearly every day. I also came in on my days off, both because I wanted to continue learning and because I didn't have anything else to do. Work was everything to me; it was my life.

I put in hours and hours of overtime, and finally Jim asked me to take Ralph's spot on the broiler when he moved on. This meant that I was in charge of my own little crew of prep guys, which was a lot of responsibility for a nineteen-year-old kid without a high school diploma. But the older guys in the kitchen respected me.

I was still doing drugs—along with everyone else in the kitchen— but I never came to work high. I knew I needed to be as clearheaded as possible in order to concentrate and keep up with the volume of covers every night. Day after day we gave our all in the kitchen, and night after night, we rewarded ourselves with a good bottle of scotch, a handful of joints, and a lot of cocaine. Six days a week, we stayed out until one or two in the morning, burning the candle at both ends. I ran home to catch a couple hours of sleep and a quick shower, and then I forced myself out of bed to get up and to do it all over again.

Sometimes I met up with Marco and Paulie and Eileen, and it was always great to catch up with them and hear what was going on in their lives. But for the most part, my focus was on climbing to the top of that kitchen ladder.

I could see a good living here. Cooking came easy to me and the pay was great—and as a bonus, I could still party. In fact, the two things seemed to go hand in hand, a perfect fit for me! When we weren't working, we spent a lot of time at a couple of little clubs downtown.

My coworkers and I would go to a club like the Orange Monkey or the Red Creek Inn, where we got to see some amazing performers like Stevie Ray Vaughan before they became big names. Often, each of us would pick out a girl who looked like she might be up for some casual, no-strings-attached sex, and then spend the rest of the night pursuing her. It was easy, fast, and fun. This was the first time since high school that I was actually in a position to pick up a girl. I was single, I had money, and I was pretty good at the game.

Rarely did I ever stop to think about what I was doing—although occasionally, I had to admit something deep in my spirit just wasn't right. Sometimes when I would wake up in the bed of a thirty-year-old cocktail waitress, head pounding and mouth filled with cotton, my heart was heavy with something that felt a little like guilt. But what did I have to be guilty about? Everyone else was doing it; why shouldn't I?

LAMB CHOPS WITH GARLIC JUS AND BOILED POTATOES

A traditional steakhouse, the Scotch 'N Sirloin was known for its prime cuts of beef, but it always featured specials that didn't include beef. Lamb chops, along with veal and pork chops, were popular. Ever since then, I've been a big fan of grilling or roasting lamb chops, which are a great alternative to chicken or beef. — *SERVES 4*

For the potatoes
12 fingerling potatoes
2 Tbs. kosher salt
5 coriander seeds
1 bay leaf

For the jus
¼ c. vegetable oil
½ lb. lamb scraps, from your local butcher
3 Tbs. whole butter
2 cloves garlic, crushed lightly
2 shallots, peeled and sliced ¼-inch thick
½ c. water
20 oz. veal or beef stock
1½ oz. sherry vinegar

For the lamb
¼ c. herb marinade (recipe below)
1 head garlic, cloves removed, skin on and crushed lightly
¼ c. olive oil
¼ c. vegetable oil
4 double-cut lamb chops, 6 to 8 oz. each
Kosher salt
Freshly cracked black pepper
2 Tbs. whole butter
2 four-inch rosemary sprigs

Herb marinade
¾ c. olive oil
1 tsp. minced garlic
1 tsp. fresh rosemary, chopped
1 tsp. lemon zest
½ Tbs. chopped parsley
Freshly cracked pepper
2 Tbs. orange juice

1. Whisk ingredients together.

TO MAKE POTATOES
1. Place the potatoes in a small saucepan and cover with cold water. Add salt to the pot with the coriander seeds and bay leaf.

2. Bring the potatoes to a simmer and cook until fork-tender. Reserve warm for service.

TO MAKE THE JUS

1. Add half the vegetable oil to the pan over high heat; once hot, add the lamb scrap meat. Cook the meat on high until it is completely caramelized.
2. Once caramelized, drain off the grease and add 2 Tbs. whole butter, allowing it to foam.
3. Add 2 garlic cloves and the sliced shallots. Allow them to cook in the butter with the lamb scraps until they begin to become soft. Do not allow the garlic or shallot to brown. Begin to scrape the bottom of the pan with a wooden spoon.
4. Once the garlic is cooked, add water to the pan and continue to scrape the bottom of the pan. Reduce the water until the bottom of pan is dry; then add the stock.
5. Bring the stock to a simmer and cook for half an hour.
6. Strain stock through a fine-mesh sieve and reduce remaining volume by one-quarter.
7. Reserve for service.

TO MAKE THE LAMB

1. Place lamb chops in herb marinade. Keep immersed for 4 to 6 hours.
2. Remove lamb from marinade; drain.
3. Preheat the oven to 400°F.
4. Season the lamb with kosher salt and black pepper and sear the flesh of the lamb until it is deep brown.
5. Place the lamb in the oven for 7 to 10 minutes, depending on your taste. Remove from oven, adding 2 Tbs. of whole butter and the rosemary. As the butter melts, baste the lamb with it.
6. Remove the lamb from the pan and allow it to rest for 3 to 5 minutes.
7. To plate, place four hot potatoes, split, in the center of the plate. Cut the lamb chop in half and arrange it with the cut side facing out. Spike the sauce with sherry vinegar, and drizzle 3 to 4 ounces on each plate. Garnish with five of the roasted garlic cloves, still in their skins.

9
STRATHALLAN

*If we confess our sins, He is faithful and just to forgive us
our sins and to cleanse us from all unrighteousness.*

1 JOHN 1:9

I'd been at the Scotch 'N Sirloin for just over two years when my dad was released from prison. Under the conditions of his five-year parole, he went to work for General Railway Signal Company.

Working the switches left him grimy and dirty every day. But prison had straightened him out in a lot of ways. He knew that if he wanted to do well on his probation, he had to change his environment, be accountable to his parole officer, and stay away from the people he'd been involved with before.

He and my mom started going to church at Sacred Heart regularly, and they even tried counseling to help them resolve their problems. After all we had been through, my dad really wanted to make things right for our family. He was serious about cleaning up his own lifestyle. He stopped smoking and started volunteering with Meals on Wheels. He also visited friends in local nursing homes, where he'd play cards with the residents. They loved him there—he could sit and talk with anyone.

Though my dad was proud of me for doing so well on the job, when he saw the way I was living my life outside of work, he couldn't help but be disappointed and angry. Finally one afternoon, my dad sat me down and told me it was time to clean up my act.

"Ricky, even though you have grown up in a lot of ways since I went away to 'school'"—which is how he referred to his time in jail—"you're still very young," he said. "You're still a kid but you are trying to live and play like an adult, and you don't have the maturity or experience to do that. You're going to end up hurting yourself or someone else if you don't change your ways."

Speaking as a typical know-it-all teenager, I assured him that I was fine, but I promised I would try to tone down the partying a little if it would make him feel better.

Later that week, I decided to head home after work instead of going out with the guys. The newness of having my dad around still hadn't worn off, and I really wanted to get to know him again and rebuild our relationship. Of course I stuck around the restaurant for a bit after my shift ended, but I only had a couple of beers and smoked a little bit of pot. I felt pretty good when I climbed into my Z28 IROC and headed for the interstate, stereo blasting and flying down the highway at 80 miles per hour as I always did.

What I didn't realize was that sometime during my shift, someone had tried to steal the Cragar rims off my car. Whoever it was had stolen all but one of the lug nuts from each wheel—the locknut that could be removed only using a specific tool. As I exited off the express ramp, the remaining locknut on the back right wheel sheered completely off and sent the tire flying. Before I knew what was happening, the axle hit the ground, shooting off sparks and sending my sports car veering off into the steep ditch alongside the ramp. A few inches farther to the right and I would have smashed head-on into the concrete light pole, surely killing myself—game over.

I barely had time to catch my breath when a police officer showed up. Even though I felt pretty coherent, he could see that I'd been drinking. Given the combination of pot and alcohol in my system, I knew I was in trouble.

But as luck would have it, the cop wasn't a New York state trooper. He was a local guy who happened to know my dad. He told me to sit down in the back of his car while he called in the accident and contacted my folks. I was shaking.

When my dad showed up a half hour later, he shook the officer's hand and thanked him for taking care of me. They talked for a while and then the cop turned to go.

"You stay out of trouble now, you hear?" he said to me as he walked toward his car. "Drive more carefully in the future."

I nodded. "I will."

My dad watched the squad car until it disappeared on the interstate and then he turned to me.

"What were you thinking?" he screamed. "I know you've been drinking and so did that cop. I know you've been doing drugs because I found roach clips in your room. You could have gotten a DWI; you could have killed someone; you could have killed *yourself*!"

As he spoke, he paced back and forth in front of me, waving his hands for emphasis. "You are going into rehab and that's all there is to it. You will either go voluntarily or I will drag you there myself."

I knew I was busted. I also knew I had a problem. I *had* been acting crazy and reckless, putting myself and others in danger. My dad was right. It was a miracle I hadn't killed myself or someone else yet. My life was all about access and excess—and yet, it still felt strangely empty.

The next day, my parents enrolled me in a drug and alcohol rehabilitation program at Rochester General Hospital. For the first few days of the program I pretty much just went through the motions, learning what answers I needed to give in order to get the approving nod, knowing when to act sad and remorseful and when to appear tough and determined to fight my addictions. But by the third week, I had to admit, some of the stuff was actually making sense. The counselors encouraged us to relinquish ourselves to a higher power, to let God release us from the bondage of drugs and alcohol.

In a way, I realized that my parents were modeling the two choices ahead of me. I thought about how my mom responded when things seemed so out of control in our lives. Like me, she was consumed with anger. On the other hand, I remembered the comfort and warmth I felt sitting in the pew next to my dad at Sacred Heart. He honored tradition and had a soft heart. Which would it be for me? Would I allow bitterness and anger to cloud everything I did, or would I choose to leave the past behind, work hard, and build a new life?

When I left rehab and went back to work, things were different. I could feel the eyes of everyone in the kitchen following me as I walked to my station and gathered up my knives. Jim Kurtz stood in the doorway of his office and watched me closely. Catching my eye, he jerked his head toward the office, indicating that he wanted to talk to me privately.

"We're glad you're back, Ricky," he said. "I'm not here to judge you. But I've been through a lot of stuff in my life and I don't want to lose you. I hope you've gotten all this taken care of and it's not going to be an issue from this point on."

I assured him that I was fine, and that he could count on me just as he always had.

"This job means a lot to me," I said. "The drugs will *not* be a problem. I promise you that."

Whether I liked it or not, I knew things had changed. I was no longer just one of the guys; now I was the kid brother whom everyone needed to keep an eye on.

I went back to finish setting up my station for that day's service, and one of the waitresses stepped behind the line, waiting for me to finish. Sally was extremely attractive, and I'd done my best to hook up with her, but until today she never wanted anything to do with me romantically. Now here she was, coming into my section of the kitchen and looking like she wanted to talk.

"Hey, Rick," she said. "I heard about what happened. I'm sorry things were so bad for you." I nodded and mumbled something about rumors always making things sounds worse than they were.

"You know, it is possible to get clean and still have a great life," Sally said. "I go to this really great church. I'd love it if you would come with me to Bible study tomorrow night."

Oh man. Bible study? In a church? That was pushing it, even for someone as attractive as Sally. But I had to admit, there really was something different about her. She always seemed to be happy, or at least peaceful, and I could use a little of whatever it was that made her that way. I told her I would think about it, and by the end of the shift I decided it was worth a shot.

When Sally picked me up at the restaurant the following night, I was both nervous and excited. I had no idea what to expect. Mostly, I hoped she would want to go out with me if I went to church with her. But there was also a small, almost hidden part of me that thought maybe this whole higher power thing was exactly what I had been looking for.

Sally pushed a cassette tape into the player, and I was immediately drawn to the music. It was heavy metal—my kind of music—but I had never heard it before.

"Who is this?" I asked, pointing to the tape player.

"It's a band called Stryper," she said, handing me the cassette case. "They're a Christian heavy metal band and their songs are about praising God, not sex and drugs."

Christian heavy metal? Seriously? I didn't know there even was such a thing, but surprisingly, I liked it.

"I have a bunch more tapes at home you might like," she said, reaching into the backseat. "Here," she said. "I got you this." She handed me a black leather Bible. Even though I'd been to church as a child, I had never owned a Bible before. And this was certainly a Bible—big and obvious and impossible to hide.

"This is the *New* King James Version," she said. I hadn't even realized there was an *old* King James Version, but I thanked her anyway.

That first night of Bible study, I was pretty overwhelmed. It seemed like these people were speaking a foreign language, and I didn't understand most of what went on. They talked about being born again, which made absolutely no sense at all. But even so, I was really drawn to the positive energy and love I felt in that little sanctuary. I liked the idea of getting right with God, fellowshipping with others, and turning my life around. As I sat in that group and listened to everyone talk, the empty feeling that always gnawed at the bottom of my soul didn't seem quite as painful.

I was ready for a change in my life, and like I did with everything else, I went at this church thing full force. I started reading my new Bible and studying everything I could find about Jesus. I attended

Bible study every Wednesday night, and I cut out the drinking and the drugs completely. I also quit smoking—even though that was the hardest addiction of all to give up.

Finally one night, the pastor started talking about the fact that God offers us all "new life in Christ." Then he asked if any of us wanted to come down to the altar and commit our lives to Christ. I definitely wanted a new life, but I wasn't sure I was ready to walk down that aisle in front of the whole group. But once everyone's eyes were closed and heads were bowed, I felt something pushing me out of my seat in spite of myself. I stood up and began to walk toward the front of the church. It was almost as if I was being drawn, like something outside of myself was making me move forward—even as the voice in my head cried out in protest, *What are you doing? Are you crazy?*

When I reached the altar, I told the pastor I wanted to be born again. He smiled broadly and patted me on the back, leading me over to the front pew. Together, we knelt in front of the pew and I repeated the lines of the prayer he told me to say:

"Dear heavenly Father, I know that I'm a sinner. Please forgive me. I know that you sent your Son to die for me and take away my sins. Tonight I accept your free gift of salvation and new life in Christ. In Jesus' name, amen."

I didn't feel much different after that, and I really wasn't sure I understood what that prayer had been all about. But I sure enjoyed the feeling I got from being around all of these positive people. I figured that being born again was just like anything else, something I would have to learn about as I went. Their social activities were so foreign to me—going to coffee shops or playing softball—but I was up for trying them.

In the coming weeks, my new group of friends did their best to keep me busy when I wasn't working. They wanted me to see that it was possible to have fun without partying. And at home, my parents were even getting along better. Mom seemed to be functioning at a higher level again—at least she was talking more, and not just to herself.

Marco and Paulie tried to help me stay away from drugs too. Now when they came over, we usually just hung out and watched TV or swam in the pool rather than getting wasted or hitting the bars. They were happy to cut back on their own partying in order to support me, although none of them wanted anything to do with my newfound faith. I was "sold out for Jesus," and they were pretty sure I had joined some sort of crazy cult.

Now that I was clean and my head was clear, I realized it was time to start thinking seriously about my future. I had learned so much at the Scotch 'N Sirloin, but I knew I didn't want to stay there forever. I didn't want to be stuck on a broiler all day and party all night with nothing lasting to show for it: no kids, no family. I was ready to take my career to the next level.

I started cooking at home for my friends and bought a bunch of cookbooks—Escoffier's *Le Guide Culinaire*, James Beard's *American Cookery*, and Julia Child's *Mastering the Art of French Cooking*. Because it was such a struggle for me to read, I had to ask people to read passages to me. I was determined to figure out what I would need to do in order to pursue a career as a professional chef. I had Italian and American cooking pretty much down, but if I wanted to make it in this business, I would need to understand French cooking.

I started watching the classified ads for a position in a French restaurant or a large hotel, someplace I could move beyond the foundations I had learned at the Scotch and really cut my teeth on culinary technique.

After weeks of searching, I finally found what I was looking for: the Strathallan Hotel in Rochester was interviewing for a line cook. This was it! The Strathallan was rated one of the best hotel restaurants in the city. Since it was a hotel kitchen, I would be exposed to room service, catering, banquets, and pastry, as well as honing my breakfast, lunch, and dinner skills. Plus, if I worked my way up, I might even be able to get some benefits.

This time when I turned in my application, I was much more confident than I had been when I applied at the Scotch. Even though I still wasn't strong at reading or spelling and didn't have my high school diploma, I did have plenty of experience in the kitchen. I told the interviewer all about my responsibilities at Wendy's and then at the Scotch, making sure to toss out a few industry terms, just to prove that I could understand "kitchen-speak."

After talking with me for about an hour, the manager sent me down to the kitchen to meet with Greg Broman, the hotel's executive chef. Greg was well-respected in the Rochester area, having earned the Strathallan numerous awards and recognitions over the years. I was excited to actually meet him face-to-face.

Walking down the stairs into the basement, I was totally unprepared for the Strathallan kitchen. Unlike the kitchen at the Scotch, this one was truly old school. Running under the entire length of the hotel, the cavernous room was lined with heavy outdated equipment and huge ovens. But even though it was old and very dark, the kitchen was perfectly organized and super clean. The place was bustling with activity. Prep cooks dressed in chef whites and perfect toques moved quickly through the aisles, arms laden with pans of produce and trays of raw meat. Line cooks hustled around the prep area, whisking up thick sauces and cleaning up from that morning's breakfast service. Five pristine gueridon carts stood along the wall, already set with linen tablecloths and tableside cooking tools.

Chef Broman's office was little more than a storage room with a desk. Dry goods lined the walls, with paper products and chef's coats stacked up on the floor next to the huge wooden desk. How could someone with such a great culinary reputation be stuck in a room like this? Greg Broman was an anomaly on every level. Like no one I had ever met before, he looked nothing like an award-winning executive chef. With curly hair and a cigarette dangling from his lips, he walked with a limp and looked like he might be in pain. His face was weathered and rough.

I liked him already. I knew that on paper, my experience must have seemed pretty limited, so I tried to tell him all that I had learned in my short time at Wendy's and the Scotch 'N Sirloin. Then I admitted that I didn't have a high school diploma or a culinary degree.

"Well, that could be a problem," Greg said. "But in this business, you can definitely learn more in the kitchen than in a classroom. Hands-on experience—*that* will be your education."

He went on to tell me about his own background. Before heading up the kitchen here, he had worked under André Soltner, the well-known chef-owner of Lutece in New York City. I had just read an article about

Soltner in the last issue of *Gourmet*, and I was blown away. If I could work under Greg Broman at the Strathallan, maybe some of what he had learned from Soltner would trickle down to me.

Greg asked me to come in the next day to do a working interview. He wanted to cook with me and see my knife skills. I definitely knew a lot about cutting down sirloins and tenderloins, but most of what I knew I had picked up by watching the guys at the Scotch. No one had taught me the finer points of using my knives. The guys at the Strath were butchering beautiful racks of lamb and loins of venison. They were also creating intricate vegetable carvings as well as huge fruit tables and ice sculptures for their buffets. I knew nothing about that kind of work.

Knowing what a daunting task I faced the next day, I went home and pulled out my books. I quickly became frustrated. As much as I tried to make sense of the words on the page, they just jumbled up in my brain. I was able to pick up some things by studying the illustrations, but it wasn't enough to master various techniques. I knew the only way I was going to learn to make the perfect dice or brunoise would be by watching someone else do it first.

The next day, I helped Greg prep for that night's service, which included two banquets. We made sauces and stocks, chopped vegetables, and trimmed meat. I managed to keep pace with Greg and really enjoyed watching him work. He was truly a master at his craft and a great technician.

I'd been in the business long enough by now to know that the best thing for me to do was to keep my eyes open and my mouth shut, help as much as I could, and most importantly, stay out of the way. If we happened to get a few minutes of downtime, I wiped down the counters or grabbed a broom and swept our work area. I liked to clean—my mom was a cleaning lady, how could I not? Plus, I wanted to make a good impression because I really wanted this job.

At the end of the day, Greg reached out his hand and said, "Well done, Rick. I see a lot of raw talent in you. We'll need to get you up to speed on some of the French techniques and terminology, but you're already ahead of the game in other areas. What you need is a mentor, someone to really show you the ropes."

He took a drag on his cigarette and blew a billow of smoke into the air around his head.

"You've got the talent and the tools, but I've seen that before. Guys with talent like yours tend to get cocky, and I won't put up with that. Here's the deal: I will help you out, but you've got to do what you're told and put in the hours.

"I'm going to be extremely hard on you, and you need to be ready for that. Think you're tough enough to handle that?"

"I am willing to do whatever it takes, Chef."

"Okay, now let's talk about your knife skills. Where is your knife kit?"

My knife kit? At the Scotch, all of our blades had been provided by a rental company that came in every week and replenished our supply with freshly sharpened instruments. I didn't know I needed to have my own.

"I don't have a knife kit, Chef," I said, embarrassed.

Greg tossed me a catalog. "Well, you'd better get one. At the very least, you'll need a twelve-inch chef's knife, a boning knife, a slicer, a serrated knife, a paring knife, and a steel. And you'll also need a knife kit to carry them in. Oh, and you'd better get yourself a good potato peeler since you're going to be peeling a lot of potatoes. Take a look at this and tell me what you can afford. I'll get it ordered for you."

I looked at the glossy pages and blinked. Knives were expensive! I had the money, but who wanted to spend it on cooking utensils? Then suddenly it clicked. Like a rock star's guitar, knives were my instruments—the tools of my trade.

I picked out the best knives I could afford and handed the book back to Greg.

"Good choices, all of them. Now don't be late on your first day. I won't put up with that."

I smiled and hurried back to turn in my notice at the Scotch. I couldn't wait to start. Even though I'd be making less money and working at a lower position, the experience and education I could gain at the Strath would definitely be worth the sacrifice.

Once I started at the Strath, I realized that my role was actually more like an apprentice than an employee, and working with Greg was like working with a true craftsman. His technical skills were brilliant. He took seriously his role as my mentor and really put me through the paces. His disciplines were the best of the best—and he expected nothing less from the people who worked for him.

When things really heated up during service, the decibel level of Greg's yelling rose to match the intensity of the situation. Every other word that came out of his mouth was a curse word, and we knew to keep our eyes open for flying plates. He was the chef—the king. He was a tough taskmaster with extremely high expectations, but he had the talent and reputation to back them up.

Greg was especially fanatical about his coolers. Sometimes out of the blue, he would walk into the cooler and just go crazy: "This is a mess; who closed last night? Why isn't this produce consolidated? This is two days old! Tramonto, get in here—*now*!"

I learned very quickly to leave my ego at the door, especially when Greg was ranting and raving. And as the low guy on the totem pole, I usually bore the brunt of his emotional outbursts. Following one of Greg's "cooler tantrums" as we called them, I'd have to go in and take everything out of the cooler and put it on the prep table. Then I would scrub the walls, scrub the floors, and relabel everything before putting it back neatly.

In addition to scrubbing coolers, I also got all the grunt work Greg could throw at me. Some might have been demoralized by his harsh words and incessant demands. Thankfully, I had already developed a pretty thick skin from growing up in my parents' house. Without it, I wouldn't have lasted a day in the Strathallan kitchen.

I vowed I would do whatever it took to make Greg glad he hired me. As I stood around the stainless steel table with other prep cooks, I studied the way they sharpened their knives and made light work of the huge pile of produce in the middle of the table. These guys could turn a mushroom or slice a turnip faster than anyone I'd ever seen. The work was ongoing, but it never felt overwhelming. I loved the camaraderie of being part of the culinary team.

Since I knew absolutely no French, I struggled to get up to speed and at least learn some of the basic terms. The Strath's kitchen was structured much like the classical French "brigade" system, which included a hot appetizer station, a fish station, a meat station, a veg station, a sauce station, a garde-manger station, and a pastry station.

Huge loading docks led into the kitchen, which allowed us to go right into the truck to check in the deliveries. We checked the quality of fish and meat from inside the truck. This way, we could make sure there were no mistakes with the order before the food even came into the kitchen.

I was able to work three times as hard as in the past because I wasn't doing any drugs. Though I was scheduled from six to six, I usually showed up two or three hours early and almost always stayed long after my shift ended. I took on extra hours whenever I could, and often came in on my days off. I began to invest in cookbooks and cooking magazines, knives, and tools. My whole focus had begun to change, though in reality, I was only trading one obsession for another: drugs for work.

Going 100 miles per hour all day, every day, I quickly proved that I was willing to do the job—and then some. I was young and energetic, and I would have run through a brick wall for Greg. He knew it too.

Though I had worked the meat station at the Scotch, I really began to hone my skills at the Strath. We were doing all the old-school stuff—French onion soup, veal piccata, beef Wellington, and Dover sole—as well as a lot of tableside cooking—rack of lamb, lobster Newberg, baked Alaska, steak Diane.

As in most French kitchens, Greg expected precision and detail. When I plated up salads or created garnishes at the garde-manger station, he reminded me that I was the one responsible for creating a customer's first and last impression of the entire meal. He made me focus on the disciplines and techniques, showing me how to choose produce, perfect my knife skills, and develop top-notch sauces and stocks. And every night he sent me home with homework.

"Tonight, I want you to go home and learn everything you can about hollandaise sauce," he told me one day. When I got home, I pored over my copy of *La Technique*, but once again I got frustrated by my inability to comprehend what I was studying. The next day I admitted to Greg that I couldn't read well. He then showed me how to make the sauce himself.

Whisking the clarified butter into the egg yolks and lemon juice, he explained the meaning of French terms like *sabayon*, *espagnole*, and *chaud-froid*. And then he quizzed me on variations, uses, and alternatives for hollandaise. From then on, Greg spent a lot of time explaining and demonstrating the principles of food science to me. It was like science class at school, only I got paid—and I frequently got yelled at.

I didn't really mind. I knew I could do this as long as I could find people willing to teach me through hands-on experience. I definitely learned better when someone showed me how to do something. Reading just seemed to make me more confused. Though I tried taking notes, often I couldn't make sense of them later. Simple drawings helped, as did my photographic memory. As long as someone showed me how to do something a few times, I would get it.

Unlike the Scotch, the Strath had a separate pastry kitchen, which excited me because I had never really been exposed to any baking or dessert making. And the pastry chef was top notch; I loved to watch her work. Gale Gand approached pastry making with all the flourish of an artist approaching a blank canvas. Whether it was a chocolate torte or an old-fashioned French soufflé, Gale's creations were always unique and amazing.

Just as impressive, she seemed to be making it in this very harsh, male-dominated world of cooking. Gale was one of only three females among the thirty members of the kitchen staff and the only woman among the five department managers.

We all respected her because we knew that none of us could do what she did. And since pastry was such a huge part of our kitchen service, the Strath couldn't afford to lose her. Pastry chefs were hard to come by—particularly ones as talented as she.

Her flair for the artistic was no accident. She already had a degree from the Cleveland Institute of Art and was still trying to decide if she wanted to be a chef or an artist. She and her husband were originally from the North Shore of Chicago, and when she wasn't at the restaurant, she was busy working on a bachelor of fine arts degree in metalsmithing from Rochester Institute of Technology.

As part of my training, I spent three weeks in the pastry kitchen, and I found Gale fascinating. Seven years older than me, she was everything I was not. Bubbly, lively, and superpositive, she had a zest for life that I craved. I wondered if maybe she was a Christian, but when I asked her, she told me she was Jewish. Wow. I had never met a Jewish girl before. I was intrigued.

Gale was well-traveled and well-read, and she was extremely knowledgeable about the food world. She had been to France many times and had eaten at many of the restaurants we were trying to emulate. She told me what cookbooks and pastry books I needed to add to my collection, and what magazines to read. She introduced me to noted French pastry chef Gaston Lenôtre, along with the chefs Auguste Escoffier and Fernand Point, both considered fathers of modern French cuisine. She had never intended to become a pastry chef—which is what female chefs were generally expected to do—but she really had the touch, and Greg knew talent when he saw it.

Even so, Gale often came over to the prep table or into the savory side of the kitchen so she could watch and learn. She was pretty good friends with one of the only other women in the kitchen, Mary, from whom I had learned a lot just by watching her work behind the line. Gale and Mary managed to hold their own pretty well with the guys in the kitchen, who could be pretty raunchy. What might be considered sexual harassment today—telling an inappropriate joke or grabbing at a female staffer when she walked into the cooler—was nothing unusual back then. But both women could put a guy in his place pretty quickly. They knew how to take the razzing—and give it right back when they had to.

We all worked long hours. Our fourteen-hour shifts included nine to ten hours of prep followed by four to five hours of service. After setting up my station, I often sat on top of the low ice cream cooler next to the pastry kitchen to eat my staff meal, rest my aching feet, and wait for service to start again. Sometimes Gale and Mary joined me as well, and the three of us would talk about the food world and which new chefs we had recently heard about.

We were hearing about the new American food revolution. Jonathan Waxman and Alice Waters had been trained by the great French and European chefs and now were putting a new twist on the classical techniques they had learned. They took classic flavor profiles—like macaroni and cheese—and developed recipes like truffle mac and cheese. Some of these American chefs were becoming prominent, and a few of them, like Waxman, were opening restaurants in New York.

"We should all go cook in New York City," Mary would say, a wistful look in her eye. "That's where all the good stuff is happening. If you want to be somebody, you've got to do New York."

I'd just roll my eyes and laugh. The idea of leaving Rochester was so far outside my scope of possibility, I couldn't even begin to think about what cooking in Manhattan might look like.

"Why do you always look so depressed and sad?" Gale would tease, poking me in the ribs. "What are you pouting about?"

"I'm not pouting," I'd say. "Just storing up my energy for what's to come. Besides, not all of us can be as happy as you all the time. Don't you ever have problems?"

I liked Gale, but as much as I was drawn to her smile and her positive attitude, I knew enough to keep my distance. Gale was extremely intelligent and she had a great passion for food. A ripe peach could make her cry. I loved that she saw the beauty and art of raw product, and I found myself intensely attracted to her.

But she was married. I knew better than to mess with a married woman, especially one who was so clearly out of my reach. Besides, I couldn't afford to lose my focus. I still had so much to learn, and my hands were full just trying to keep up with Greg's demands.

At first, I was so engrossed in the work of studying and training and cooking, I didn't even notice how hard-core the other guys in the kitchen were about their drinking and their drugs. Right from the start, I had made it pretty clear to them that I was a born-again Christian and was trying to keep my nose clean. Most of them thought I was crazy and mocked me by calling me "Jesus Freak" or "Bible-Thumper." I didn't mind it at first, but when Jimmy Swaggart's infidelities were publically exposed and then Jim Bakker's *PTL Club* imploded a few months later, I really took a lot of heat.

"See," Greg laughed at me. "I told you it was all a scam. These guys just want your money. That Christian stuff is nothing but a waste of time."

I was embarrassed and confused. I had no idea how to deal with this, and then about that same time, the pastor of the little church I had been attending announced he was having an affair with one of the congregants and stepped down.

Still young in my faith and knowing very little Scripture, I was totally unprepared and unequipped for something like this. Though I couldn't see it then, my faith had largely been in a pastor and a church rather than in Christ and the Bible. I realized that Greg was probably right: I had been sucked into a cult. I decided my newfound faith was all bogus. The Catholic church seemed to have more integrity, and I wondered why I'd wandered away from it. But instead of reexamining my faith, I walked away from God altogether.

I decided I didn't have anything to lose by joining the guys after work for a beer once in a while. But what started as a single drink and maybe a cigarette on the weekends quickly turned into four drinks and a couple of joints every night, and before long, I was right back in the middle of the party.

Sometimes Gale would join us for a glass of wine after work, and I found myself pouring out my frustrations to her. She had such a great way of making things look better than they were.

Gale and I began sharing our stories and eating our dinners together every night on the ice cream cooler. She told me about what it was like to be Jewish and explained her faith's culture and belief system. She talked about going to college and growing up on the North Shore of Chicago. I told her about what it was like to be Italian and the importance of food and family meals as I was growing up. I also confided in her about dropping out of high school and my dad's Mafia past. She told me about her marital problems, and I told her about my time in rehab. Her family was in the music business, and she was impressed by my knowledge of the music industry and its history.

When she told me she was thinking about leaving her husband, I decided it was time to pour on the romance. Though I didn't have a lot of experience in wooing women—just sleeping with them—I knew that cards and flowers were usually part of the deal. But given that I usually worked from six o'clock in the morning until eleven or twelve at night, those things weren't so easy to come by. So I made do. I'd pull out a blank sheet from the day's produce order pad and write my own cards, trying to communicate through poems and short notes. I carved little roses out of radishes and scallions and left them on her car after work.

My handwriting and spelling were atrocious, so much so that sometimes Gale had to ask me what I had written. One morning, she brought me a card I had left in her locker the day before.

"Rick," she said, holding out a folded piece of paper. "Where did you get this poem that you wrote for me?"

I blushed. As much as I tried to be creative and original, sometimes the easiest way to express what was on my heart was to steal the lyrics from a rock song.

"That's from a Journey song," I said. "I know it's not my own words, but it's exactly what I feel: 'Here I am with open arms, hoping you'll see what your love means to me . . .'"

She smiled. "I do see, and I love the card. Thank you."

I nodded and she turned to go, but then stopped.

"Rick, do you know what dyslexia is?"

I shook my head. Never heard of it.

"It's a kind of learning disability, and I have it to some degree," she said. "I think you might have it too."

What? I tried to process what she was saying. Why would she think I had a learning disability? Just because I had stolen a couple of lines from a song?

"Why do you say that?"

She held out the card. Yes, my handwriting was awful, but a lot of people had bad writing. When my doctor wrote me a prescription, I couldn't even make out his instructions.

"See this word here?" She pointed to the third line. "Not only did you mix up these two words and put 'means' before 'love,' you also switched the letters: M-A-E-N-S."

At first glance I thought she was mistaken. The words looked right to me. But when I studied it closer, I realized she was right.

"I don't know how I did that. I was looking at it the whole time I was writing it down," I said. "And I definitely never thought I might have a learning disability. You say you have this thing too?"

"Yep. It's called dyslexia and it's pretty common. Even teachers can miss it though. They usually just try to push kids through the system and figure they will catch up along the way."

That had certainly been the case for me. Only I never caught up. I just gave up. Gale was the first person since Marco to realize what a struggle it was for me to do simple academic tasks like writing a note or reading a recipe. She was appalled that no one had caught on to the source of my struggles in school or tried to help me. She'd been brought up to believe education was very important. The fact that she cared and wanted to help me learn to read and spell better meant the world to me.

We started spending more time together after that, and often Gale would help me figure out how to convert a recipe or read through an order guide. I hated when one of us had a day off, because it meant being away from each other. I started coming up with excuses to call her at home. Pretending that I was trying to work on my pastry skills, I would call and ask her questions about frosting or batter thickness— anything just to talk to her.

I really wanted to be with Gale, especially now that she and her husband were talking about divorce. I knew we made a good fit, and I told her so. She admitted that the feelings were mutual, but she insisted that even if she left her husband, she wouldn't be staying in Rochester.

"This is the perfect time for me to find work in New York," she said. "I've been talking to Mary about it for months now. If I am going to do something with this pastry thing, I can't stay. I need to work in a bigger city with some of the top chefs."

I knew she was right. Greg had told me the same thing about my own career.

"You have huge natural talent," he told me after I'd been at the Strath for about a year. "If you aren't going to go back to high school or to culinary school, you are going to have to do it the hard way—the very hard way. You have to move around to major metropolitan cities and apprentice again and again and again under well-known chefs in many different regions. The chefs in California are cooking differently than the chefs in Maine or in Chicago. They are working with different regional preferences and types of produce. You'll need to spend time learning different types of cuisine—Italian, French, Mediterranean. That will become your apprenticeship program.

"Every time you start with a new chef, you will have to start over and take a step down because you'll be learning a new cuisine and will be last in the pecking order. Give yourself a good eight to ten years to work up the ladder and learn your craft well. Don't take any shortcuts. It won't be easy, but it will be worth it."

When I had first started down this road, I had no idea how long the journey would be. It didn't matter that I could hold my own in the kitchen. What mattered was having the means, the business savvy, and the connections. Without those things, I'd never make it in the food world. I didn't know how I was going to get to the next level, but I didn't think too much about it. I knew exactly where I wanted to go. I wanted to have my own kitchen and create my own style of food. I wanted to play in the big leagues. I wanted to be a chef.

ROASTED STUFFED VEAL LOIN WITH PROSCIUTTO, FONTINA, SPINACH, AND OVEN-DRIED TOMATOES

At the Strathallan, Greg liked to showcase old-world-spirited dishes like beef Wellington that could be carved tableside and served on big silver platters. This is a good example of such a dish.

The soul of this dish, however, is my mom's. She roasted stuffed veal on the holidays and always on my birthday, cooking it as my grandmother had taught her, who had learned it from her mother. This recipe is inspired by hers, though I have enhanced it with oven-dried tomatoes and truffles.

I wrap the veal in caul fat, an old-fashioned, old-world technique. It effectively adds moisture, and since it renders during cooking, it does not add a lot of fat. Ask your butcher for caul fat, which is the membrane that encloses the paunch of hogs, sheep, and veal calves. Caul fat comes in a roll, often packed in salt, and resembles sausage casing. — *SERVES 6*

One 3- to 4-pound loin of veal, trimmed of fat and sinew
12 paper-thin slices prosciutto di Parma
1 c. spinach, blanched
1 c. grated fontina cheese
½ c. oven-dried tomatoes (see page 5)
8 oz. caul fat (see introductory note above)
¼ c. olive oil
6 russet potatoes (about 2 lb.)
3 Tbs. kosher salt
½ c. heavy cream
10 Tbs. unsalted butter
24 icicle radishes

1 c. water
Kosher salt
Freshly ground black pepper
1 c. red wine sauce (recipe follows)
1 c. white truffle emulsion (recipe follows)
Chopped black truffles, for garnishing

1. Preheat oven to 375°F.
2. Slice the loin nearly all the way through the center so that you can open it like a book. Gently pound with a meat tenderizer until it is an even thickness. Lay the prosciutto slices over the loin. Spread the spinach over the prosciutto and sprinkle with grated cheese. Spread the oven-dried tomatoes near the bottom of the loin in a single row. Beginning with the edge nearest you, roll the veal into a log.
3. Lay the caul fat in a single layer on a work surface. Put the veal log on the fat and wrap the fat around the veal. Tie the roll with kitchen twine at ½-inch intervals.
4. Heat the oil in a large, ovenproof skillet over medium-high heat and sear the veal on all sides until it is golden brown. Transfer to the oven and roast for 12 to 16 minutes or until medium rare.
5. Meanwhile, peel the potatoes and cut them into equal-size pieces. Transfer the potatoes to a large saucepan and add enough cold water to cover by about 3 inches. Add salt. Bring to a boil over medium-high heat, reduce the heat, and simmer for about 20 minutes or until tender. Drain the potatoes in a colander, then press them through a ricer. Press potatoes through a tamis (cloth strainer) or fine-mesh sieve into a bowl.
6. In a small saucepan, heat the cream and 8 Tbs. of the butter over medium-low heat until the butter melts. Gently fold the cream mixture into the potatoes, and season to taste with salt and pepper. Cover to keep warm.
7. Cut the radishes into quarters. In a sauté pan, heat the remaining 2 Tbs. of butter and 1 c. of water over low heat. When the butter melts, add the radishes and cook for 10 to 15 minutes or until tender. Drain and season to taste with salt and pepper. Cover to keep warm.
8. In a small saucepan, heat the red wine sauce over medium heat until heated through.
9. To serve, spoon some of the mashed potatoes into the center of each plate. Place 4 of the radishes on the potatoes and then arrange 2 slices of the veal on each plate. Drizzle red wine sauce over the meat and potatoes. Spoon some of the truffle emulsion around the veal. Garnish with chopped truffles.

Red Wine Sauce
2 Tbs. olive oil
½ c. chopped carrots
½ c. chopped celery
⅛ c. chopped shallots
1 head garlic, root end cut out
12 oz. dry red wine
1 sprig fresh thyme
2 c. veal or beef stock

1 Tbs. butter
½ orange
½ Tbs. fresh tarragon, chopped
Kosher salt and freshly ground pepper

1. Heat olive oil over medium heat in saucepan. Add carrots, celery, shallots, and garlic; cook until lightly browned and softened, about 8 to 10 minutes.
2. Add wine and thyme and bring to boil over high heat. Lower heat and simmer 10 to 20 minutes until bottom of pan is almost dry.
3. Add stock and simmer over medium heat. Lower heat and simmer 30 minutes or until the liquid is reduced to about 2½ cups.
4. Strain through fine-mesh sieve into clean pot. Whisk in butter and juice from half an orange. Simmer 3 to 5 more minutes. Just before removing from heat, add tarragon. Season to taste with salt and pepper. After allowing sauce to cool, cover and refrigerate for 4 to 6 days. Freezes well for up to 2 months.

White Truffle Emulsion (makes about 2 cups)
3 Tbs. unsalted butter
5 shallots, thinly sliced
3 fresh thyme sprigs
1 bay leaf
2 tsp. black peppercorns
1 c. vermouth
1 c. dry white wine
2 c. heavy cream
Ice and ice water for an ice bath
2 Tbs. white truffle oil
Kosher salt
Freshly ground white pepper

1. In a medium-size saucepan, melt 1 Tbs. of the butter over low heat. Add the shallots, thyme, bay leaf, and peppercorns, and cook for 5 to 7 minutes or until the shallots are softened but not colored. Add the vermouth and white wine and bring to a boil over medium-high heat. Reduce the heat and simmer for 25 to 30 minutes or until most of the wine has evaporated and the bottom of the pan is almost dry.
2. Add the heavy cream and bring to a boil. Remove from the heat and let cool slightly. Strain through a chinois or fine-mesh sieve into a bowl. Set the bowl in a larger bowl containing ice and ice water. Stir for about 10 minutes or until completely cool.
3. When cool, use the emulsion immediately or cover the bowl and refrigerate it until needed.
4. When ready to use the emulsion, combine 2 cups of the chilled mixture with the truffle oil over medium heat and heat. Add the remaining butter and cook until the butter melts, taking care the liquid does not boil. Remove the pan from the heat and season to taste with salt and white pepper.
5. Using a handheld immersion blender, whip until foamy. Use the foamy top of the truffle emulsion immediately.

PART III

CULINARY COLLEGE

Early 1980s through late 1980s

10
NEW YORK CITY

A man's heart plans his way,
but the LORD directs his steps.

PROVERBS 16:9

Gale came behind the line one morning and waited until I finished setting up the station. I could tell by the look on her face that something was up.

"It's official," she said quietly. "I'm filing for divorce and I'm moving out."

This was the news I had been waiting for.

"What now?" I asked.

"Mary and I are heading to Manhattan this weekend to look for jobs and an apartment. Do you want to come with us?"

My heart sank. As much as I had tried not to think about it, this was really happening. Gale was really going to leave. Even so, there was no way I could join her. How would I ever make it in New York City? Sure, I had managed to do pretty well for myself thus far, but without a high school diploma, I was pretty sure I would be eaten alive in those big-city kitchens. Then there was my family to consider. My parents had recently filed for bankruptcy, and my mom was still struggling emotionally. I'd never considered leaving Rochester before either. Besides, wasn't I lucky just to have stayed alive and out of jail?

"No," I snapped. "I'm staying here. You guys go ahead and pursue your dreams."

Undaunted, Gale shrugged her shoulders. "Oh, well. It's too bad you won't be joining us," she said as she returned to her station.

The next three days seemed to drag on forever. Without Gale, the kitchen was void of energy. I slogged through my shifts, feeling sorry for myself and taking it out on everyone who came near me. I tried to kill the pain with drugs and alcohol.

When the girls returned on Tuesday, they were positively glowing. Gale rushed over to me and wrapped her arms around my neck.

"You won't believe this," she said, barely able to contain her excitement. "We both found jobs and an apartment!"

"Wow, aren't you lucky," I said, making no effort to mask my sarcasm.

"Yep, everything just came together, like it was meant to be, and our place is just perfect! But here's the thing. It's still really expensive, so we will need to get a third roommate. I really want that person to be you. You could come with Mary and me and find a job and start your life! When are you going to stop living in the mess your parents have made?"

The walls I had been working so hard to maintain began to crumble. How could I say no to Gale? I loved her and wanted to be with her. For the first time since we'd started talking about it, I allowed the idea of New York into my realm of possibility.

But I'd been at the Strathallan for two years now, and I owed Greg a lot. If Gale, Mary, and I all resigned at once, we'd really be leaving him in a bind. If I wanted to be a chef, though, I knew I had to work in New York. Surely Greg would understand; after all, turnover is common for just that reason.

At the end of my shift, I took off my apron and sat down in Greg's office.

"I'm thinking about going with Gale to New York," I said. "You've always told me I need to apprentice under a big-time chef and I think it's time. If I don't do it now, I never will."

Greg was quiet—an uncommon reaction for him. He squinted at me.

"If you're just doing this to follow after Gale, you're making a big mistake," he said. "You have to really want this, because it's not going to be easy. You're going to have to go back to square one. Start over. You'll be doing all the garbage work again. Are you ready for that?"

I nodded. I had no idea what to expect or even if I had what it took. But I sure wanted the chance to try.

"Well, I guess I can't stop you, can I?" Greg asked. "You've managed to hold your own here. Let me know if you need a recommendation. I'll help you in any way I can."

That was as close to a blessing as I was going to get from Greg, and I took it.

Now I needed to figure out a way to break the news to my folks. I decided my best option was to use Gale as a buffer. My parents loved Gale. Not only was she sweet and respectful to them, she was also a good influence on me. They knew she had a good head on her shoulders, and they trusted me when I was with her. So although they were heartbroken at the thought of my leaving, they were glad that at least I would be with Gale.

Not long after, I took a train to the city to see what I could find. Gale met me at Grand Central Station, handed me a subway map, and said, "Learn this. You'll need it. Mary and I are both working tonight, but tomorrow we will take you around and show you the sights."

And with that, she was off to work, leaving me on my own in the Big Apple. Standing on the corner of Forty-second Street and Park Avenue, I couldn't help but be in awe. The sheer enormity of the place literally took my breath away. Although I felt completely overwhelmed and unprepared, I knew I wasn't going to find a job just standing here. So I hit the pavement.

Gale and Mary had been able to find work so quickly—Gale was working for Jonathan Waxman at Jams, and Mary was over at An American Place with Larry Forgione—and I hoped I would have the same luck. Fortunately, all the big places were hiring. I filled out applications at Windows on the World, the Ritz-Carlton, the Four Seasons, and the Tavern on the Green.

Well versed in the culinary culture by now, I managed to do pretty well at all of the interviews. As is customary, I was invited to come back as a *stagiaire* in all three kitchens. A *stage* (pronounced *st-ah-ge*) was like a working interview, a chance for me to get a taste of each place while at the same time giving the chef an opportunity to assess my skills.

I must have made a good impression, because I was offered a job at both Windows on the World at the top of the Twin Towers and at the Tavern on the Green. As much as I liked Windows, I decided to take the prep cook position at Tavern on the Green—mostly because it paid the most. I skipped my stage day at the Ritz so that I could start work immediately at the Tavern.

After that whirlwind weekend, I headed back to empty my bank account and start packing up my things. Gale had warned me to bring only the bare necessities.

"Our place is decent, but it's really, *really* tiny," she had said. "Just bring some clothes, your cookbooks, your knives, and maybe your stereo. That's about all we'll have room for."

When the time came for me to leave, my dad and Uncle Paul drove me and my stuff to Manhattan in a rental truck. The three of us then carried my belongings up the five flights of stairs into my new home at West Tenth Street and Sixth Avenue. We had sublet the tiny apartment from a French pianist who spent six months of the year in Los Angeles. Gale was right. The sixth-floor walk-up was so small that we barely had room to turn around once the three of us all got inside. We had a tiny kitchen, an even tinier sitting room, and one decent-size bedroom. Unfortunately, the owner's upright piano took up most of the bedroom, so she had built a loft bed over the top it. Between the floor, the pullout couch, and the loft bed we all had a place to sleep.

Despite its drawbacks, the apartment's location was great—right across the street from the Joffrey Ballet School. At any given time during the day or night, music poured out into the street and our apartment. At night we could sit on the fire escape and look directly into the sixth floor, a brightly lit loft where the dancers practiced. If we tired of that, we could look down into the Texarkana, a Cajun/Louisiana–inspired restaurant, on the first floor. Thanks to its large plate window, we could watch workers bustle around the kitchen. With my limited budget, I savored the restaurant smells and the sight of the ballet dancers performing. It was like my own early version of Bravo meets the Food Network.

Unfortunately, the Tavern on the Green was located in Central Park—nowhere near my West Village apartment—so I had to take two different trains across town to get there. I really hated not having my IROC to get around in. In order to arrive at work on time my first day, I had to be up and out the door before the sun rose to catch my train. Packed in like sardines with the other commuters, I held my breath against the stench of urine and garbage that hung in the air. It wasn't even seven o'clock yet, and already the temperatures inside the tunnel were nearing 85 degrees. Inside the train, it felt even hotter. I could barely make out the conductor's words as he called out each stop, and though I managed to make the switch between my first and second trains, I missed my final stop, forcing me to double back and show up for work thirty minutes late.

Of course the chef had little pity for a punk kid who couldn't even bother to be on time his first day on the job. He warned me that if I was ever late again, I shouldn't bother coming in at all. Overwhelmed and exhausted, I felt like I had just worked a double shift, and I hadn't even punched in yet. What had I gotten myself into? But there was little time for feeling sorry for myself. Before I knew what was happening, someone wheeled a fifty-five-gallon trash can filled with onions over to me and said, "Here, peel and dice."

I didn't have much choice but to roll up my sleeves and get to work. Fortunately, it didn't take me long to get into the rhythm of the kitchen once again. After peeling and dicing onions, I moved on to carrots and then celery so we could make the day's stock. As I worked, I took a look around the kitchen. The amount of food being prepared was staggering. I knew that one thousand covers a day was the norm here—a number I could barely get my head around. But having never been a part of such a fast-paced environment doing such huge volumes, I couldn't imagine how they did it.

It didn't take long to figure it out. Unlike the Strathallan, this was not high-end cooking; it was more like a production line where we cranked out the same thing over and over and over again day after day after day. In my other positions, I had always been driven by the lure of learning new things. Here it was more like working in a factory or a sweatshop.

The Tavern's kitchen was unlike anything I had ever seen—or heard—before. The extensive line of twenty-five or thirty cooks was managed by six expediters who shouted orders into their microphones as fast as they came in. The sheer volume of the chaos and insanity was deafening: pots and pans slamming, people yelling, music blaring. More often than not, I left with my head pounding and the sound of dishes clanging still ringing in my ears.

Almost from the start, I dreaded going in to work. Every day, it was the same thing: peel, clean, scrub, peel, clean, scrub. We made gallons and gallons of stocks and sauces, with eight or ten pots going on the stove at any given time. We handled thousands of lobsters a week, so many that I would have to ice down my hands—swollen from being poked by the sharp edges and pointy ends of the shells—before I could unbutton my chef coat at the end of the shift.

As much as I hated it, I knew I had to stick things out for at least a year if I wanted to build a quality résumé. I also needed at least three hundred dollars a week to pay my expenses, and the Tavern's popularity pretty much guaranteed a steady paycheck.

Our restaurant was definitely a tourist destination, and it was especially packed during Sunday brunch when even the New Yorkers would come. Renovated in 1976 by restaurateur Warner LeRoy, the Tavern on the Green had been part of New York's history since the late 1800s. Somewhat eccentric and always theatrical, Warner had managed to really turn the place around, making it *the* place to see and be seen in New York City.

Tourists and celebrities alike flocked to the Tavern, enticed by the restaurant's spectacular setting, eclectic menu, and lavish decor. Everything about it was over the top, from the polished brass and stained glass to the soaring ceilings and glittering chandeliers. Every day we seemed to be hosting some kind of prominent event: political fund-raisers and charity balls, Broadway openings and movie premieres—we did it all.

The parade of celebrities through the Tavern never seemed to slow down—Kim Basinger, Farrah Fawcett, Burt Reynolds, Kevin

Bacon, Sophia Loren, Danny DeVito, Chevy Chase—we served them all.

As exciting as the celebrity sightings and elaborate parties were, nothing could make up for the monotony of the work and the unsavory working conditions.

Discouraged by my situation, for the first time in my life I didn't go all out for my job. I stayed only as long as I had to every day, getting in and out as quickly as I could. Rather than working through my breaks or showing up two hours early, I avoided the kitchen as much as possible, taking every single smoke break the union allowed. Whenever possible, I ate my lunch in Central Park. The fresh air and beautiful surroundings helped rejuvenate and reenergize me just enough to go back in and finish out my shift.

Whenever we happened to have a day off together, Gale tried to educate me about New York. She really wanted us to be part of the city's cultural fabric, so we started by doing all the touristy things: the Statue of Liberty, the Empire State Building, and the Met. We also tried to sample new foods, whether in Little Italy or Chinatown or from street vendors, and take in some art on our days off. Gale could spend all day in a museum or gallery, and she could spend hours talking about the intricacies of a particular technique or style. It sounded like a foreign language to me, and frankly, I found it to be a little boring. But the last thing I wanted was for Gale to think less of me, so I just kept my mouth shut, nodding and agreeing whenever it seemed appropriate.

Gale was good for me. She stretched me and helped me move outside my comfort zone in so many ways. And above all, she understood and shared my passion for cooking and all things food-related. The eighties were an amazing time in the culinary world, and we were right in the middle of it all. Influenced by a variety of cuisines, fusion cooking combined French, Latin American, Californian, and Southwestern cuisines with Asian flavors in a whole new way. New American restaurants were popping up all across the city and some of the up-and-coming new American chefs were really starting to make a name for themselves: Wolfgang Puck, David Bouley, Alfred Portale, Alice Waters, and Daniel Boulud, to name a few.

Gale's and Mary's jobs gave them direct access to this incredible food scene, and more than anything, I wanted to be a part of it as well. After listening to me complain night after night about how much I hated it at the Tavern on the Green, Gale finally had enough.

"Just quit, already," she said, throwing up her hands. "There are hundreds of restaurants in New York, and plenty of jobs. If you hate working there that much, then do something about it!"

When Gale opened the latest copy of the *Village Voice* and started pointing out all the open positions, I realized she was right. I had put in my time and learned a lot in the last six years. And here I was in New York, one of the culinary centers of the world. It was time to stop doing grunt work and start focusing on my passion for food. That's what I had come here to do.

GORGONZOLA PICCANTE WITH CONCORD GRAPE SALAD

I'd like to see a renewed respect for cheese courses at fine-dining establishments. A cheese cart, usually offering about 25 different cheeses with crusty bread and condiments like jellies and relishes, is a treat for diners. I also have made many staff meals from the ends of cheeses that didn't make it on the cart! The grape garnish in this recipe makes a refreshing addition to a wonderfully powerful cheese.

At home, use leftover cheeses in omelettes and cheese spreads, or melt for fondues and cheese sauces. — *SERVES 4*

4 oz. Gorgonzola piccante
¼ lb. Concord grapes, peeled, split in half, and seeded
2 leaves mint
2 Tbs. extra-virgin olive oil
Pinch lemon zest
1 Tbs. crushed toasted hazelnuts
Pinch of kosher salt
Freshly cracked black pepper

1. Cut the Gorgonzola into 1-oz. pieces and place on a plate.
2. To peel the grapes, take a small spoon and pinch the skin between the top of the spoon and your thumb, using the stem end as an entrance point. Gently roll the grape along the contour of the inside of the spoon, keeping the skin on the top of the spoon with pressure from your thumb, while pushing the grape around with your index finger. The skin should come right off.
3. Split the grapes and remove the seeds. Place the grapes into a small mixing bowl. Julienne the mint and mix with the grapes, along with the olive oil, lemon zest, hazelnuts, salt, and cracked pepper.
4. Spoon a quarter of the salad on each plate.

11

FRENCH COOKING 101

To Him who is able to do exceedingly abundantly
above all that we ask or think,
according to the power that works in us.

EPHESIANS 3:20

I'd done my time at Tavern on the Green—eight long months—and I was ready to move on. This meant stepping outside my comfort zone, figuring out who was the best of the best, and going to work for those people. I started asking around and talking to some of Gale's and Mary's coworkers about possible opportunities. Again and again, the conversation always came back to the same thing: I had to get some experience in a French kitchen. The Strathallan had been a good start, but Greg wasn't French. Only someone who knew the French culture and language could teach me what I needed to know about authentic French cooking. I needed the kind of experience you get from cooking with a French grandmother and shopping in French markets.

Thankfully, I had a lot of options here in New York: Lutèce, La Caravelle, La Grenouille, Le Cirque, La Côte Basque; any of them would be a great place to start. I put my résumé together, got dressed, and headed to the first place on my list: La Côte Basque, owned by Chef Jean-Jacques Rachou. A friend of Gale's from Jams knew the sous-chef there, so I figured I at least had a foot in the door.

I showed up at 6:00 a.m. to seek a two-day assignment as a *stagiaire*—

I knew better than to show up during the lunch rush—and asked for Kye, the sous-chef. After introducing myself, I asked if he was looking for a *commis*, or apprentice. Kye turned and said something to the chef in French; I didn't understand a word of it. Then he told me to come back at 4:30 the next morning.

For the first time since coming to New York, I was excited to walk into the kitchen again. I had heard so much about the importance of working under a French chef, and now I was working under a world-class French chef. I couldn't wait to take my training to the next level of difficulty, discipline, and structure.

The kitchen at La Côte Basque was very serious. In the center of the room, six or seven cooks were getting ready for the day. With their toques sitting straight on top of their heads, perfectly starched chef coats, and crisp aprons, they were the picture of decorum and class. No one said a word; they simply watched as we made our way through the kitchen and Kye quietly pointed out the various stations.

The level of discipline and technical skills I observed were far superior to those at any place I'd worked before. "One thing that's different here from other places you've probably worked is that talking behind the line is prohibited. The only voice you should hear is the chef screaming or the sous-chef calling orders," he said with a half-smile. "And the only thing you should ever say in response is '*Oui*, Chef.'"

I was excited to show my stuff. But it didn't take long to see that I was definitely in over my head. Unable to speak French, I had no idea what anyone was saying or what the chef needed from me. I ended up looking pretty incompetent—a real disaster.

Over the next few weeks, I repeated the process at La Caravelle and Lutèce, getting a little better at it each time, but never quite good enough. At Lutèce, they threw me into prep, cleaning lobsters and tournéeing vegetables. Thankfully, I had plenty of experience in both and managed to at least hold my own and not screw up too badly. In terms of technique, I knew I could go head-to-head with the best of them, but not knowing how to speak or read French was killing me.

"We don't have time to teach you the food *and* the language," the sous-chefs would say dismissively at the end of the day. "We need someone who can step in and start working right away. Come back when you have more experience—and when you learn to speak French."

Sometimes I didn't even get that much.

"Out! Get out! Get out of my kitchen!" the chef would scream, using the only English I had heard all day. I didn't need a translator for that.

Finally one night, Gale came home with great news.

"My friend Rona's husband works in the kitchen at La Grenouille," she said. "He wants you to come in for a stage tomorrow *and* he said he'd stick by you to make sure you understand what the chef is saying."

Renny's translating turned out to be just the ticket I needed to prove myself in the kitchen, and by the end of the day I was offered a job as a lunchtime *entremetier*—vegetable cook. The pay was the same as I was getting at Tavern on the Green, but in terms of my culinary education, I felt like I had just graduated to the next level of learning.

One of Midtown's most successful French eateries, La Grenouille was known throughout the city for its elegance and ambiance. Owned by the Masson family, the restaurant was famous for its classic French cuisine, an extensive wine list, wonderful service—and flowers. The place was always filled with fresh flowers, and the smell was heavenly. Standing in the center of the dining room, surrounded by beautiful artwork and perfectly set tables, I couldn't imagine a more perfect environment in which to work.

La Grenouille had capitalized on the affluent, career-driven lifestyle of the eighties, serving up multicourse "power lunches" for many of the city's most successful business leaders. These people were spending serious money with us as they brokered and negotiated and signed huge business deals over martinis and caviar.

With Renny by my side, I felt a lot more comfortable in this unique culture known as a French kitchen. Every day I watched and listened and tried to pick up every little detail and nuance I could, and every night I went home and pored over the pages of Escoffier's *Le Guide Culinaire* and Montagné's *Larousse Gastronomique*, trying to educate myself about French technique, tools, ingredients, and creativity.

I can't say it was ever easy. I had enough trouble with reading comprehension when the words were in plain English. Trying to understand words and concepts translated from French into English was nearly impossible.

With a little effort, I might be able to read the menu, or make out the basic ingredients in a recipe, but usually I was just figuring things out as I went. And with the chef screaming behind me the entire time, rattling off one curse word after another, I really had to work hard to stay focused.

The first bits of French that I learned were commands and swear words, roughly translated: Close the door! Change your apron! Move faster! Hurry up! Be quiet! After a while, I began to recognize some of the terms and knew that *fermez la porte!* meant I had left the walk-in door open—again—and better shut it immediately!

In order to get a jump on the day, I always came in much earlier than my 6:00 a.m. start time. Roasting veal bones, lamb bones, beef bones for stock—all the grunt work fell to me. Prepared in fifty- to sixty-gallon steam jacket stockpots, the finished stock was dispensed through a water spout into buckets, which we then chilled in sinks. Once the pots were empty, I had to shovel out all the bits of meat and other solids at the bottom of the pots before scrubbing them clean.

One of the first things I did every morning was to roast off all three or four pans of lobster shells for our bisque. After roasting the lobsters and allowing them to cool slightly, we would crush the shells through the grinder to extract all the flavor from them. We were then ready to begin making the stock for our bisque, cooking on flattops rather than burners.

More than once I over-roasted lobster shells so the stock was bitter, resulting in the sous-chef yelling at me and telling me to throw it away and start again. I knew this was all part of the education process: watching, trying, messing up, asking questions, and trying again until I finally got it right. But the chefs were demanding and tough. In their minds, there wasn't any room for mistakes.

But even though the environment was like a pressure cooker and the learning curve was extremely steep, I thrived on the challenge and I loved every minute of it. This was the first three-star restaurant I had ever worked in, and the food we were putting out was nothing short of mind-blowing: glistening duck à l'orange, potted smoked trout, roasted skate with fresh fennel and lemon. Everything was done with such precision and perfection, made with only the freshest ingredients, and the end result was amazing, award-winning cuisine.

Over time, both my technique and my French began to improve. I was finally starting to feel more at ease and comfortable with everything that was going on around me. I could communicate with the chef, at least enough to understand what he was asking me to do—or *not* do, as the case may be.

After working for about a year, I told Renny I would really like to move to nights if anything became available. Gale and Mary were both on nights, and since I was working days, we rarely saw each other anymore. Unfortunately, La Grenouille didn't have any night spots open, nor did they anticipate any in the near future. Since it was such a high-profile place to work, people rarely left.

Renny told me he had heard that La Reserve was looking for help, so on my next day off, I set up a stage in that kitchen. At the end of the shift, I was immediately offered a spot as the nighttime veggie guy, along with the promise that a fish position would be opening soon. This was exactly what I had been looking for: the opportunity to not only gain more French cooking experience, but also to move up the ladder a bit as I went. Renny understood when I gave him my notice.

La Reserve's kitchen was spread out over three separate levels. The finishing kitchen was on the first floor, prep was on the second, and all the pastry and baking were done on the third. A spiral staircase ran down the center of the kitchen, which really took a toll on my knees and my lower back. It was the most physically demanding space I'd ever worked in, but I didn't care. I was thrilled to be in the middle of the game and studying food again.

I spent the first three weeks on the job working over-the-top, crazy hours, trying to prove myself. Every single dish we served was garnished with a carved vegetable of some sort. I spent every waking minute making stock, doing prep work, and turning veggies: carrots, celery, turnips, zucchinis. You name it, I turned it, carving the vegetables into various shapes. And I never, ever seemed to be able to catch up. Even on my breaks or while eating my employee dinner,

I would stand and turn buckets of veggies; I simply couldn't afford to fall any further behind.

Everything we did at La Reserve was extremely labor-intensive, and even the most experienced guys struggled to keep up. We did a beautiful ratatouille stuffed baby Japanese eggplant that was really difficult to perfect. But somehow, I managed to nail the dish and earn the chef's respect very early on. Within a short period of time, he rewarded me with the fish spot, which was the position I wanted anyway.

Now I was really cooking! Because of all the techniques I was using, La Reserve is where I was able to really refine my knife skills. The culinary arts were finally starting to make sense to me now too, and I was catching on to a lot of the subtleties that I hadn't been able to pick up just by reading my cookbooks or cooking at home. From day one, I began to learn all these classic fish dishes: scorpion fish, monkfish, beautiful sea brines with apples and aromatic vegetables, wild salmon en papillote. As the fish guy, or *poissonier*, I had a couple of *commis* from the local culinary school assisting me, which really helped. We were responsible for every piece of seafood from the time it came in the back door until it was placed in front of the customer—cleaning it, cooking it, and arranging it on the plate.

I found that I truly loved working with fish. There was just something really precise about deboning a fish that suited me. As much as I enjoyed butchering meat—beef, pork, lamb—a fish was a lot more delicate with a lot less room for error.

I still had my eye on the goal—to be a chef in my own place and create my own food—and in order to get there, I needed to continue my apprenticeship by putting in at least a year with each of the chefs I had a chance to work with. After that year, though, I had to move on. There wasn't much turnover, so I couldn't advance very quickly in any one place.

Each job gave me a brief opportunity to gain all that I could from these top-notch French chefs. What frustrated me the most was that, back then, a lot of these guys, with all of their talent, refused to share their knowledge with an American like me. I had no other choice but to keep my eyes open and my mouth shut, and hope to catch a little of what they knew.

Thankfully, the American culinary community at large was actually a pretty tight-knit group. We helped each other out and shared news and information whenever we could. Once I began to gain a little confidence in my French, I started looking for opportunities to expand my repertoire and add to my résumé.

On my days off, I tried to do as many other stages as I could, working in some of the best kitchens in the city. I spent a few days at the River Café in Brooklyn and another day at Lutèce. I also did stages at Valentino's and La Caravelle. All were amazing experiences. I looked at these extra stages as extra-credit classes in my culinary schooling.

A friend of mine had recently started working over at the Gotham Bar and Grill, a new restaurant in Greenwich Village—two blocks away from my apartment—and the chef was getting a lot of buzz around town. Chef Alfred Portale had recently returned to the States after working in some of France's best kitchens, like Jacques Maximin's, Michel Guérard's, and the Troisgros brothers. He was known for creating breathtakingly original dishes using fresh, seasonal ingredients and for his architecture-like plating presentations and beautiful towering salads, which seemed to stand up by magic.

When I learned they were looking for line cooks, I immediately set up a stage with Chef Portale. The Gotham was a 200-seat restaurant, and its kitchen, which was in the basement, literally shone.

Alfred and I hit it off immediately, and within minutes, we were talking comfortably. He was one of the first chefs I had met in New York who actually shook my hand and looked me in the eye when he talked to me. And he spoke English!

"I see you're the *poissonier* at La Reserve," he said, looking at my résumé. "That's a pretty good spot. Why would you want to leave?"

I told him I was looking for a kitchen where I could learn from someone experienced in French cooking, but without the language barrier and the French head games. He seemed to know exactly what I was talking about.

"I've done my time in the French kitchens," I explained. "Now I think I'd get more from an American chef who studied in France and knows how to apply those disciplines and techniques to American food. I am looking for someone who can teach me, not just scream at me all the time in French."

Alfred laughed. He was looking to put the Gotham on the map as a three-star restaurant; he wanted to build a team he could count on. He noticed I was from Rochester and said he was from Buffalo. We talked a bit about the long winters we both knew from our childhoods in upstate New York, and then he asked me about my culinary background.

I admitted that I had not gone to culinary school, or even finished high school. He seemed to ponder that news for a while, not quite sure how to respond. But as I told him more of my story, he understood.

"I'm intrigued by you," he said finally. "It's rare to see someone with a résumé like yours without a culinary degree. It's obvious you've been to a much tougher school than that: the school of life. I think we can definitely find a place for you here. Why don't you come back for a stage?"

He told me he would throw me on the appetizer station, and then pointed out these great goat cheese raviolis the crew was making for that day's service. Each serving was placed in a beautiful little white bowl and topped with fresh herbs and a bit of crispy pancetta—much like my grandma used to make. This was right up my alley!

Of course, on the day of my stage I made sure to come in early so I could help make the homemade pasta. As I cut the long strands of squid-ink pasta, I couldn't help but think about all the times I had made pasta with my grandmother. And then when Alfred showed me how to make his squid-ink black fettuccine in a lobster and tarragon sauce, I was blown away to realize I was already familiar with a lot of his technique—thanks to my time at La Grenouille and La Reserve.

This signature dish turned out beautifully. After blanching the fettuccine, we turned the pasta with a long-tong fork, creating a long cylinder into which the lobster meat could go. After placing the lobster's head and tail in the appropriate places at the top and sides of the pasta body, we drizzled lobster sauce over all of it.

I couldn't have asked for a better fit at the time. Finally, I had found a fine-dining restaurant serving pasta! Alfred was all about new American cuisine with Mediterranean flavors, but his cooking was based on great classic French technique. I was in my element.

I had come in at 9:00 a.m. and stayed through closing. After helping to prep the next day's produce, I moved on to scrubbing down the flattops and cleaning up the line. Finally at 1:00 a.m., we walked out the kitchen door. I think I got Alfred's attention at that point.

"You did a great job tonight," he said, again shaking my hand. "I would love to give you the opportunity to join our team." Sitting in the locker room off the kitchen after he left, I felt happy and relieved. After living through some hard knocks, I felt I had finally accomplished something and landed in the right city with the right chef and the right food.

I was so excited to get going that I immediately gave my notice at La Reserve and started picking up shifts at the Gotham on my days off. This gave me the opportunity to learn my station ahead of time so that when my first day rolled around, I was already one step ahead of the game.

Though Alfred had trained in France, the Gotham's kitchen was set up more like an American hot line than a French island where everyone faced each other. I started on the hot app/pasta station, learning how to make Alfred's signature black fettuccine, goat cheese ravioli, and hot appetizers, and after a couple of months I moved over to the grill station.

Alfred wasn't afraid to try something new; in fact, he was one of the first in the industry to create architectural cuisine and take his food vertical. His seafood salads rose up six or eight inches off the plate, all held together by delicate leaves of lettuce and calamari. He would use a ring collar to get the height he wanted and then remove it so the salads looked like skyscrapers on the plate. It wasn't uncommon for waiters to bring back a plate—or two or three—because they had wrecked the presentation on their way out to the table.

Thankfully, the atmosphere at the Gotham was lighthearted and fun—unlike anyplace I had ever worked before. Though he ran a tight ship, Alfred did it without screaming or intimidation. Like anyone who's been in the business for very long, Alfred definitely had his moments: times when he let the stress get the better of him and would fly off the handle. After all, as an American trying to establish himself as a world-class chef, the stakes were really high for him. But for the most part, he was much more levelheaded and calm than anyone I had ever worked for. He really knew how to lead and inspire a brigade, and even though he was very strict in terms of kitchen discipline, he was always respectful toward his employees. I found this kind of leadership to be both refreshing and extremely motivating.

In all my years of cooking, this was the first time I had ever been in a kitchen where there was a little bit of laughter. Although Alfred's standards were just as high as anyone else's, he really made us feel like we were human. His point was well taken: the chef doesn't necessarily have to act like a jerk in order to create awesome food or lead an award-winning kitchen.

Now that I actually spoke the same language as the chef and could understand what the guys in the kitchen were saying, I tried to learn more about the actual management of a kitchen. I knew I could learn a lot from Alfred, so I began to pay very close attention to the way he managed the crew, kept his cool under pressure, and dealt with difficult situations. I often came in on my days off to work the line and get exposure in other areas of the kitchen, including receiving, ordering, and other prep work.

After I had been at the Gotham for about six months, I approached Alfred. "I know you've been looking for a good pastry chef," I said. "I think I might have just the right person for you."

Alfred agreed to meet with Gale, and when he did, he hired her on the spot. Like Greg, he knew true talent when he saw it. Now that Gale and I were working together at jobs we both enjoyed, I couldn't imagine life getting any better.

And then it did. After a late night of service, Alfred and Gotham owner Jerry Kretchmer called the whole staff together for a meeting. We all liked Jerry a lot. He had a real head for business and an eye on the future of New York dining. In addition to the Gotham, he was also working on opening a new restaurant with a guy named Bobby Flay. If he wanted to meet with all of us at once, we figured he must have big news.

"You guys have really been working hard and doing a great job here at the Gotham," he began. "Alfred has done exactly what we asked him to do: put out a quality product that gets attention. And all your efforts are about to pay off. I just received word that in tomorrow's *New York Times*, Bryan Miller will be giving the Gotham a three-star review."

A cheer went up across the room. Three stars! This was huge news. Alfred was grinning from ear to ear, and Jerry began to hand out envelopes of bonuses, a "small token of his appreciation" for all we had done. Soon, champagne corks were popping and together we toasted our success.

Nothing could have prepared us for the craziness that was about to hit us. Within hours of the *Times* release, the Gotham's reservation line began to buzz. Within a week we went from doing 120 covers a night to well over 300. Now, instead of doing one turn in the dining room, we were doing two and three turns every night. Fridays and Saturdays were booked many months in advance.

With a single review, life had changed for all of us. Alfred suddenly became very famous, as did those of us on his crew. Wherever we went, we were recognized for working at the Gotham; I found the recognition to be both exhilarating and daunting. Somehow those three stars made us special and changed our lives. And we weren't alone. All across the city, new chefs were emerging and making names for themselves. We were a fairly small community of like-minded folks, all sharing the same passion for creating crazy food and growing our careers, and everyone had worked with everyone else at one time or another. What we didn't realize at the time was just how big this cooking thing was going to get. Food Network wasn't yet around, and even if it had been, none of us would have had time to watch it since we were all so busy just trying to keep up with the row of orders hanging across our lines.

For the next year, I continued to watch and learn from Alfred. I was amazed at the way he leveraged the media in order to advance his career and reputation. He seemed to know exactly what people were looking for, and he gave it to them. Every day, we put out amazing dishes, always pushing the envelope and wowing diners and critics alike. As exhausting and physical as the work was, I loved every single minute of it and couldn't wait to get to work every day.

And then one afternoon out of the blue, I got a call from Renny. "Hey, Rick, I was just calling to let you know that Joe Baum is getting ready to open a new place over on Forty-ninth Street," he said. It was going to be called Aurora, and Joe had brought in world-class architect Milton Glaser to design the restaurant. He had also hired two-star Michelin chef Gerard Pangaud to come in from France to run the kitchen.

Renny was going to be the executive sous-chef, and he needed to build a team of key players for Chef Pangaud. He wanted me to be his head garde-manger. I couldn't help but be intrigued by the offer. Part of me wanted to stay and keep learning from Alfred, but part of me also wanted the chance to do an opening and work with Chef Pangaud. I might never get a chance to work for a two-star Michelin chef again.

I talked to Gale about it, but she had some reservations. In fact, she thought I was crazy to consider going back to work for another French chef. "Why would you want to leave now?" she asked. "Do you really want to go back to that? Things are great here. If it ain't broke, don't fix it." I pointed out that this opportunity was a way to learn from a French chef without actually going to France.

I knew Gale had a point though: I had already had my fill of the French kitchen environment. Did I really want to go back into that insanity? On the other hand, I had never been involved in an opening. That would certainly be an important piece to add to my repertoire.

Alfred encouraged me to go.

"If you really want to devise your own apprenticeship as a way to learn to be a chef, you need to work in eight or ten kitchens and gain a wide variety of experiences, techniques, and disciplines from lots of different chefs," he said. "I've given you what I know, and it's been great. Now it's time to continue your journey and learn something new."

So with Alfred's blessing, I took the next step in my career and joined the new crew at the French restaurant Aurora.

CINNAMON-ROASTED PUMPKIN SOUP WITH WILD RICE AND RABBIT CONFIT

I naturally think of pumpkin soup whenever I am creating an autumn menu. I lay colorful autumn leaves on plates for garnish and ladle the soup into hollowed-out mini pumpkins set atop the leaves for a dramatic, pretty presentation. Garnished with wild rice and rabbit confit, this soup makes a fall dish fit for a king. In fact, rabbit and confit (which simply means cooking the meat in its own fat) are both very old-world European. — *SERVES 6 TO 10*

1 medium sugar or other cooking pumpkin (about 3 lb.), seeded and quartered
1 Tbs. ground cinnamon
3 sprigs fresh thyme, chopped
¼ c. maple syrup
4 c. chicken stock
4 c. heavy cream
3 sticks cinnamon
Kosher salt
Freshly ground black pepper
1 c. wild rice
2 c. water
1 Tbs. olive oil
1 Tbs. finely diced leeks
1 Tbs. finely diced carrot
1 Tbs. finely diced onion
½ c. rabbit confit (recipe on next page)

1. Preheat the oven to 300°F to 325°F.
2. Arrange the pumpkin quarters, flesh side up, in a large roasting pan. Sprinkle with cinnamon and thyme, and drizzle with maple syrup. Cover securely with aluminum foil and roast for about 1½ hours, or until the pumpkin is soft. Set aside to cool slightly.
3. When the pumpkin is cool enough to handle, scoop out the flesh from the shell. Transfer the flesh to a blender and add chicken stock. Puree until smooth. Strain the puree through a chinois or fine-mesh sieve into a clean saucepan. Add cream and cinnamon sticks; season to taste with salt and pepper. Bring to a simmer over medium-low heat. Turn off the heat and set aside so that the cinnamon sticks have time to infuse the soup.
4. Meanwhile, combine the rice and water in a medium-size saucepan and bring to a boil over medium-high heat. Reduce the heat and simmer, uncovered, for about 25 minutes or until all the water has been absorbed.
5. While the rice cooks, heat the olive oil in a sauté pan set over medium-high heat. Add the leeks, carrots, and onions. Cook, stirring, for 2 to 3 minutes or until vegetables begin to soften. Stir the vegetables into the rice and season to taste with salt and pepper.
6. Remove the cinnamon sticks from the soup and discard. Reheat the pumpkin

soup over medium heat. Ladle into bowls and garnish with a generous spoonful of wild rice and a little rabbit confit.

Rabbit Confit

Legs and shoulders from one 4 to 5 lb. rabbit
1¼ c. sugar
1¼ c. kosher salt
15 juniper berries
4 star anise
12 to 15 black peppercorns
5 bay leaves
1 qt. of duck fat (or more if needed)*

1. Combine the first seven ingredients in a nonreactive bowl; coat evenly. Cover and cure the meat for 8 to 12 hours in the refrigerator. At the end of the curing time, wash the rabbit meat under cold running water. Pat dry.
2. Remove duck fat from the refrigerator, and place in an oven-safe pot. Over medium heat, warm the duck fat until it is liquid and reaches a temperature of 300°F to 350°F. Place the rabbit meat in the hot duck fat, making sure it is completely submerged in the fat. Cook slowly at 300°F to 350°F for approximately three hours or until the meat is fork tender and just starting to fall off the bone. Check occasionally to be sure that the rabbit is completely submerged in the fat. (You may need to add more fat or oil.)
3. Remove the rabbit from the fat and place on a cooling rack over a cookie sheet to cool. When the rabbit has cooled, remove the meat from the bones and pull into small pieces. Refrigerate until needed.

* You can order duck fat from your butcher. Refrigerate until ready to use. Vegetable oil, lard, or olive oil can be substituted.

12

THE BIG TIME

Oh, give thanks to the LORD! Call upon His name;
Make known His deeds among the peoples!

PSALM 105:1

Gale and I made a great team, both professionally and personally, I thought. We had forged a strong bond of shared interests and mutual respect for one another. I knew I wanted to marry her. Gale, however, wasn't ready.

"We can't lose our focus right now," she said. "I've already done the marriage thing, and I just don't think I'm ready to do it again. We need to keep our eyes on our careers. Things are good between us. Let's not ruin it but instead concentrate on being culinary partners."

I understood where she was coming from, but I continued to pester her anyway, promising that one day I would whisk her away to Paris and propose under the Eiffel Tower.

"You won't be able to resist me then," I said. "You'll have to say yes."

We both had to laugh at that one. Even though we were so busy working and trying to get ahead in our careers, we didn't have any money. We also had very little free time. We couldn't even break long enough to get back to Rochester, let alone Paris.

While I wouldn't have minded flying to Paris, I had no desire to return to Rochester anyway. I was just starting my life, and I was excited about what the future held. The idea of going back home only brought me down. Nothing much had changed there. Dad was still working for the railroad, and Mom was still cleaning for the school district.

I knew life was tough for them and finances were tight. They had downsized their life as much as possible, moving into a one-bedroom apartment in a not-so-great neighborhood. Their most elaborate furnishings were a Formica table and a cheap couch. My dad was driving a used car.

But even if I wanted and could afford to go home, I probably wouldn't have been able to get the time off work. I was putting in seventy to eighty hours a week and working every weekend and every holiday. New York City never stopped—and we were all running at a pretty good clip just trying to keep up.

The first day I walked into Aurora, I was blown away. Joe Baum had spared no expense in creating his dream. With seating for about 125 people, the dining room literally sparkled, from the glass globes that hung overhead to the marbled floors underfoot. This took the beauty of La Grenouille and La Reserve to a whole other level—from floral arrangements to linens to drapes to glassware, everything was immaculate.

And the kitchen! Joe had made sure his world-class chef would have a state-of-the-art environment in which to work his magic. All of the equipment had been imported from France, and we lacked for nothing. This, by far, was the coolest kitchen I had seen up to this point. Everything was brand new and state of the art. With a million-dollar wine cellar, ultraexpensive crystal and china, and the very best staff money could hire, Joe was going for four stars right out of the gate.

I felt lucky just to have been invited along on the ride and for the European experience I knew I was going to get.

When I first arrived, there was still much work to be done in order to get things ready for the opening. Renny handed me a folder of recipes and said, "Here, this is your training manual."

I flipped through the pages. This was high-level stuff, and I couldn't wait to get started. We spent the next several days just going over the menu step-by-step, prepping, cooking, tasting, and adjusting again and again as we went. I had to work closely with Renny to find out exactly what garnishes and sides he wanted on each plate. And then I had to pass that information on to my own garde-manger team.

This was the first time I was a chef de partie with people working for me at my station. We had to prep up our own dishes: potted smoked fishes, pâtés, head cheese, canapés, and mousses. We created specialty salads—baby greens tossed with fresh mango and icicle radishes—warm grenouille potatoes smothered with a killer vinaigrette, veal pâtés, and oysters minuet. We would also be doing a bit of cured meat work, so we made sure we had everything we needed for that, including intricately carved miniature ice displays.

In addition to making sauces, stocks, and dressings that could be stored until opening, we also took several practice runs at the fifty-layer salmon tureen with cream cheese, alternating paper-thin slices of smoked salmon with fifty smooth layers of whipped cream cheese. We used an icing or palette knife to layer the cheese very thin. We prepared passion fruit gelée cubes, along with a petite salad for garnish, to accompany the salmon tureen.

And when we were finished with all that, we built shelving, unpacked china, and organized the walk-ins. We also cleaned up construction dust, moved tables, and labeled items before putting them where they needed to go. For many weeks, work was a combination of cooking and construction—we spent about half a day on each.

Our days usually started around 6:00 a.m. and didn't end until well past midnight. Each day seemed to run into the next. But that didn't matter. When you are part of a restaurant opening, you realize you are essentially giving up eight months to a year of your life. The adrenaline rush made the time just fly by. The French sous-chefs and American team members were united as we worked toward the same goal. I also noticed that I was treated with more respect now that I was running my own team. So far it was great.

And then executive chef Gerard Pangaud showed up. One day we were told he was coming directly to the restaurant from the airport, where he'd just flown in from France. Everyone had knots in their stomachs as we waited. It was early one afternoon, and I had already been on my feet for nine hours. Sweating and covered in packing dust, I was standing at my station, wiping down some side plates that had just arrived that day. A sudden hush in the kitchen caused me to look up just in time to see Chef Pangaud stroll in, followed by four other somber-looking gentlemen. None of them said anything; they simply surveyed the kitchen and the staff. You could have heard a pin drop.

This was Chef Gerard Pangaud! A nondescript, stocky fellow, Chef Pangaud had a reputation that far surpassed his appearance. At only twenty-eight years old, he had been the youngest chef ever to receive two stars from the prestigious Michelin Guide, as close as you can get to culinary knighthood in France. He had created and operated numerous award-winning restaurants throughout Paris, earning a steady stream of recognition and esteem along the way. I just couldn't believe we were going to get to work with this guy.

Finally, Renny moved forward and reached out his hand.

"Welcome, Chef," he said. Chef Pangaud seemed reluctant to take Renny's hand, but he finally gave it a quick squeeze.

"Allo," he said, his accent thick. Gerard Pangaud was definitely a culinary rock star of the highest pedigree, and even though we were all completely intimidated, each person in that room hoped to catch a ride on his wave of success. He quickly put us in our place. While he had greeted the sous-chef with a handshake and "Allo," when he came around the line to meet the rest of the kitchen, he walked quickly by us, grunting a brief "Allo" along the way.

Over the coming weeks, it became obvious that Chef Pangaud was brilliant, a true master of his ingredients, recipes, and specialty dishes. He had an almost encyclopedic knowledge of the culinary arts that was reflected in everything he prepared.

But even as news of our opening spread among New York's foodies, and the reservation book started filling up, we began to suspect that something was very wrong with this picture. Quite literally, Chef Pangaud was a wild man in the kitchen, far worse than any of the arrogant French chefs I had worked for at La Grenouille or La Reserve. Not only was he a hard-core French chef who had come up through the brash school of culinary etiquette, he appeared to me to be an out-of-control alcoholic. Every other word I heard come out of his mouth was a curse word.

Aurora had been open for only a few weeks, but already I knew I had made the biggest mistake of my life by leaving the Gotham. Chef Pangaud struck me as just plain mean-spirited and angry. He didn't seem to care that his people were working seven days a week, sixteen hours a day to get *his* restaurant up and running. He was a big-time chef from France who demanded perfection, even if it meant throwing something at you or throwing away the food you'd prepped in order to get it. His demand for discipline was fine, but I chafed at the way he demanded it—in a rage and usually under the influence.

Our hot lines were set up in an L-formation, and Chef Pangaud liked to position himself right at the outside of the pass during the dinner rush. This seemed very strange to me. Rather than working the dining room, tasting the food, and overseeing the sous-chefs, he wanted to expedite every order, which just seemed to create more and more chaos every day. And he was never happy. I watched him throw plates back across the line or toss entire trays of food onto the floor, screaming and cursing at the sous-chefs to do it all again—and do it right this time. Half the time, we weren't even sure what we had done wrong, nor did we have time to ask since we now had to cook and re-plate everything we had just worked so hard to prepare. We never seemed able to catch up.

Every day it was the same: work like crazy to keep up, try to stay under Chef's radar, and always be ready to dodge random cookware that might be aimed at your head.

After months and months of sleep deprivation and craziness, I had become a walking zombie. I was working seven days a week and putting in hours and hours of overtime, still trying to learn the systems and perfect the extremely complicated menu items. This was made even more challenging by the fact that Chef Pangaud would speak only French to his sous-chefs, who would then have to translate his commands into English. I found it strange that Chef didn't even make an effort to learn English and refused to speak directly to those under the sous-chef level.

Like everyone in the kitchen, I was more focused on trying not to trigger Chef Pangaud's rage than anything else. I couldn't help but think back to my childhood days when we all walked on eggshells around my mom, praying that she wouldn't lose her temper and send a plate sailing across the room.

But even though I was totally beaten down and struggling just to function, I was determined to stick it out. All around me, people were walking out, but I held on. This was such a huge opportunity, I refused to throw it away. Since I'd left the Gotham to take it, I was even more determined to stay.

One afternoon, Renny stepped behind the line and showed me that night's *amuse-bouche*. This single bite-size "gift" from the chef served when diners first sit down is meant to "amuse the palate," from which its name comes. Renny gave me instructions on preparing and plating it. This one was especially complicated because it was made up of a number of different pieces. I didn't have a lot of time, so I immediately went to work prepping 150 of them.

Each amuse started with a delicate piece of toast topped with a beautiful fresh shrimp salad, a sprig of chervil, chopped egg, and a black caviar vinaigrette. Preparing them would have been easy enough to do, but I also had all of my other setup and prep to finish. Finally, after several hours, I managed to prep and set up all 150 amuse-bouche and line them neatly on several large sheet trays.

Turning my attention to the rest of the evening's prep, I was thankfully able to get everything done just before opening. That night's service started. As I lined up my *mise en place*—all of the ingredients necessary for that night's service—I caught a glimpse of Chef Pangaud heading my way. My heart jumped into my throat as I silently prayed that he would just walk by. I kept my head down and kept working.

But of course, I couldn't get that lucky. The next thing I knew, Chef Pangaud was ripping through my station, moving things around, peering into stockpots, going through reach-in coolers, and ranting in French about who knows what. The scent of alcohol and cigarette smoke surrounded him, and he had that wild look in his eye that meant trouble for everybody. Leaning over the caviar vinaigrette I had prepared for the amuse, he dipped a small tasting spoon into the opaque mixture and lifted it to his lips. Wrinkling his nose, he turned to me.

Out of character, he yelled and cursed at me in English, ordering me to remake it.

"*Oui,* Chef." I knew that was the only response I could make.

I quickly moved the container of vinaigrette out of his reach. The last thing I needed was to spend the next twenty minutes cleaning up dressing from the floor of my station.

As he turned to leave, the tray of amuse caught his eye.

He began to scream at me, berating me for placing the chervil in the wrong spot and ordering me to remake them.

Renny jumped in and tried to take responsibility.

In French he explained, "I'm sorry, Chef. I was the one who told him where to put the chervil. We'll fix it. Don't worry."

But it was too late. Chef Pangaud's anger had already exploded. He couldn't let it go. Screaming and cursing, he began to dump the amuse, tossing it and everything else at my station onto the floor or in the trash. As he did, the rest of us sprung into action, trying to salvage what little we could before he got his hands on it. In a blink of an eye, a whole day's work was gone. I was speechless.

Meanwhile, orders had already begun to come in. As I hurried to replenish a good part of my station, I was careful not to slip on the broken glass and oily sauces that now lay strewn all over the floor.

As Chef Pangaud stomped away, the rest of us just stared at him in disbelief. Service had already started and our first course was now sitting at the bottom of a trash can. Was this guy for real? I'd never had a chef put service so far into jeopardy before.

Frustrated and fed up, Renny followed after him and began shouting to him in French. Shouting became screaming, and soon they were verbally dueling it out.

As the two of them went at it in French, the rest of us scrambled to keep up with the incoming orders while at the same time trying to come up with a quick replacement for the now ruined amuse-bouche.

As I worked, a couple of the other sous-chefs joined in the argument with Renny. By now, I could understand enough French to pick up a few details.

"You can't keep doing this!" Renny shouted. "Word is getting out about you and your temper. You're going to sink this ship if you don't stop acting so crazy!"

But Chef Pangaud was oblivious. His face red with rage, he simply increased his volume and continued to scream.

That's when I knew we were really in trouble. Renny was right. This ship was going down fast and there was no way to plug the leaks. We had all tolerated Chef's insanity because he was such a brilliant chef. But instead of bringing us along on his ride to success, he was pulling us all down with him.

Things didn't get much better the rest of the night. We never got ahead, and building amuses to order was nearly impossible. Somehow, we managed to finish the shift, and by the time I finally boarded the train for home, I could barely see straight. Exhausted and broken, I leaned my head against the window and tried not to lose it. I had been through a lot in my life, and I considered myself pretty tough skinned. But this night had truly been horrific.

Trudging up the six flights of stairs to our apartment, I reached the top and simply could not take another step. I sat down on the landing, buried my face in my hands, and started to sob.

"Rick! What happened? What's wrong?" Gale had recently left the Gotham in order to work for Richard Krause at Batons. Although she usually worked days, for some reason she had stayed late on this night and was just now getting home. She dropped her bags and sat down beside me.

"I can't function like this anymore," I told her. "No matter how great Chef Pangaud is supposed to be, I just can't take the abuse for one more day. Even Renny is barely holding it together."

"You know what? You should talk to the guys at Batons. We've got a daytime sous-chef position open. You'd be a great fit."

My spirits immediately lifted. I liked the sound of that. Gale loved working with Richard Krause and Jonathan Eismann. And since Batons wasn't open for lunch, a daytime position would be focused on butchering all the meats, making all the sauces, and filleting all the fish. Running a large prep team without the pressure of doing service was new and odd for me.

I decided I would go see Chef Krause the next day. But before that, I stopped in at the Gotham to ask Alfred if he had any openings. First, I filled him in on my situation.

"I've definitely heard rumblings about the chaos going on over there. I was wondering how you were holding up," Alfred said.

My parents didn't take many photos when I was growing up; this picture of my first Christmas is the only baby picture I have.

Getting ready for a gig with my high school band Star Struck. We were one of the only bands in town serious enough to get hired to play events, so we were really popular. We even had roadies!

You'll see some faces you recognize in this photo at a James Beard dinner in 1991, taken on the back kitchen steps at Charlie Trotter's restaurant. That's Charlie at the far right in the third row—look how young we all were!

I had met Emeril before, but the James Beard dinner was the first time we ever cooked together. We hit it off from the start, and our friendship continues today.

The beautiful main house at the Stapleford Park hotel, during one of the Cotswold Hunts. Afterward, the riders would gather for tea or cocktails, and we'd cook the grouse, pheasant, or hare that they brought back.

I was proud to work with this "Michelin team" at the Stapleford Park hotel. Our kitchen staff came from all over the world, but we shared an incredible passion and tenacity for the job. It was one of the most driven teams I'd ever had the privilege of working with.

This was the first of six times I've cooked at the James Beard House—it's so inspiring to work in the house where he lived and cooked.

The famous Trio medicine cabinet shelves and floor tiles that we used as plates when we didn't have enough money for china!

One of our many Tru partners' meetings. Rich Melman often joined Gale and me for tastings; because he's so knowledgable and well traveled, he was a great palate to have at the table.

Plating an amuse-bouche in the Tru kitchen—lots of attention to detail and concentration required!

Tru's kitchen on opening day—it's like a work of art. (You should have seen the "before" shot—we gutted the original structure down to the studs and cinder block walls!)

The beautiful Osteria di Tramonto dining room, described at the beginning of this book.

It was such an honor to call Julia Child my friend and be part of culinary history by cooking with her at her home in Cambridge.

Visiting with Wolfgang Puck in Chicago during his first book tour. We've been friends for more than twenty years, and he's always been a good sounding board and inspiration to me.

Alain Ducasse and I in Monaco, where I toured his kitchen and enjoyed one of my first three-star Michelin meals. One of many moments as a young chef where I was in the right place at the right time—and got to experience culinary history as it was being made.

This shot was taken during a Citymeals-on-Wheels event in New York City in 2003. The amount of talent gathered in this one place to celebrate a great cause blows me away. Can you spot some of the famous chefs?

Tom Colicchio and I, years before we would appear together on *Top Chef*.

This photo still cracks me up. When Mario Batali had dinner at Tru during his book tour for *The Babbo Cookbook*, he arrived to find all seventy of our staff members wearing his trademark orange clogs. That was the spirit of Tru—fine dining with a sense of humor.

Bobby Flay and I, after breakfast at Osteria. I have always been grateful to Bobby for introducing me to the world of cookbook publishing and my longtime book agent.

Even though I worked behind the line with Dave Thomas at Wendy's years ago, I never got a photo of the two of us—so I seized the opportunity to pose with this life-size cutout of Dave when visiting the Wendy's headquarters in Ohio. What a great guy with a great legacy.

Tru was one of the first restaurants to host a benefit dinner after the World Trade Center fell. Here, Michael Lomonaco, executive chef of Windows on the World, tells his heart-wrenching story of watching the north tower fall with some of his staff still inside. There was not a dry eye in the house.

Katie Couric and I on the *Today* show in Chicago. That morning, I had just flown in from Russia after being inducted into the Relais and Châteaux Relais-Gourmand list of chefs (one of the youngest ever). I literally walked off a plane, into a car, and onto the set. What a trip!

I'm in the construction pit that would eventually become my home. Little did I know that a year after this was taken I would have a whole new life with Eileen.

It seemed right to have our small wedding with 25 guests in the (finally finished) house. Here Eileen and I are cutting the cake.

Pastor Dickow and I take a moment after the ceremony to talk to Gio and Brian about this new stage in our lives, and to pray for our family as it comes together.

This photo was taken on the day Sean left for college. This was a big deal for me and Eileen, since we didn't go to college ourselves and I wasn't able to get my GED. We were so proud and excited for him.

Brian, Gio, and I at the Epcot Food & Wine Festival in Disney World. We used to take them to Disney every year for this event; sometimes they'd help out and wear their own little chef coats.

John Folse and I really bonded while we were helping to feed the rescue workers and refugees in New Orleans after Katrina. We prepped food for hundreds in this Korean convent—there were men, women, and kids everywhere, sleeping in the hallways and stairwells. I was so impressed with the city's culture, traditions, and resilience.

Back in New Orleans a few years later, with artist Michael Israel and some of the country's greatest chefs at Chef's Ashore, a charity event to bring awareness to the Gulf oil spill and raise money for the families whose livelihoods were threatened or destroyed by the disaster.

John and I in Jackson Square, New Orleans, after announcing our new restaurant and company ventures together.

With my family on the set for John's PBS special *After the Hunt*—we went shrimpin', froggin', and cooked up some turtle at John's studio in Baton Rouge. We are looking forward to our new life in this amazing city.

I shrugged. "I don't know. There's a part of me that loved it, believe it or not. Chef Pangaud is nothing short of amazing. I can see why everyone is so impressed by him. But when he's drinking or gets in one of his raging moods, he acts insane."

Alfred shook his head. "Hey, I wish I could take you back, but I've already filled your spot and I don't have anything else open right now." He confirmed what Gale already told me: Batons had a sous-chef position open, and he encouraged me to pursue that.

I chuckled at his suggestion. "What a coincidence. I was headed down to talk to Chef Krause right now."

Alfred wished me luck.

My interview with Chef Krause went much better than I could have anticipated. He was super laid back with a demeanor that screamed L.A. When I introduced myself to him and called him Chef Krause, he asked me just to call him Richard. I told him about my experience at Aurora and he laughed.

"It's not how many times you get knocked down, it's how many times you get back up. And with the French, you have to keep getting up. I'm well aware of that French kitchen craziness," he said. "You wouldn't get me back inside one of those places for anything."

Richard was clearly all about the food and was known for taking risks and pushing the envelope. He walked me through the open kitchen, where they were blanching fresh, whole ducks in honey, vinegar, and water. We watched as the chefs used air compressors to separate the skin from the meat before the ducks were hung in the coolers to dry. It was fun watching the ducks blow up like floats in the Macy's Parade. In the back, prep cooks were unwrapping FedEx boxes filled with beautiful produce—all miniature versions of traditional vegetables: baby carrots, baby corn, baby turnips. I had heard that restaurants on the West Coast like Wolfgang Puck's Spago and Chinois were using Asian-inspired ingredients, but Richard, who had been a protégé of Puck's, was one of the first to bring the trend to New York.

Everything about Batons was more casual: from the paper table liners to the relaxed atmosphere and informal staff uniforms. Rather than starched white chef coats and crisp aprons, the kitchen crew all wore baggy pants and fun hats in a variety of prints and colors.

Though it seemed a little sloppy to me, I had to admit these guys looked like they were having a blast, and there was no doubt about it: they were cooking their tails off.

Richard offered me the job and asked me to start right away. I didn't have to think twice. The money was great and the working conditions ten times better than where I had been. Since the restaurant was just a block away from my Greenwich Village apartment, I'd also be able to walk to work. I rushed back to Aurora to give my two weeks notice, but Chef Pangaud just waved his hand at me.

"Get out!" he shouted. "I have no use for you."

And with that, I was free to go. I started working at Batons the very next day and immediately knew I had found a home.

And as the daytime sous-chef, I really got a lot of hands-on time with Richard and Jonathan Eismann, the executive sous-chef. In addition to doing all the prep work and butchering, I was able to be there while Jonathan was handling a lot of the managerial tasks of running the kitchen. We often sat down and went over scheduling or ordering or budgets. Even though I didn't have a lot of experience with this side of the business, I was pleasantly surprised to find that I had a real knack for it.

I loved working in an open kitchen, right in the middle of the action. I enjoyed hearing the buzz from all the chic people who were watching me cook—I felt as if I were part of live theater. Batons was extremely popular with the in crowd, its edgy, black-and-white decor more urban than elegant. Celebrities from TV, film, and music, like Larry King, Sylvester Stallone, and Mick Jagger, found their way through our doors, happy just to hang out and enjoy the atmosphere. Loud eighties music constantly pumped through the dining room and kitchen, giving the place a club-like feel. People just seemed to like being there.

Most of the staff had come in from California, and they shared Richard's passion for great food *and* laid-back living. For these guys, life itself was a party and every night was a weekend. Once we wrapped things up for the night, we'd head out for the clubs. I had been so focused on my career for such a long time, I couldn't remember the last time I had partied. But like riding a bike, I picked it back up in no time. Eventually I was going out every single night, not getting in until two or three o'clock in the morning, and somehow managing to catch a few hours of sleep before heading into work for the next day's shift.

Everything seemed to be working out the way it was supposed to. My job was great and I was learning so much. I finally knew beyond a shadow of a doubt that I could make a good living at this. More important, I realized I was passionate about food and committed to becoming a chef and cooking for the rest of my life. I no longer felt quite so hindered by my lack of formal education.

My relationship with Gale was great. We were connected personally and professionally, and I was pretty sure things were only going to get better from here. But in spite of all these good things, if I were really honest with myself, I had to admit that something was missing—something I couldn't quite put my finger on. I couldn't possibly work any more than I already was. And I couldn't party any harder either. Somehow, no matter how many hours I put in or how many joints I smoked, I couldn't erase the nagging sense of emptiness deep in my soul.

And then we got the call: Greg wanted us to come home.

ROASTED PORCINI-STUFFED LAMB SADDLE WITH FIVE-BEAN RAGOUT

This is a great example of the cooking style developed by great American chefs in the 1980s, when they began layering foods (such as a three-beet salad with a five-bean ragout). The advent of the farm-to-table movement also came in the eighties.

This is definitely comfort food, and I liked to serve it for the element of the surprise it brought to the more sophisticated, contemporary food we served at Tru. I also like to make this for Sunday dinner when I cook for my family. — *SERVES 6*

6 Tbs. olive oil
½ c. sliced porcini mushrooms
2 tsp. minced shallot
1 tsp. minced garlic
Kosher salt
Freshly ground black pepper
One lamb saddle (2 loins; 6 to 7 pounds with bone; 2 to 3 pounds boned)
12 oil-packed sun-dried tomatoes
6 whole fresh basil leaves
1 lb. caul fat (see recipe introduction on page 93)
3 c. five-bean ragout (recipe follows)

1. Heat 2 Tbs. of the olive oil in a medium sauté pan over medium heat until hot. Add the mushrooms and sauté for 7 to 8 minutes or until mushrooms are tender and golden brown. Add the shallots and garlic; cook for 2 to 3 more minutes. Season to taste with salt and pepper. Set aside to cool to room temperature.

2. Using a boning knife, remove the loin from the saddle of lamb, making sure to keep the flap intact. Remove the tenderloin from the opposite side. Reserve the bones for another use. (You can ask the butcher to do this for you.)

3. Making sure to keep the flap attached to the loin, trim the flap so that it's 4 to 5 inches long. Pound the flap with a meat mallet or the bottom of a small, heavy skillet until it's about ¼-inch thick and tender.

4. Place the loin on a work surface with the flap facing away from you. Position the tenderloin in the crack between the loin and the flap.

5. Lay the sun-dried tomatoes in a single layer over the top of the loin. Top the tomatoes with basil leaves. Place the mushroom mixture between the loin and the tenderloin.

6. Carefully roll the loin toward the flap to make a roll about 2 to 3 inches wide.

7. Lay out the caul fat in one even layer. Place the rolled loin at one end and carefully wrap the loin in the caul fat. Put on a tray, cover with plastic wrap, and refrigerate for at least 30 minutes and for up to 8 hours.

8. Preheat the oven to 375°F.

9. Tie the loin securely with kitchen string.

10. Heat the remaining 4 Tbs. of olive oil in a large ovenproof sauté pan over medium-high heat until hot. Sear the lamb on all sides until golden brown.

11. Transfer to the oven and roast for 8 to 12 minutes or until medium to well done. Transfer to a plate and allow to rest for 5 minutes.

12. To serve, spoon some of the bean ragout on the center of a plate. Slice the loin into 2- to 3-inch-wide slices and place a slice on top of the ragout. Repeat to make 5 more servings.

Five-Bean Ragout *(makes about 3½ cups)*
½ c. dried white beans
½ c. dried cranberry beans
½ c. dried flageolet beans
3 Spanish onions, diced
3 carrots, diced
3 bay leaves
3 sprigs fresh thyme
½ c. haricots verts (green beans)
½ c. yellow wax beans
2 Tbs. unsalted butter
2 Tbs. chicken stock
¼ c. finely diced fresh tomato
Kosher salt and freshly ground black pepper
1 Tbs. parsley, chopped
½ Tbs. tarragon, chopped
1 Tbs. chives, chopped

1. Put the white beans, cranberry beans, and flageolet beans in three separate bowls. Add enough cold water to each bowl to cover the beans by 2 inches. Soak the beans for at least 6 hours or overnight. Drain and transfer each to a separate pot.

2. Cut three 10-inch squares of cheesecloth and mound a third of the onion and a third of the carrot in the center of each of the squares. Add 1 bay leaf and 1 sprig of thyme to each. Bring the corners of the cloth together and tie the sachet with kitchen string.

3. Add enough cold water to each pot to cover the beans by about 2 inches. Add a sachet to each pot. Bring to a boil over high heat; reduce the heat, and simmer gently for 45 minutes to 1 hour, or until the beans are tender and cooked through. Add additional water as needed to keep the beans covered.

4. Drain the beans in a colander. Remove and discard the vegetable sachets. Transfer the beans to a large bowl and set aside at room temperature.

5. Meanwhile, in a large pot of lightly salted boiling water, blanch the haricots verts for 4 to 8 minutes or until just tender. Remove with a slotted spoon and immediately submerge in ice cold water. Drain and spread on paper towels to dry.

6. Blanch the wax beans in the same pot of boiling water for 4 to 8 minutes or until just tender. Drain and immediately submerge in ice cold water. Drain in colander.

7. In a large sauté pan, melt the butter over medium heat. Add the white beans, cranberry beans, and flageolet beans; stir in the chicken stock. Add the diced tomatoes, haricots verts, and wax beans and season to taste with salt and pepper. Cook until heated through. Mix in chopped parsley, tarragon, and chives. Cover to keep warm.

━ 13 ━
COMING HOME

The fear of the LORD is the beginning of knowledge,
but fools despise wisdom and instruction.

PROVERBS 1:7

After years of successfully running the kitchen at the Strathallan, Chef Greg Broman had finally decided to open his own place in downtown Rochester. He had named the restaurant Chapel's in honor of French chef Alain Chapel.

"I really think now is the time for this," he told me. "Rochester is primed and ready for something new and high end. I'm trying to pull together the best opening crew that I possibly can, and I want you and Gale to be part of it."

Gale and I didn't know what to think. We were both doing well in New York and had come so far since our days at the Strathallan. But lately, Gale had been feeling it might be time to move on. Although she ultimately wanted to end up in Chicago so she could be closer to her family, Gale respected Greg and had liked working for him.

The more I thought about it, the more I had to admit that the idea of going home to work for Greg was appealing. Maybe that would allow me to get some rest, clean up my act, and dry out again. Plus Greg promised to share all of the opening experience with us so we could learn how to open our own restaurant someday.

And if Gale really was thinking about leaving, I wasn't about to let her get away. I would have followed her anywhere. I still wanted to marry her, and I was counting on the fact that if I asked her enough times, she would eventually soften to the idea and say yes.

After talking about the pros and cons for several weeks, we finally decided to go back—at least long enough to help Greg open his restaurant and get it off the ground. I owed Greg that much; he had really done a lot for me, taking a chance on a rough-looking kid with little experience and no formal training.

As I pulled up to my parents' place after making the decision to move back, I realized just how much I had missed my family and friends. It had been several years since I'd left, and in that time I'd made it back only a handful of times.

I hadn't seen Marco or Paulie since moving to New York, but I had managed to keep up with Eileen through occasional phone calls and letters. She had even come to visit Gale and me once. We had taken her to all the top tourist spots and to some of our favorite bakeries and diners. But mostly we had just hung out, enjoying the time together and catching up on one another's lives. Gale and Eileen had connected right off the bat, which made me happy. Eileen was such an important part of my past, and I really wanted her to be part of my future as well. I didn't have many close friends or family members left anymore; Gale and Eileen *were* my family.

Gale and I began looking for a place to live in the Tenth Ward, my old stomping grounds. One of the first places we looked at was a beautiful old Victorian home that had been divided into two apartments. With lots of old wood and intricate detail work, the place had so much character that we instantly fell in love with it.

Once we'd signed our lease, we headed back to New York to give our notices to Richard at Batons. Two weeks later we rented a moving van to bring our few belongings home to Rochester. We settled in quickly and immediately got down to business at Chapel's. With only two months until the opening, we had a lot to accomplish in a very short amount of time.

Greg had brought a lot of the old Strath team back together, so it was pretty easy to get back into the groove. We spent about two months cooking through the menu and getting ready for the opening. Everything was classic Greg. As always, he was very organized and disciplined, still serving classic French cuisine but now with some contemporary items thrown in as well. He had designed the kitchen to be both practical and efficient and filled it with brand-new equipment. Unlike the opening at Aurora, I felt so much more involved and appreciated here. I had a little more insight this time around too.

I was the *poissonier*. We also had a sauté chef, a vegetable chef, and a garde-manger. Gale ran the pastry department on her own, with only a culinary student for an assistant. We did five lunches and six dinners a week with that skeleton crew. We couldn't even call in sick because we knew there would be no one else to cover our station.

Although it was bare bones, Greg had really put together a quality team. We all understood how much this meant to Greg, and we were willing to do whatever it took to help him succeed. Because there were so few of us, we were supposed to work splits, which meant we would go in at seven in the morning to set up for lunch, do lunch service until two, set up for dinner, and then take a few hours off before coming back for dinner at five. Unfortunately, once we opened, we never stopped, usually working straight through until ten or eleven at night.

The schedule was insane. I was working all the time, and I was exhausted. I felt almost frail. Sometimes I managed to grab a couple hours of sleep in the banquet room between shifts; the rest of the time I was usually running solely on speed and caffeine.

We were working harder than we ever had in New York. Thankfully, that paid off, and Chapel's managed to get great reviews right off the bat. A lot of that success was the result of Greg's attention to detail and insistence on quality old-world scratch cooking.

One of his signature dishes was a trout au bleu, an old-world classic dish that Greg had reworked and that required us to start with a live fish. In France or the larger U.S. cities, it was not uncommon for a restaurant to have a live trout or shellfish tank somewhere on the premises. But we didn't have that luxury. Instead, we purchased our trout from a local fishery and kept them in a plastic baby pool just inside the walk-in cooler. When an order came in, I'd have to grab the keys to the cooler and then head back there with my net. Once I snagged one,

I'd carefully lift it out of the net by the gills. Then with my free hand, I'd slide my knife into the trout's underbelly, slicing in a straight line right down the middle. With minimal handling, I quickly gutted and cleaned the fish before plunging it in a pot of simmering fish fumet. As the fish poached, it would turn a beautiful sky blue color.

Even with all of my experience thus far, I found that because Greg was so focused on his craft, every step required intense concentration. Everything we did was really, really complex and really, really difficult. I had notes all over my station just to help me remember stuff.

When I was still in New York, I had begun to feel in my knees the effects of standing all day. Now I was starting to feel it in my back as well. I was about forty pounds overweight by this time, and carrying all those extra pounds was taking a toll. I wasn't eating well—mostly just getting by on a quick employee meal here and there, and relying on alcohol and pharmaceuticals as my main fuel source. I wasn't alone. While all the guys in the kitchen were extremely talented, they were also all really big partiers.

After we'd been back in Rochester for about six months, I started to push Gale again about getting married. Still, she wasn't ready.

Gale was always upbeat, the exact opposite of me. She was into the journey, enjoying the adventure. She had always been like that. I thought back to all the times back in New York when she would say, "Let's take the train to the Upper East Side or Harlem and just see what kind of treasures we can find." We never had a plan or a destination. And if we got lost along the way, she thought that was even better.

I, on the other hand, hated the not-knowing. I was the planner, always in search of the sure thing, something I could really sink my life into that would remain solid and strong and never crumble underneath me. So far I had not found it.

I was tired and frustrated and in pain, and I'm ashamed to admit that too often I made Gale the target of my discontent. Although I had initially been drawn to her easygoing nature, now it was starting to bug me. I couldn't understand how she could always be so happy and just roll with the punches; it sometimes made me feel like she didn't care, even though that wasn't true.

We hadn't fought very much at all when we lived in New York.

We had rarely gotten frustrated with each other because we both knew what the mission was: to become chefs and to run our own restaurants. That's why we were in New York. That's why we worked as much as we did, missing many family holidays, birthdays, weddings, and other special occasions. We fueled the fire for each other. We were struggling artists, trying to learn our craft. It wasn't easy, but we were doing it together.

But now that we'd been together for more than a few years, Gale was beginning to see the darker side of my personality. I definitely had my mom's temper, and like her, I didn't care who I hurt when my rage reached its peak. I was so goal-oriented that being nice was simply not an option for me. I still struggled with my dyslexia—just writing out a recipe could take me twice as long as everyone else. I felt stupid and inferior to everyone around me, especially Gale. She was so intellectual and bright. She possessed all the qualities I lacked, and that frustrated me all the more. The anger, bitterness, and resentment gnawed at me constantly, driving me to work harder and longer than everyone else.

The more stressed out I got, the more neurotic I became: labeling everything and becoming very obsessive about organizing and cleaning. If something was out of place, I simply couldn't function. Overwhelmed by a rising sense of panic, I would have to stop whatever I was doing and make things right. Once everything was in its place, I figured I must be okay. It's the only way I made it through the day sometimes—that, and drugs.

On the first New Year's Eve at Chapel's, we were booked solid with two full seatings. The New Year's Eve menu was even more complex than usual and the energy in the kitchen was intense. Already sweltering from the heat of the flattops and the grill, we were all pumped up. This was our first New Year's, and we needed to make a strong impression. You could cut through the tension with a knife.

Greg knew we were all hyped up.

"You guys need to chill," he said. "You're going to do great. Anybody want to celebrate New Year's with a trip?" A couple of the guys shook their heads no, but others joined in. I figured I might as well join the fun since I'd often used acid recreationally back in my high school and Wendy's days and had always functioned pretty well, even while tripping. I stuck out my tongue and Greg dropped a square of blotter acid right onto it. He handed me a second sheet for later.

The drug's effects had already kicked in by the time the first order was called a few minutes later. Giggling and horsing around, we had a great time busting our tails to get things out on time and in order. The drugs helped alleviate the stress, and we quickly got into the swing of things. Halfway through the first seating, I looked around and realized that we were doing it! We had managed to put out a fantastic lineup of food and the customers were raving. Knowing we had only one more seating to go, I figured I was on the downside now. This was New Year's Eve, and I was in the mood for celebrating. I took the second hit.

I should have known better.

We got into the second seating, and we were doing great. But I could tell something wasn't quite right. I felt like I was doing a real hard-core workout at the gym. Sweat poured down my face, and I couldn't slow my breathing. Every time I turned my head, color streams and light trails blurred my vision. I couldn't get my eyes to focus on the salmon I was preparing on the grill in front of me. I started to laugh and then couldn't stop. Greg came over and put his hand on my shoulder.

"Looks like you need to go to the back for a minute to focus," he said. "Go get your head together and then get back out here."

I grabbed a beer from the cooler and headed toward the back alley. I was flying so high—too high—and no matter what I did, I couldn't bring myself back down. Popping open the beer, I took a swig and then lit a joint, hoping the pot would settle me down and stop my heart from racing so fast.

Nothing worked. I finished off the beer and went back into the kitchen. Unable to stand on my own, I fell against the wall and stumbled into Greg's office. Immediately, Greg, Gale, and a guy named Blaine surrounded me.

"Rick, you need to snap out of this," Greg said, smacking the sides of my face. I burst out laughing, spewing spit in his face, which only made me laugh harder.

"What did you do?" Blaine demanded, clearly disappointed. "We need you out there, man." Blaine was such a cool guy. Super intelligent and super talented, he never drank or did drugs. Like Gale, he was a perfectionist who refused to let anything interfere with his work. I liked Blaine a lot and always found his New Age ideas fascinating. I hated the idea that he might think less of me.

Suddenly I was laughing again uncontrollably.

Blaine grabbed me by the shoulders and looked me in the eye.

"Don't mess with me," he shouted, his face just inches from mine. "I am the center of the universe."

Blaine was very intelligent. He had always been the philosopher in our group and was known for saying off-the-wall things. Usually we laughed it off and ignored him. But on this night and in this frame of mind, I couldn't do that. He looked like Satan himself, and he was talking directly to me, staking his claim as the center of my life.

Panic rose up in my throat. Searching wildly for a way to escape Blaine's clutches, I caught a glimpse of my own hands; the skin was melting away, leaving only blood and tendons and bones. The room was suddenly very dark and filled with evil, demonic forces.

"Take him home," Greg said to Gale, and she quickly led me out to the car. As she drove me home, I watched out the back window as fleets of demons chased after our car. Completely overwhelmed, I realized this was *my* trip—a reflection of the horror and misery and mess that was *my* life. I made Gale pull over so I could throw up.

Once we got home, Gale put me into bed and tried to get me to calm down. But it was no use. I was hyperventilating and getting paranoid. I couldn't stop the melting and the scratching and the thrashing. I could see the panic in her eyes. After all the years of doing drugs and feeling I had it down, I couldn't believe I was losing control.

Finally after twelve hours, I fell asleep, but the nightmares were horrific. And when I woke up, I was still tripping. When would this ever end? Was I going to be like this forever?

Gale leaned over me, wiping my forehead with a damp cloth. "I can't believe those drugs are still in you," I heard her say, just before I slipped back into a coma-like sleep.

Two days later, I finally woke up and felt some sense of control once again. I was still shaking and my thoughts still rushing, but it wasn't as bad as it had been. Gale fed me soup and tea, hoping to flush the acid out of my system. I called in sick to work, knowing I was still

unable to function there. What if I had done too much damage to
come back this time?

Fear gripped my soul. Had I ruined everything with this one splurge
of a drug trip? Was all that hard work for nothing? *Please, God, don't let
that be true.* I thought back to the images I had seen: Blaine's face, the
demonic forces chasing our car. Had I brought on that evil?

I thought about my life, my addictive, over-the-top, all-or-nothing
way of doing things. I thought about how reckless I had been for all
those years and how many stupid chances I had taken with my life and
the lives of others. I should have died so many times in the past, but
for some reason, I was still here. *Why, God—why am I still here?*

I knew I didn't deserve it, but I cried out to God anyway, begging
for one more chance. *I promise I won't ever touch drugs again,* I vowed.
I knew if I ever did, I would be dead. I also realized that most people
don't believe in miracles until they need one. This was the moment I
needed one. *Please get me out of this state of mind. Please save me.*

I thought about a passage of Scripture I had learned during my days
at Sally's church: "Put on the full armor of God so that you can take your
stand against the devil's schemes. For our struggle is not against flesh and
blood, but against the rulers, against the authorities, against the powers
of this dark world and against the spiritual forces of evil in the heavenly
realms. Therefore put on the full armor of God, so that when the day
of evil comes, you may be able to stand your ground, and after you have
done everything, to stand" (Ephesians 6:11-13, NIV).

I knew I had been living without protection, almost inviting bad
things to happen to me. I was afraid I wasn't going to be able to recover
from this. But if I could, I promised God I would begin to live and act
more responsibly. I was true to my word—I never did drugs again.

The day after turning to God, I returned to work, finally able to
function and think clearly. I figured I had really blown it and that Greg
would tell me to pack up my knives and move on. He didn't. But he
did pull me aside. "You really need to clean up your life," he said.

I nodded and promised I would. Then I quickly got down to the
business of the day. I knew Greg would be watching me pretty closely
over the coming weeks, and I couldn't afford to mess up again.

For Gale, however, that trip proved to be a real turning point.

About three weeks later, she sat me down one evening and said, "Rick, I think it's time for me to take a break. I need to be alone for a while, and I think I need to do it now."

I blinked, trying to process what she was telling me.

"Are you breaking up with me?" I asked.

"No, I wouldn't call it that," she said. "I just need some time away. I've never really been on my own. I went straight from living with my parents to being married to being with you. I just need to be on my own with no attachments. I'm going back to Chicago, and I want to go alone."

I could certainly understand why she would feel that way, and I can't say that I blamed her. She knew I wanted to marry her, but considering the way I had been acting over the past few years, and especially the past few months, I was clearly in no shape to be anyone's husband.

As I watched Gale pack up her things, I felt my world beginning to crumble around me. I had really blown it this time: my job, my relationship, my life. I desperately wished I could hit "rewind" and start over. My life was in shambles again, and it was my own fault. I needed to get back to ground zero; I would start at Sacred Heart.

The following week, I showed up for Mass twenty minutes early. I dipped my fingers into the holy water and made the sign of the cross before sliding into the pew. I felt safe here. It was comfortable and easy, like a pair of well-worn slippers. I knew when to stand and when to sit, when to put money in the basket, and when to go forward. The statues and the stained glass and the Communion and confession brought a sense of relief to my soul I had not felt in a long time.

In the weeks to follow, I made it a point to attend Mass as often as I could, usually followed by dinner at my parents' house. It was better than going home to my empty apartment or going out to get wasted, but I could see the worry in their eyes and hated that I was bringing my darkness into their world. I couldn't help but wonder what Gale was doing. Had she found someone new? Was she missing me?

I was a wreck. I wasn't drinking or doing drugs, but that almost made things worse. With nothing to numb the pain, my heart was like a raw, gaping wound. The only way I could function was to keep my head down and do my work. At least that was the same.

ROASTED SPICY ARTICHOKES

We did lots of vegetable work at Chapel's. That meant lots of cleaning and turning vegetables. In fact, we brought in fresh vegetables by the case, and four or five of us would stand around a table, getting them ready for the various teams in the kitchen. This is one of my favorite artichoke dishes, and I think you'll love it too. Just be sure to wear plastic gloves as you prep so your hands won't turn black. (If you've never cleaned an artichoke, it would be good to read up on it before preparing this dish.) — *SERVES 4*

8 medium globe artichokes, cleaned
6 lemons
3 garlic cloves, cut in half
1¼ tsp. red chili flakes
3 c. white wine
½ gallon water or vegetable stock
1 Tbs. kosher salt
½ bunch parsley stems
¼ tsp. peppercorns
1 bay leaf
½ c. olive oil
1 clove garlic, minced
2 Tbs. parsley, chopped
2 Tbs. chives, chopped
2 c. seasoned Italian bread crumbs
½ c. Parmesan cheese

1. Be sure artichokes are cleaned correctly—peel the stem, remove the outer leaves and inside choke. Be sure to trim bottom of choke stem so artichokes will stand upright while roasting. Hold artichokes in acidulated water to prevent browning.
2. Sweat the garlic cloves and ¼ tsp. red chili flakes in a large saucepan for 2 minutes. Add wine, vegetable stock, and salt; bring to a boil.
3. Add the juice from one lemon, parsley stems, peppercorns, bay leaf, and artichokes.
4. Simmer artichokes for about 30 minutes. Remove from broth; reserve 1 c. of this poaching liquid.
5. Whisk together olive juice a, juice from one lemon, 1 tsp. red chili flakes, garlic, parsley, and chives. Toss artichokes in mixture.
6. Pour reserved broth into baking dish. Stand up artichokes in dish and sprinkle each with ¼ c. bread crumbs.
7. Bake at 350°F for 15 minutes. After removing from oven, sprinkle artichokes with Parmesan cheese and garnish with lemon quarters.

14
CHICAGO

Rejoice in the Lord always. Again I will say, rejoice!

PHILIPPIANS 4:4

Just when I thought things couldn't get any worse, I got a call from Gale. She had found a job, moved back in with her parents temporarily, and started hanging out with her old friends, including old boyfriends. She thought we should be free to date other people.

What could I say? I didn't have any hold on her; it's not like we were engaged. I had no choice but to say okay.

Now, in addition to my depression and other neurotic behaviors, I began to obsess over Gale and what she was doing. I thought about her all the time, wondering who she was with and if she was falling in love with someone else. I began to send her cards and flowers and candy, calling her ten times a day, apologizing and begging for her to forgive me.

Though she was always sweet and polite, careful not to hurt my feelings, I was pretty sure my stalker-like behavior was only pushing her further away from me. But even so, I couldn't stop.

Never had I wanted a drink or to get high so badly, but I had made a promise to God, and there was no way I was going to risk that lightning bolt. Fear can be a beautiful thing. It kept me clean and focused.

I finally decided that I needed to see Gale face-to-face so I could stop obsessing and decide what was going on with our relationship. I had never been to Chicago, and I had no idea what I was doing, but I bought myself a plane ticket and flew in to O'Hare. Amid the rush of the crowds and chaos, I made my way to a pay phone and called Gale. I had timed my arrival so that it was her day off.

"Hey," I said when she picked up the phone. "What are you doing right now?"

"Not too much, just hanging out with my mom and dad."

"Oh good. I need a ride. Can you come pick me up?"

"What do you mean?"

"I'm at the airport and I need a ride—and probably a place to crash tonight. Can you come get me?"

I knew Gale well enough to know she was probably smiling on the other end of the phone.

"Rick, you are crazy! I can't believe you are here. Hang on; I'll be there in an hour."

I breathed a sigh of relief. So far, so good.

When she pulled up to the curb in her little silver Nissan, I tossed my bag into the backseat.

"I am so sorry I've been such a jerk," I said. "Please give me another chance. I'd like to try to work this out with you."

Gale looked up, her eyes glistening with tears.

"Okay," she said quietly. We spent the weekend hanging out and driving around the city. We cooked together and just enjoyed checking out the restaurants in Chicago.

When it was time to head back to the airport, I didn't want to leave. Gale promised to come to Rochester to visit soon, which made it a little easier to say good-bye.

I went back to work with a spring in my step and a renewed sense of hope for the future. I had kept my promise to God to clean up my act, and now things actually seemed to be going in the right direction with Gale as well. I needed to make her visit one she would never forget.

I went out and bought a framed poster of the Eiffel Tower that we hung over table 21 in the dining room at Chapel's. And then I went down to Zales in Long Ridge Mall and picked out the best engagement ring I could afford. It wasn't much, but I thought it was beautiful. I hoped Gale would agree.

When Gale arrived in town, I was ready. I had to work the first seating and at least get the orders out for the second, but after that, I was free to go. Excited and a little nervous, I couldn't put out the food fast enough. When things finally slowed down enough that I felt comfortable leaving, I slipped into the office where I exchanged my spattered chef's coat for some clean clothes. I splashed a little cologne on my cheeks, knowing it was probably pointless. The smell of fish was so deeply embedded in my pores, I never really got rid of it.

Gale and I sat down together at a two-top toward the back of the dining room. A few other guests were still lingering over their desserts and drinks, but for the most part, we had the place to ourselves. Since it was such a rarity for the two of us to sit down and just enjoy a good meal together, I told the server that we wanted to do all six courses. But as the third course was arriving, I couldn't contain my excitement any longer.

"Gale, I am sorry things got out of control over New Year's, but I'm committed to you and to our careers. I am done with drugs and all the excess of that old lifestyle."

I pointed to the poster above our table. "I promised you that one day I would propose to you under the Eiffel Tower. It may not be Paris, but it's the best I can do right now. You are the best thing that's ever happened to me. We make an amazing team. What would you think about spending the rest of your life with me?"

She smiled and shook her head as if to say, *I give up*. I could tell from the look on her face that she was done fighting me.

"Yes," she said quietly, reaching across the table and taking my hand.

Finally! I had never felt so happy in all my life. Even though I had spent the last seven years focusing on my professional future, I had to admit that Gale was really the main motivation for everything I had done to this point. I would have done anything to keep this relationship. Now I felt like I was finally crossing the finish line after completing a marathon. No, make that a triathlon.

Gale had gotten a great job working at Carlos' in Highland Park with Chefs Roland and Mary Beth Liccioni, and she didn't want to leave. That was fine with me. I was willing to go back to Chicago with her.

Chapel's was doing great, so I wasn't worried about leaving Greg in a bind. I turned in my notice and started packing up the apartment. I planned to move to Chicago as soon as possible, but we decided that since I had such a big family, we would come back to have the wedding in Rochester. Gale had already done the big traditional wedding, so we figured we would have a second, smaller reception in Chicago after we were married. We set the date—October 1, 1988—and then headed to Chicago so I could find a job.

We knew we didn't want to work together this time, so I hit the pavement, starting with Le Francais in Wheeling. I interviewed with Jean Banchet for over half an hour. He was impressed with my New York résumé but not with the way I looked. My hair was long, hanging halfway down my back, and I had three piercings in each ear and a number of tattoos. That look didn't work in a kitchen like his.

I went back to the classifieds. I saw an ad for a new restaurant called Scoozi!, owned by a company called Lettuce Entertain You. They had an opening for an executive sous-chef.

I set up an appointment with the corporate chef, Russell, of Lettuce Entertain You, and he asked me to come in to do a tasting. I did my homework so I knew what they were looking for: high-quality, scratch Italian cooking. This was my forte: good Italian food and lots of it. I went nuts: I made linguini with garlic and anchovy crumbs with lemon zest; pounded salmon with a crisp fennel salad; osso buco with saffron risotto; whole, roasted bronzini with truffled polenta; a white pizza with spinach and roasted garlic (and another with Swiss chard and mushrooms). They wanted comfortable Italian; I would give them comfortable Italian. I was the epitome of comfortable Italian.

The chef loved it. After tasting all of my dishes, he sat me down and said, "Okay, we're going to open Scoozi! in two months. We anticipate at least six hundred covers every day for lunch and maybe up to eight hundred each night for dinner—"

"Whoa, whoa, whoa—what?" I had worked in some busy places before, but I knew that with this volume of cooking, a restaurant had to make concessions. "How many seats do you have again?"

"Three hundred fifty. Why?"

As much as I hated to admit it, I had to tell him I really didn't want to do that much volume right then. Visions of Tavern on the Green floated through my head, and I knew I would never be happy just cranking out huge amounts of food every day. It pained me to tell the chef that I was going to have to pass.

"I'm sorry to have wasted your time," I told him. "I just don't think this is for me. I'm really looking for something a little more refined with a little less volume."

I started to leave and he said, "Wait a minute, before you go, I want you to meet the president of the company, Rich Melman. Let me make a phone call and see if he's available to meet with you."

I checked my watch. I was flying back to New York that afternoon to pack up the rest of our things, and if I wanted to make my flight, I knew I needed to get on the road.

But the chef was already on the phone with Rich. He put his hand over the mouthpiece and said, "Don't worry. Rich will take care of changing your flight."

I wondered what kind of power this guy had. No one had ever done anything like this for me before. Part of me definitely didn't trust the situation—why would they go out of their way to make these kinds of accommodations for a nobody like me? But the chef set up a meeting between me and Rich at the Lettuce corporate offices the next morning, and when I got home and told Gale, she freaked out.

"Do you know who Rich Melman is? He's one of the most successful restaurateurs in the country. And they are bringing you in for a one-on-one with him? This is huge; this is a really big deal."

I didn't have a car yet, so the next morning, we got up and Gale drove me to the Lettuce corporate offices, which were on the first floor of a huge glass-and-mirrored building. Gale dropped me at the entrance and said she'd wait for me out front.

"I'll see you soon," I said. "I shouldn't be more than a half hour or forty-five minutes."

As I entered the lobby, I was immediately struck by the quirky decor. A woman sat at the reception desk, with a huge head of lettuce painted on the wall behind her. Offbeat statues and funky photographs lined the walls, as well as numerous articles touting Rich Melman's success in the Chicago market. It was such a playful environment, I couldn't help but grin.

While I waited for Mr. Melman, I sat and watched the traffic of people moving in and around the office. While certainly a busy city, Chicago had a completely different feel than New York. It seemed more down to earth, more comfortable for some reason. I could definitely see myself settling here if the right opportunity came along.

I turned to see a good-looking young guy in blue jeans and a baseball cap coming toward me. He held out his hand.

"Hi, Ricky," he said. "I'm Rich Melman. It's nice to meet you."

"It's nice to meet you, too, Mr. Melman," I said. I was thinking, *No one but my parents call me Ricky. What a nice, personal way to address me.*

"Please, enough with the 'Mr.' My dad was Mr. Melman. Call me Rich."

I couldn't believe this was *the* Richard Melman that Gale had gone on and on about. There was nothing pretentious or arrogant about this guy whatsoever. In the restaurant world, where power and prestige and position made all kinds of bad behavior acceptable, it was unheard of for someone at this level to be so warm and personable—let alone show up for work in blue jeans and a baseball cap.

"We have a phrase here: 'bases loaded, out of the park,'" Rich said. "My chef tells me you really knocked the tasting out of the park yesterday. I love food, and I love working one-on-one with chefs who love food."

"I'm glad to hear that," I said. "I'm sorry about Scoozi! I just don't think I want to do that kind of volume right now."

"I completely understand that. Come on, let's go into my office where we can talk."

Rich's office was big and inviting. I sat down on a soft leather sofa, and Rich sat across from me in a huge overstuffed chair. His walls were covered with articles and reviews for the Pump Room, Ambria, and R. J. Grunts. Awards lined the shelves amid rows and rows of cookbooks and culinary magazines. Surprisingly, I felt completely at home here. It was as if Rich and I had known each other our whole lives. I liked him immediately.

We got right down to business as Rich pulled out my résumé and started perusing my work history. He was familiar with all the places I had worked, including the Strathallan. When he saw I had worked at the Gotham, he said, "That's one of my favorite places to eat. I love anything Alfred does and try to go there when I'm in New York."

And then he asked me to tell him about working at Tavern on the Green. I started at the beginning, explaining what it was like to work in the heat of that kitchen producing such a high volume of food every day. And then I went even further back, telling him about my Italian childhood and the food I had grown up preparing and enjoying. I even told him about my dad going to prison and how that had affected me both personally and professionally.

Rich understood. He told me about working in his family deli in Skokie, and how he had spent much of his life striving to earn the praise of his father. Surprised that he was opening up like this, I felt like it might be safe to lower my guard and tell him a little more. I explained that I had dyslexia and had not finished high school. I described my struggle to educate myself and learn everything I could about the world of professional cooking.

The more I talked, the more comfortable I felt. Rich continued to nod and smile, clearly not judging me or thinking less of me because of what he was hearing. We shared our stories for quite some time, until I happened to look down at my watch. We had been talking for two and a half hours. And poor Gale was still hanging out somewhere out front, waiting for me to finish.

"I have really enjoyed talking to you, Rich," I said. "But I'm going to have to get going."

Rich stood up. "I can tell you would be a great fit for this company," he said. "I definitely understand your hesitancy about the volume at Scoozi! I'm thinking you might do better at Avanzare, which is an upscale, more contemporary northern Italian restaurant. We average about three hundred covers down there. What do you think?"

"That sounds perfect. It's probably more my speed."

"Yeah, I think you're right." Rich nodded, rubbing his chin. "You and Gale need to go have dinner down there and check it out. It'll be on me. And then I want you to do a tasting with me and our head chef, Joe, and maybe Marvin and Fred, a couple of the partners."

Ten minutes later, I was outside the building and dodging traffic as I made my way to Gale's car. I'm sure I looked like a fool as I ran between cars, grinning from ear to ear, but I didn't care. I was in a great city with an unbelievable opportunity with one of the best restaurateurs in the country. I really started to see my future.

After enjoying a fantastic dinner compliments of Rich, I did my best to wow the team at the next day's tasting. I had worked through my menu until two in the morning—a goat cheese ravioli with wild mushrooms, a pounded salmon with a fennel salad, ricotta and basil stuffed chicken breasts and roasted delicata squash with orange and vanilla, and a roasted bistecca with pistachio pesto. Although I should have been nervous, I felt surprisingly calm about the whole thing.

After the tasting, Rich and I sat down in one of the booths.

"Great job today," he said. "Everyone is really impressed and excited to have you join the Lettuce crew. How soon can you start?"

"I need to give my two weeks notice and move to Chicago."

When I climbed into the car with Gale, I was smiling like crazy.

"I got the job! He loved it!"

Later that afternoon, I finally boarded my flight back to Rochester, excited to pack up my things and get started. Being part of the Lettuce Entertain You machine was a whole new ball game for me. This wasn't just one restaurant and one owner; this was an entire corporation.

Avanzare was extremely popular, and we were busy all the time, usually averaging between 250 and 300 covers for lunch and 350 to 400 for dinner. I helped develop the specials and fine-tune the menu. It was almost as if this role had been custom-made for me. Rich had based the Avanzare concept on modern Milanese Italian cooking. Starting with classic dishes like eggplant parmigiana, lasagna, and fettuccine, we dressed them up with contemporary techniques and served them on beautiful china. The base cooking went back to my childhood. I could do this kind of cooking in my sleep. Avanzare had been earning high praise even before I got there, including a number of three-starred reviews, so my main job was to maintain the high standards that had already been set as well as move Avanzare ahead by keeping the menu fresh and changing with the seasons. I was having the time of my life.

The month I came on board, Robert De Niro and Kevin Costner happened to be in town shooting *The Untouchables*. The cast and crew spent a lot of time in our neighborhood, and they often ended the day with a meal at Avanzare. I liked to joke that I was helping De Niro put on all that weight for the movie. After that, we became known as a real celebrity hangout.

After about a year and a half on the job, I was able to broaden my reach a bit. The restaurant was running quite well on its own, and I was able to slip away occasionally to help Rich out at the corporate offices. He'd often call me and other members of the team in for tastings or to develop menu ideas, especially when he was working on new stuff for Scoozi!, the Pump Room, Foodlife, or Hat Dance. Rich was a great conduit when it came to bringing together a group of chefs to work on singular dishes and find the best one.

Working with Rich was truly enlightening. If Rochester had been my culinary high school, Chicago was easily culinary college. Lettuce was the next step—an entrepreneurial-driven but very large company with multiple concepts. It combined the best of both worlds: great food *and* great business sense.

Everything we did was very methodical and organized. Lettuce Entertain You tracked inventory in all of its restaurants very carefully. We created daily, weekly, and monthly product reports; calculated food and labor costs down to the penny; and generated detailed buying guides for every kitchen. It was all about making operations as efficient as possible.

Surprisingly, I was totally digging the business side of things. Up to this point in my career, everything had been about the food and the service: the quality, the quantity, and the speed. Now, I got a whole new perspective as Rich taught me to look at these same issues with a focus on profit. He poured the same passion into the business side as the operations side. Whenever I got the opportunity, I peppered him with questions about the business, trying to mine the depths of his wisdom and get everything I could from my time with him. So many chefs in my past had taken me under their wing—Jim, Greg, Alfred—but I loved the one-on-one time I had with Rich. He was inspiring and someone I wanted to emulate: smart, discerning, and generous with his time and means. He also had great integrity and was an all-around good guy. Although his company was extremely successful and large, Rich was more focused on being the best, not the biggest, and it was all about the food and touching the customer. Corner Bakery, Maggiano's, Big Bowl, and Wildfire—all are mainstream concepts Rich and Lettuce Entertain You developed and later sold to even bigger corporations.

The more time I spent down at headquarters, the more people I got to know, including a couple of the founding corporate partners, Charles Haskell and Fred Joast. When they learned I did not have a high school diploma and struggled to read everything from a profit-and-loss statement to a recipe, these two guys personally decided to oversee my education. Charles taught me how to cost out recipes and build a successful budget. Fred was a hard-core disciplinarian of Austrian descent who had a heart of gold. I knew he loved old-school cooking, so I cooked that way for him. Together we would pore over the Avanzare menu, always looking for ways to improve our dishes. At Lettuce, we would bring in five different kinds of clams, taste each one, and then do a comparison among those varieties. It wasn't uncommon for us to bring in other chefs from New York or Los Angeles or Italy in order to find the best, whether it was the best sausage maker or best cheese producer.

Meanwhile, Gale and I were planning our wedding and trying to buy a house. As an only child from a large Italian family, I knew that having a big Italian wedding was really important to my parents. As much as I wanted to get married, we did have several issues to work through right from the start.

Since I had no siblings, passing on my family name was important to me. But Gale had always been Gale Gand. She had spent so much time cultivating her brand, I understood why she would want to keep her last name, but even so, I wondered how that would play out if we ever did have children.

In addition, she was Jewish. I had no intention of converting, nor did she have any desire to join the Catholic church. Even though I was not a practicing Catholic, I still believed in the Son of God. I believed in his birth, his death, and his resurrection. It would have been nearly impossible for me to turn my back on that belief and become Jewish. And anyway, Gale didn't necessarily want me to convert; she just didn't want me to push her to become Catholic.

I always used to say that Gale was Switzerland. She just wanted everyone to get along. From the very beginning, our relationship was all about compromise and finding the middle ground. So in that spirit, we decided to have our ceremony at the Unity Church in Rochester.

We invited 325 guests, nearly all from my side. Six bridesmaids and six groomsmen stood up for us, including Marco, Paulie, and Eileen, whom Gale now considered a friend. After the ceremony, we put on a huge spread with tons of killer food. My aunts cooked for days just getting ready for the festivities. Gale made the cake and set up an amazing dessert table, and my cousins made up all the Italian cookie trays. It was a great party.

And then Gale and I hopped on a plane and headed for Europe for our honeymoon. We rented a car and proceeded to eat our way through Paris and Rome. Our goal was to eat at as many three-star Michelin restaurants as we could. We had read so much in preparation for this trip and made a list of all the places we wanted to try. Jamin was the first on our list.

When we landed in France, we immediately headed there. We had a 1:00 p.m. reservation, and even though we were totally jet lagged and hungover after two days of partying with my family, we were both really excited to eat at this restaurant.

We were seated at an elegant table near a window. Everything from the china to the crystal to the silverware was gorgeous. The chef, Joël Robuchon, was like a rock star to me.

Just a few minutes later, the waiter approached our table and set a tiny china dish in front of each of us. On each plate was a delicately prepared raw scallop topped with caviar and vinaigrette.

I was immediately impressed with this special little gift from Chef Joël Robuchon, and I vowed right then and there that I would one day have amuse-bouche in my own repertoire. (Who'd have guessed back then that one day I would write a whole book about amuse-bouche?)

Gale and I spent the next four weeks going to chocolate shops, bakeries, produce markets, fish markets, and three-star Michelin restaurants. Our entire honeymoon was centered 100 percent around food and foodstuff. We started what we called our "dream file," in which we documented every single experience, taking detailed notes on every meal, saving every menu, photographing every restaurant, both inside and out. This was a practice we would continue for the next ten years, and it served us well.

We also began a "wish file," filling it with pictures, notes, and ideas of what we might one day want to include in our own restaurant. We jotted notes about china patterns we liked, decor ideas we thought were particularly unique, and even an amazing dish we ate at Jacques Maximin and Alain Ducasse on the French Riviera. We figured that one day all of these things would help jump-start our thinking when it came time to plan, design, and decorate our own place.

When we got back home, we were deeply in debt, but rich in experience. With all that I had seen, eaten, and taken in, I felt better prepared to go into an interview and play the game at a much higher level. I had always been told that I needed not only to apprentice, but also to travel, to see, to work, and to eat. I still try to get to Europe once or twice a year as part of my continuing education.

About this time, I got a phone call from a headhunter. The folks who ran Mama Mia Pasta in Chicago's Loop were looking to do a contemporary Italian restaurant called Bella Luna, and they wondered if I could help them get it off the ground. In addition to helping to design the place, I would be the executive chef of this full-service restaurant—my first gig as head chef. I asked Gale to be my head pastry chef. This was the first time we would be working together as a married couple, and I hoped I would be able to handle it better than I had at Chapel's. I didn't want to blow the opportunity to be both a chef/pastry chef and husband/wife team.

Sometimes when I looked at Gale, I had to shake my head and wonder. She always seemed so sure-footed, never showing any doubt. Of the two of us, she was definitely the one with the grander plan; she knew exactly where she wanted to go and what she wanted to do. She never doubted that she would one day reach the top.

I was never quite as sure—or secure—as she was. I doubted myself every single day. It seemed I was always fighting an uphill battle, one that she had already climbed. Being in Chicago, Gale definitely had the hometown advantage. She was even beginning to get a bit of press and notoriety within Chicago's restaurant community. But I had to wonder, what about me? Would I end up as *Mr. Gand*?

Admittedly, Gale never held her success over my head. She made it clear that we were in this together: fifty-fifty. Our goals were exactly the same: buy a house, be chefs, write cookbooks, own a restaurant, maybe even have kids one day. We slid right back into things at Bella Luna, working side by side and always in sync, just like old times.

We both loved Bella Luna. It was a cool little Italian restaurant with an open kitchen and wood-burning ovens. We had a lot of freedom when it came to creating the menu and building a team. We put together a great staff of people, including a couple of kids from Lettuce and Levy, another Chicago enterprise.

We asked Eileen to come out and help us with the pizza. She had worked in a few pizzerias since leaving Wendy's, and I wanted her expertise in bringing a great New York–style pie to the Windy City. Eileen had already moved to Chicago, where she worked as a manager at a Domino's Pizza. That meant she knew the science, equipment, and operations of a pizzeria. I also trusted her work ethic, which would help us get through the opening.

As with any new venture, the stress level was high—really high. This was the first time I was truly accountable for everything. I was young and still trying to figure out the mechanics of running the business side of things.

I knew this time around it would be *my* name in the press, for good or for bad. If I messed this up, I might never be able to salvage my reputation. With that in mind, I worked twelve hours a day, six days a week. My day off was spent running errands and doing laundry. I also tightened the controls and ran the kitchen in much the same way I had seen other head chefs do it: by screaming, throwing things, and breaking dishware. I was like a drill sergeant, ruling with an iron fist. There was no room for mediocrity or mistakes. I knew this kind of tactic would result in daily casualties of war, but

I believed it was worth the cost. Driven by fear of failure, every day felt like life and death.

During our first week of opening, the general manager overbooked one of our first lunches and slammed the kitchen. As hard as we worked, we couldn't get the food out quickly enough. The waitstaff was scrambling. As lunch was finally starting to wind down, the stress got the better of me. I marched out to the hostess stand and started screaming at the manager, berating him for being so stupid and putting us in such an impossible position. Oblivious to the full dining room of people now staring at me in horror, I turned to the phone and began to rip it from the wall, wires and all. I threw the entire contraption onto the ground, smashing it into a thousand pieces.

"Now try to overbook us!" I screamed. "It's not you they are going to write about when they talk about the horrible food and service. We need to get this right, and you are making it impossible for me to do my job."

I was like a bull in a china shop, and I'm sure my staff thought I was either the ultimate jerk or completely insane. I mimicked the hard-nosed chefs I knew from New York, and people put up with it, just as I had put up with the abuse when I was in their shoes.

This was the first time Eileen had ever seen this side of my personality. I was such a lunatic in the kitchen, screaming at her, screaming at Gale, screaming at everyone. I knew I was being mean and irrational, but I didn't care. Looking back, I think I may have been meaner to Gale and Eileen than I was to anyone else. I guess I felt like they would put up with it because they *had* to. They were family.

Plus, that was just how I ran my kitchen; if people didn't like it, they could leave. And that's exactly what Eileen did, right around Christmas. Eileen had decided to meet her family in Florida, booking a flight for the day before Christmas Eve.

"Oh no, Eileen, you can't go just before Christmas," I told her. "With all the last-minute holiday shoppers, it's going to be crazy here. Change your flight."

Eileen rescheduled her flight to Christmas Day. Traffic was heavy at Bella Luna the night before. After finishing her work and staying for a few hours to help the dishwashers out, Eileen got ready to leave.

"Where do you think you're going?" I demanded, throwing in a few curse words to let her know I was serious. "Can't you see the dishwashers need your help? Get back in there!"

Seething, Eileen ignored my tirade and walked out of Bella Luna. One of the first things she did when she got to Florida was call me. The conversation was short and not so sweet. "I quit," she said.

I couldn't believe that she of all people would quit. I was furious. "Fine," I spat at her. "Leave. I don't care. We don't need you here."

Eileen found another job at a restaurant in Lake Forest. We no longer talked, but about a year later I heard through the grapevine that she had moved back to Rochester and married. I was not invited to the wedding.

As difficult as I was to work for, no one could argue with the results. I invited Rich in to eat, and he raved over what we had done. We were getting great reviews and national attention, including *Food & Wine* magazine and *Bon Appétit*. In fact, the very first issue of *Food Arts* featured Gale's and my second wedding reception, which we held at the restaurant for all of our Chicago friends and Gale's family.

And then out of nowhere, we showed up to work one day, only to find padlocks on every door. No lights, no cars, no sign. Nothing. Just an empty, locked up building. Apparently, one of the partners in the group had been caught embezzling money, and suddenly we were done.

I couldn't believe it. We had put so much time and energy into getting this place up and running. And just when we seemed to be hitting our stride, we ran straight into a brick wall. Somebody, somewhere, definitely had it in for me. Now what?

With bills to pay, Gale and I had no choice but to hit the pavement. Thankfully, we both managed to land spots quickly at a new restaurant called Bice, which we knew from our New York days. In addition to their Chicago and New York locations, they also had establishments in Milan and London. My position was chef de cuisine.

Gale and I were brought on just in time for the opening, and we were immediately sent to New York and Italy for a few weeks of intensive training. Fortunately, Italian food came easy to me, and we both really enjoyed the training period.

Back in Chicago, our crew was mostly Italian, and they were all crazy. Since the expediter spoke only in Italian, I was extremely frustrated as I tried to make sense of the orders and keep up with what was going on. These guys had their own culture and dialect, and they followed the old-world practices of smoking in the kitchen and drinking red wine while working behind the line. From the very start, I always seemed to be butting heads with someone.

One afternoon, I was upstairs getting ready for a party. Just as I was putting the last garnitures on the plates, the maître d' came in and starting filling a tray with the plates.

"Whoa, whoa, whoa, where are you going?" I stopped him as he headed out the door. "I'm not done."

"It looks fine," he said, turning back toward the door.

"No, they're not fine; they're not done. Bring them back."

"No, it's fine."

We continued to argue back and forth, playing tug-of-war with the tray like two little kids in a sandbox.

Finally, I had had enough. I grabbed the tray in both hands and threw it at him, completely trashing his two-thousand-dollar Armani suit. The fight turned physical, and I knew I would kill him if I didn't get out of there.

I walked downstairs back into the kitchen and said to no one in particular, "I'm leaving and I won't be back. I've had enough." Then I turned and marched out the back door, my anger raging. Visions of my mom's rages flashed through my head.

Half my guys followed me, but Gale stayed behind. Always the peacemaker, she wasn't about to join in a revolt just because I couldn't control my temper.

I was so angry, I was literally seeing red. As I marched down Michigan Avenue, I looked down and realized I still had my apron and side towel on. I must have looked like an idiot. The guys who had followed me slowly peeled off as I continued to walk. Some ducked into nearby bars; others headed home; and still others slunk back to Bice, hoping the chef hadn't noticed they were gone.

After walking for what must have been an hour to blow off steam, I stopped and finally looked up. I found myself standing in front of Charlie Trotter's restaurant, which had been open for about two years.

The restaurant had been making a huge splash in Chicago and was even starting to get noticed nationally. Charlie and I had done a few local events together, and though we didn't know each other well, he was a colleague of sorts. I went to the back door and knocked.

Charlie was standing at the line in the middle of the kitchen, sorting through a pile of kale with his dog resting at his feet. I hadn't seen a dog in the kitchen since our travels in Europe. Charlie looked up when I entered, clearly wondering why I was knocking at his back door in the middle of the day. "Hi, Rick. What are you doing here?"

I blurted out, "I just quit Bice, and I need a job."

He invited me in, gave me a cup of coffee, and then just waited until I calmed down a bit. We talked for a while and I told him what had happened. Without saying a word, he stood up, walked over to the phone, and dialed.

"Gale, I've got Rick in my back room having an espresso and chilling out," he said. "I just wanted you to know he's here and he's okay."

He talked for a few minutes more and then turned to me.

"Come in at seven o'clock Monday ready to work. I need an a.m. sous-chef, so let's give it a shot."

Suddenly, a huge weight lifted off my shoulders. This guy, whom I respected so much, was doing me a monstrous favor, one that I clearly didn't deserve. I was also amazed to consider that out of all the places in Chicago where I could have ended up after my anger-fueled walk, I had found myself at Trotter's.

"Thank you so much, Charlie. I'll see you Monday." Then I started the hour-long walk back to my car.

When I walked in on Monday, the chef de cuisine was standing at the big stainless sink, washing a stockpot. "The first thing you need to know is that we don't have a dishwasher during the day," he said. "We self-wash, and we do a lot of cleaning around here."

Wow. That was going to be interesting. There was rarely enough time to get things done when we *had* dishwashers. This was definitely going to add pressure to the schedule. Fortunately, I was already used to coming in two hours early and staying two hours late, so I was up for the challenge.

Things were different in Charlie's kitchen, and I had to learn the

"Trotter culture." He was a masterful chef, and his kitchen was very strict and disciplined. We would spend all day prepping, butchering, cooking, and cleaning. Sometimes the morning crew stayed to work service just so we could watch the kitchen in action. It was so controlled that no one spoke. Charlie's *mise en place* was tedious and refined, and his food was precise and technical. Whether we were washing pots or setting a table or creating a tureen, everything we did was done with the highest attention to detail and quality. Charlie constantly challenged us to do things right, even if it was just mopping the floor. There was always a "Trotter way" to do it. More than anyone else I had ever worked for, he reflected passion for excellence, drive, and authenticity. This guy was heading for culinary royalty, and even though none of us was making very much money, we felt lucky just to be part of the journey.

The longer I studied under Charlie, the more convinced I became that I needed to get to Europe. I had completed my culinary high school and culinary college. The only thing left was graduate school, and I needed to go to Europe for that. By the time my year at Trotter's was complete, I was thriving on the structure and discipline, which replicated the fine-dining establishments in Europe. I wanted more of that, and Charlie inspired me to get that experience as a stepping-stone in my career.

"You've worked for a lot of great chefs who have studied under even greater chefs in Europe," he said. "Now you need to work for some of those chefs as well. That experience will surely help you reach the top."

I wasn't sure I wanted to leave Chicago, but I knew I needed to study abroad. It was the only way I would really be able to pick up the techniques of people like Michel Guérard, Pierre Gagnaire, and Frédy Girardet, all of whom I admired and respected.

I set up an appointment with Rich Melman and told him what had happened at Bice and about my experiences working under Charlie at Trotter's. Rich understood the struggles, and he encouraged me not to take the Bice thing personally.

Then he asked, "If you could do anything right now, what would it be?"

I told him I really wanted to go into fine dining and definitely spend some time in Europe to study with some of the greats.

"I think it would be a really good idea for you to study abroad," he said. "I will put some feelers out and see what I can find."

Gale and I also figured we'd keep our eyes open and start trying to build a nest egg so we could make our way overseas. What we should have known, however, was that when Rich Melman puts out a call, it doesn't take long for someone to answer him.

TRAMONTO'S SIGNATURE PIZZA (PIZZA DEI TRAMONTO)

Pizza, of course, was one of the mainstay dishes at Bella Luna. Of the many outstanding variations on our menu, I consider this my signature pizza. In fact, this recipe followed me all the way to Osteria di Tramonto, where it became a hit.

Notice that I recommend using a thin crust. Though I spent about two decades in Chicago, I still favor New York–style pizza. — *SERVES 4*

1 pizza crust (recipe follows)
2 Tbs. garlic oil (recipe follows)
1½ Tbs. roasted garlic puree (recipe follows)
2 oz. mozzarella, sliced
1½ tsp. red wine vinegar
1 tsp. truffle oil
⅓ c. arugula
¼ c. seeded and diced Roma tomatoes
¼ oz. Gaeta olives, pitted
Kosher salt and freshly ground black pepper
1 lemon, quartered

1. Position the oven rack in the middle of the oven. If you have a pizza stone, put it on the rack to heat up. Preheat the oven to 450°F.
2. Roll out the dough to a circle 12 inches in diameter and ¼- to ½-inch thick. Work on a lightly floured cutting board so you can slide the pizza onto a baking sheet or the pizza stone.
3. Brush the crust with half the garlic oil and spread the garlic puree over the crust to cover it generously. Top with the mozzarella slices.
4. Transfer the pizza to the oven and bake about 15 minutes or until the sauce bubbles. Gently lift it up and peek at the bottom. If it is golden brown and solid, it's done. If it's still pale and a little soft looking, let it cook a few minutes longer.
5. Meanwhile, in a small bowl, stir together the vinegar, truffle oil, and remaining garlic oil. Add the arugula, tomatoes, and olives. Toss lightly to make a small salad. Season to taste with salt and pepper.
6. Cut pizza into 4 wedges; top each wedge with salad and a lemon quarter.

Pizza dough (makes 2 crusts)

This authentic Italian pizza dough will perform beautifully for you if you make it with really good olive oil and don't overwork the dough. Roll it as thin or as thick as you like. I like thin-crust pizzas, so I roll the pizza dough so that it's ¼- to ½-inch thick. You could go thicker (and increase the baking time a little).

¾ c. water, room temperature
¼ oz. of fresh yeast (or ½ package of active dry yeast)
2 c. all-purpose flour
2 tsp. kosher salt
1 tsp. sugar
1 tsp. extra-virgin olive oil

1. In the large bowl of an electric mixer fitted with the paddle attachment, gently stir the water with the yeast by hand and set aside for about 10 minutes. (As an alternative, you can mix by hand.) The mixture will bubble and foam.
2. Add flour, salt, and sugar to the yeast mixture; mix on low speed for about 3 minutes or until the dough comes together in a cohesive mass. Increase the speed to medium and mix for about 10 minutes or until the dough is smooth and elastic.
3. Transfer the dough to a lightly oiled bowl; cover the bowl with a well-wrung, damp kitchen towel, and set aside in a warm, draft-free place for 30 minutes or until the dough rises and doubles in size.
4. Turn the dough out onto a lightly floured surface and knead it a few times to expel the air from the dough. Divide the dough into 2 balls. Brush each ball with oil and set it on a baking sheet. Cover the dough with plastic wrap and set aside for at least 2 hours, but no longer than 12 hours.

Garlic oil (makes about 1¼ c.)
2 c. extra-virgin olive oil
6 cloves garlic, minced

1. In a glass jar or similar container, combine the oil and garlic. Cover and set aside for at least 24 hours to give the oil time to steep.
2. The oil will keep for four days if stored in a cool, dark place.

Roasted garlic puree (makes about 1½ Tbs.)
12 unpeeled garlic cloves, lightly crushed and with top ends cut off
½ c. extra-virgin olive oil
1 tsp. kosher salt

1. Preheat oven to 300°F.
2. Lay a large sheet of aluminum foil on the countertop and put the garlic cloves in the center. Drizzle with the olive oil and sprinkle with the salt. Fold the foil into a sealed package. Set the package in a small baking pan and bake for about 35 minutes or until the garlic cloves are tender.
3. Open the package and let the garlic cloves cool a little. When they are cool enough to handle, squeeze the soft garlic pulp from the skins into a small bowl. Discard the skins.
4. Mash the garlic pulp with a fork to make a puree. Use immediately or cool to room temperature. To store the puree, put it in a small dish and cover it with olive oil. Cover the dish with plastic wrap and refrigerate for up to 5 days.

PART IV

CULINARY
GRAD SCHOOL

1990s

---- 15 ----
EUROPE

Command those who are rich in this present age
not to be haughty, nor to trust in uncertain riches but in
the living God, who gives us richly all things to enjoy.
I TIMOTHY 6:17

One afternoon I came home from work to find the message light on
our answering machine blinking. I hit the play button and immediately took a step back as a big, booming voice echoed out from the
recorder:

"Hi there, Rick and Gale, this is Bob Payton. I got your name from
Rich Melman and a few other people around Chicago. How would
you like to come to sunny Leicestershire, England, and cook for the
rich and famous?" He laughed.

I was immediately intrigued. Although I wouldn't know until
much, much later that Leicestershire gets only about five sunny days
a year, Bob Payton was definitely painting an inviting picture. "I own
Stapleford Park Country House Hotel," he continued, "and I'm looking for an American chef to come help me run things. I'm in Chicago
for a couple of days, and I'd like to talk to you about joining our team.
Give me a call, and let's see if we can make a deal!"

I immediately called Rich and asked him what he knew about Bob
Payton. He assured me that Bob was definitely legit. A former advertising
executive with J. Walter Thompson, Bob had great marketing instincts

and had been the first to bring Chicago-style deep-dish pizza to London with his Chicago Pizza Pie Factories. The UK had never seen anything like it, and the franchise took off like wildfire. Bob quickly followed up his success with a series of equally strong theme restaurants: Chicago Rib Shacks, Chicago Meatpackers, and Henry J. Bean's Bar and Grill.

In a very short time, Bob Payton had become Europe's own version of Richard Melman, running an international megarestaurant conglomerate that stretched from London and Paris to Barcelona, Madrid, and Edinburgh.

Apparently, Bob had recently purchased Stapleford Park, a sixteenth-century estate that had belonged to Lord and Lady Gretton, owners of the Bass Brewers. He immediately gutted and remodeled the deteriorating mansion, turning it into a fifty-five-room luxury country house hotel.

"He's gotten rave reviews from all the travel magazines and guidebooks," Rich said. "I think everyone likes the idea of an American entrepreneur turning a crumbling country manor into an American-style hotel. Unfortunately, the reviewers love the house but hate the food. I think you could really help him out in that area."

I thanked Rich for the insight and quickly called Gale.

"Don't hang around after your shift tonight," I told her. "Have I got some news for you!"

Once she got home, I filled her in on the details of my conversations with Bob and Rich. We pulled out all of our culinary magazines and files and tried to find out as much as we could about Stapleford Park and Bob's work. Other than news briefs about his restaurants, we couldn't find much about the hotel itself. We did know, however, that competition in this area of England's countryside—two hours from London—was tough. Michelin-starred chef Raymond Blanc was doing some great things in Oxfordshire. The Michelin-starred Roux brothers were also out in the area, which would make it difficult for anyone—especially an ad man from the United States—to compete. We did a little research on other country house hotels—Gidleigh Park in Devon and Chewton Glen in New Forest, Hampshire—and after discussing it for most of the evening, we decided we didn't have anything to lose by talking with Bob. We made an appointment for the next morning.

We both had to be at work by nine, so we showed up at the Drake Hotel at 6:00 a.m. in our chef's whites. When Gale told the maître d' that we were there to meet Mr. Payton, he knew exactly who we were talking about, and he indicated a table in the corner. Although we could tell that someone was sitting there, his entire body was blocked from view by the *New York Times* he was holding up in front of him. As we approached the table, Bob put the paper down and stood to greet us with a huge smile. As he stood, our eyes followed him upward. Standing over six feet tall, Bob Payton was a sight to behold. Wearing a brown polyester tracksuit, red sneakers, and oversize reading glasses, he certainly made a lasting impression.

"Sit down," he boomed jovially. Waving the waitress over, he ordered a large stack of blueberry pancakes and another Diet Coke with two lemons for himself. And then he pointed to Gale and me and said, "Order whatever you want. Eat up!"

Ten minutes later, as we scarfed down bacon, eggs, waffles, and pancakes, Bob spread a bunch of glossy brochures all over the table.

"*This* is Stapleford Park, my dream," he said. "I've put my heart and soul—and fortune—into this place. Everyone loves the design, the service, and the amenities, but we are just getting hammered on the food. I've brought in chefs from England, Germany, and France, but none of them understand what I'm trying to do. They just don't get it. I want big, comfortable American breakfasts and fun, casual American picnic basket lunches, but I also want to do Michelin-rated fine dining for dinner. I just haven't been able to find anyone who knows how to meld the two cultures and do it well. I finally realized that I need an American chef and pastry chef to come help me get things moving, preferably a team like yourselves."

We gave Bob our résumés and told him a little bit about our credentials. But we also explained that working for another American wasn't really on our radar right now.

"We are both at the stage in our careers where we need to work under some of the great chefs in Europe if we want to move to the next level," I said. "As great as it would be to work for you, I just don't see how it would help us to accomplish that goal."

"I am going for a Michelin star here, kids, and we will do whatever it takes to get there. If you could get me that, it could be the start of a long, great career for each of you," he replied. "Plus, I know everybody, especially all the people you want to apprentice and stage with, like Anton Mosimann, Raymond Blanc, and the Roux brothers. I can get you into all of those places if you want to move on after Stapleford. I have flats all over the world, and I'm always happy to help fellow foodies."

And then he made us an offer we couldn't refuse: an awesome salary—twice what we were making here in the States—free housing, our own car, four weeks vacation every year, and full health benefits.

Wow. It seemed like a no-brainer. We agreed to fly over for a tasting with Bob and his board of directors as soon as possible, neither one of us really believing it was for real. But a couple of days later, a FedEx box showed up on our doorstep with two plane tickets, an itinerary, and contacts so we could order our food for the tasting. We realized this was no joke; we'd better get ready to go!

Two weeks later, we jumped on a plane and flew to London. Bob sent a car to pick us up from Heathrow and make the two-hour trek deep into the English countryside. As we drove farther and farther from the city center, I was awestruck by the beauty of England's rural pasturelands. Sheep and goats grazed along the grassy hillsides, and fields of wildflowers stretched out for miles and miles. We weren't in Chicago anymore.

And then we turned the corner. In the distance we saw it: an incredible Elizabethan structure rising up from a well-manicured lawn, a Rolls-Royce parked in the circular drive in front. The place was breathtaking; it seemed like a picture straight out of a travel magazine.

As we drove down the winding road toward the hotel, we passed an old stone church and a cemetery off to the left, and a little farther down, a number of small thatched-roof cottages on the right. These dwellings, known as grace and favour cottages, had been built for longtime staff who could live there until they died. In fact, many of Bob's staff members had been employed by the estate their entire working lives. At the time, the elderly former gardener and head housekeeper lived in two of the cottages; the third, the chef's cottage, had been set aside for us. In addition, the driver told us, Stapleford included tennis courts, several walled gardens, a proper riding school, and its own helipad.

Pulling up in front of the hotel, we were met at the door by an older gentleman carrying a burlap sack.

"Hello there," he said, reaching out his free hand to shake mine. "You must be the chefs we've been waiting for. I'm Malcolm, the gamekeeper here. Just let me know what kind of meat you will need, and I'll be sure you get it."

I wondered if the bag he had slung over his shoulder contained that evening's supper, but before I could ask, he continued in his thick English accent.

"You'll also find that most any kind of produce you need is grown right here on our grounds or in the near vicinity. The Stilton cheese factory is just a few miles from here, and we have a miller just down the road who stone-grinds all the flour we use in our bread. Let me know if you need anything else. I'm happy to help."

Gale and I looked at each other. This was truly a chef's dream.

We made our way into the entryway and were immediately struck by the sophisticated warmth of the decor. Bob had certainly outdone himself in blending the tranquility of the English countryside with the elegance of a five-star hotel.

As we took in our surroundings, Bob's loud voice echoed through the corridors: "You made it! You're here! Welcome." Chuckling, he added, "Come on in. I'll show you around our little place, and we'll have a diet Coke."

As we toured the hotel, I just couldn't get over the amount of detail and thought that had gone into it. Room after room was filled with warm, inviting fabrics and patterns and furnishings. Bob had brought in famous designers from all over the world to decorate and furnish each of the rooms and suites in their own unique style and brand. Designs included Wedgwood, Crabtree & Evelyn, Lady Jane Churchill, and others. Apparently, it had become quite the competition between the companies to see who could create the most beautiful, most luxurious room of all. I could see why all the travel magazines had rated Stapleford so highly.

The kitchens were another story.

"Don't let first impressions fool you," Bob said as he showed us around. "I haven't found the right team to run the food part, so I haven't really put any money back here yet. But don't you worry. If you agree to take this gig and can help get Stapleford Park on the food map, I will give you your dream kitchen and let you design it."

We assured him that we had indeed seen and worked in worse, and that we could certainly make do until the time was right to renovate. We dropped our bags in one of the guest rooms, and after a tour of the grounds and a quick bite to eat, we decided to turn in for the night. Gale and I were both up early the next morning, ready to get started with our prep work. We were pumped. We had chosen some of our favorite dishes for the tasting, confident we could turn this place around and make a name for ourselves throughout Europe.

But surprisingly, even though we did everything right, our stuff just wasn't turning out the way it should—especially Gale's pastries and breads. After retracing our steps and making sure we hadn't forgotten anything, it dawned on us: many of the basic ingredients like flour weren't ground the same way here. Also, the butterfat content was much higher than in the States, meaning the fat content in the cream was much higher as well.

Once we figured that out, we were able to readjust our recipes and were relieved when things started coming out of the oven looking like they should.

On the third day, we served our twelve-course menu to the six-member board of directors. Starting with multiple amuse-bouche we moved on to tuna tartar with caviar, lobster tails poached in vanilla butter, and braised veal shank with black truffle sauce and chanterelle risotto. Gale finished up with four courses of desserts, chocolates, and petits fours.

We tried hard not to get our hopes up, but it was clear from the looks on their faces that everyone was truly enjoying the meal. And at the end of the evening, Bob came back into the kitchen to congratulate us.

"Brilliant, kids, just brilliant. You two blew them out of the water," he said, patting me on the back. "You rocked it! I knew you would; I just didn't know you'd do it so well!"

Gale and I looked at each other and smiled. This was really happening!

The next day, we sat down with Bob to close our deal and plan our move. Unlike moving from New York to Chicago, this job change was going to be a little more complicated. We figured it would take about six weeks to get our working visas, turn in our notices, and figure out what to do with our house in the Chicago suburb of Buffalo Grove.

After talking to our families and employers about our plans, we didn't really have anyone else to tell—except our friends. I made a point to call Eileen because I knew her mother was from Liverpool, England. Also, I still felt bad at the way I'd treated her and the way things had ended between us at Bella Luna. I was pretty sure she didn't want much to do with me; still, I felt like I owed her a phone call to let her know we were leaving. After all, I had known her since I was fifteen, and she had come to Chicago because of me.

When I called her, she answered on the first ring.

"Hey," I said.

"Hey yourself."

"I heard you got married. Thanks for inviting me."

She laughed. "Yeah, sorry about that. I didn't think you'd want to come."

"Well, I just wanted to let you know that Gale and I are moving. We got a job offer in England. We're leaving next month."

"Wow, that's really great. I've already moved: to Michigan."

"Oh, okay. Well, good luck."

"Yeah, you too. Bye."

As I hung up, sadness and remorse swept over me. Other than Gale, Eileen was the one person in my life who had always believed in me. She was such a great person. I really hoped she was happy.

Gale was more than ready to give notice at Bice, but I was nervous about telling Charlie. Thankfully, he completely understood my desire to further my education in Europe, and he fully supported our decision to go.

Since we wouldn't have any expenses in England—housing was provided—we decided not to sell our house and cars. We wanted to leave things in the house here just as they were, right down to the socks in the dresser drawers. That way, when we came home a couple of times each year, we were truly coming home to a life.

Bob would have preferred that we sold the house. I think he hoped that once we got to England, we would fall in love and never want to leave. Though we weren't ruling out the possibility of settling there eventually, we decided to keep our options open with a two-year contract and a two-year option. We packed up just enough clothes and cookbooks to fill a few trunks and set out on the next leg of our journey.

Once in England, we stayed in the hotel for a couple of months. We couldn't move into our little stone cottage right away because Bob wanted to do some repairs and get it cleaned up from the last chef. This was fine by us; it gave us a chance to get a feel for all of the different rooms, the service, the atmosphere. We spent a lot of time exploring the hotel: the salon, the library, the billiard room, the conference room; and the three dining areas, which included a large formal dining room where dinners and special events were held, a breakfast room, and a lunch area.

It didn't take us long to get our feet on the ground and feel like we knew what we were doing. Thankfully, we had a full kitchen staff that were all well trained and a joy to work with. Others on the hotel staff helped out as well. If we ordered rabbit, Malcolm the gamekeeper brought us fresh rabbit—the whole rabbit, fur and all. We could tell the gardeners what to plant for the next season; for instance, we might ask them to provide pumpkins for our fall menu. We were also able to pick herbs from the estate's walled garden.

In the midst of all the tradition we knew we wanted to make changes, yet we also knew better than to mess with things that were working well: full afternoon tea, picnic lunches, Sunday afternoon barbecues. The guests really seemed to get a kick out of eating something as informal and American as barbecued ribs in such a pristine setting.

The trick of combining two cultures as well as combining formal and informal dining was a challenge, but somehow I knew we could do it. After all, I was the guy who could just as easily throw together foie gras as burgers. I could definitely do this.

Remembering the huge stack of fluffy pancakes Bob had ordered at the Drake, we decided to start an American-style breakfast. We added items like pecan waffles with maple syrup, banana pancakes, three-egg omelets, and stuffed French toast, but we offered traditional English fare as well: soft scrambled eggs, sausages, and grilled tomatoes and mushrooms.

After we got breakfast up and running the way we wanted, we moved on to lunch. We had decided to tackle dinner last because we wanted to hold off until we could get the kitchens redesigned.

We spent the first year at Stapleford developing the menu, figuring out how to adapt and convert our recipes, training the staff, designing the kitchens, and just building a reputation as a respectable establishment. And then we got great news: we had earned a red M from the Michelin guide! The "M" rating, a requirement for earning a star, set the press abuzz and upped the stakes almost overnight. Every day new articles and feature stories appeared, highlighting our work and praising the Stapleford team. Gale and I became known as the "American chefs who are making a name for themselves at Stapleford Park." And just as we had seen at the Gotham, when you have a great product, you need the media to get the word out. Suddenly, we were on our way to making our reputations as celebrity chefs, and everybody wanted to write about us.

Reporters and travel writers filled the reservation book. Wealthy travelers changed their vacation plans so they could stay at the Stapleford. Other chefs—including Raymond Blanc, Anton Mosimann, and Marco Pierre White—even made the trip out to Leicestershire to check us out. We loved the chance to "talk shop" with fellow chefs, and sometimes we would end up sitting in the salon until the wee hours of the morning, sharing stories and talking about our kitchens.

Always the businessman, Bob saw how important these relationships were to getting the word out about the hotel, so he began to encourage us to reciprocate. Talk about a chef's dream! Sometimes it was just a quick train ride to Paris for lunch and dinner at L'Ami Louis on Rue du Vertbois or Brasserie Flo. Other times, we'd take the helicopter and spend a couple of days at different country house hotels around the region. Everywhere we went, we brought along our wish file and took notes on everything we experienced: things we tasted, flavor profiles we liked, and everything else we wanted to remember for the future: the service, the decor, the place settings, even the music and the landscaping.

Bob was such a great mentor. He poured his wisdom and knowledge into us, giving us as many opportunities to grow as he could. The more he mentored us and helped us build our careers, the bigger his business became. It was a win-win for all of us.

But as much as we loved the work and Bob and his wife, Wendy, things weren't always sunny. In fact, things were rarely sunny in Leicestershire. Though Bob had sold it differently, this place was more like "rainy and cloudy Leicestershire." He hadn't mentioned that this area of England was predominantly dark, dreary, and cold—all the time.

And along with the gloom, the dark side of my personality eventually returned. I enjoyed the work, but we worked *all* the time, seven days a week, forty-eight weeks a year. And because we lived where we worked, we never really got a break. For me, living so far away from any kind of city life was a lot tougher than I had thought it would be. No television, no social life, no movie theaters, no pizza delivery, no nightclubs. The closest town, Melton Mowbray, had only a cheese shop, a bank, a pub, and a few other small stores.

In addition, my dyslexia made it nearly impossible for me to drive in England. After several attempts to learn, Gale and I both agreed it was *not* a good idea for me to get behind the wheel. This made me feel even more frustrated and isolated.

Everything was different here: the money, the measuring, the telephones, the cooking, even the products we were used to working with. We had to readjust all of our processes and all of our recipes, which required a lot of trial and error until we got it right. Once again, I felt like the slow kid in the class, always one step behind everyone else and never really able to catch up.

Gale, on the other hand, didn't share my frustrations. Instead, she embraced the experience with her typical positive attitude and loved everything about being in England. She especially adored our stone cottage, which seemed right out of a fairy tale with its thatched roof, beautiful tea roses, and coal-stoked fireplace for heat. She didn't seem to mind that we could never seem to get it warm enough, and she even made peace with the bats that flew around inside. She became friends with our neighbors in the other grace and favour cottages, including the former head housekeeper, Mrs. Essum, who was ninety.

Gale didn't even mind that we were so far away from the hustle and bustle of the city. She took riding lessons on the hotel grounds, and really took a liking to the sport. We even got ourselves a dog, Rootie, to keep us company. But for me, it was just not enough.

"What's it going to take to make you happy?" Gale chided me. "Look around at all that we have here. A great place to live, a great job, plenty of freedom to do what we want. What more could you possibly want?"

She made a good point. Bob had really given us all we could ask for, and our careers were soaring. We were in Europe, mingling with the wealthiest people in the world. Why did I still feel like that young kid back in Rochester, searching for something to fill the void in my life?

I started to get short-tempered with the staff and even with Bob. Always a friendly guy, Bob tried his best to lift me out of my mood, but it didn't matter what he did, I was always frustrated and upset. I just couldn't get out of my funk, and finally one afternoon I had had enough. I marched into Bob's office and threatened to leave.

"Rick, I just don't know what to do for you anymore," Bob said. "I don't want you to go, but clearly you are no good to me here if you are this unhappy. What can we do?"

"I need some civilization," I said. "I feel so isolated out here. I need the energy of the city to keep me going."

Bob thought about it for a minute, and then he made me a proposition.

"What if I found you something in London? I'd still expect you to oversee things here, but you've built a great team. They can handle the day-to-day without you having to physically be here all the time. You can go back and forth and that way you'd get your city fix and I'd get to keep you."

It seemed like a perfect plan. Even Gale agreed that it might be just what we needed to reenergize our efforts and help lift me out of my depression.

The next week the three of us headed down to Piccadilly Circus where we met with Rocco Forte. Rocco owned a line of luxury hotels, resorts, and restaurants—Trust House Forte—and he was in the market for someone to help him develop a new concept for a historical building right in the square.

Rocco wanted to reopen an American-style brasserie in the Criterion building, and he wanted us to do it for him. We could live in one of Bob's apartments above Henry J. Bean's in Kensington while we worked toward the grand opening. We would still be able to go back to Stapleford on weekends to oversee the kitchen during busy times, but for the most part our focus was now on getting the Criterion Brasserie reopened and on its feet.

Redesigning the kitchen, developing the menus, hiring the staff—suddenly, we were back in the game. Like New York, London was a twenty-four-hour city. Everything we needed was at our fingertips, and we dove right in. When we weren't working, we took advantage of all the city had to offer: movies, tourist attractions, museums, theater, concerts. We had the opportunity to see Eric Clapton perform at Royal Albert Hall. We even managed to snag tickets to Wimbledon.

Life was good again! We worked closely with Rocco and Bob to create a wonderful restaurant in this seventeenth-century building. The setting was almost palatial, with a mirrored marble hall, gilded ceilings, and imposing arches. We created a menu that was simple but luxurious, including everything from American favorites to classic Parisian and Mediterranean dishes.

From the very start, the London crowd embraced us. The opening went off without a hitch, and within a year the place was virtually running itself. This definitely worked to our advantage, since we were still traveling between Leicestershire and London every week.

And whenever we had the chance, we tried to *stage* for some of the better-known chefs in the region. I did, after all, still consider myself to be a chef-in-training. During this period, I had amazing opportunities to work with some of the greatest chefs of all time, including Michel Guérard, Pierre Gagnaire, Nico Ladenis, Anton Mosimann, and the Roux brothers.

We had the best of all worlds: opportunity, resources, and experience. Celebrities—including Madonna, Michael Caine, and Mick Jagger—often found their way into the restaurant or out to the country house. Because we knew how to take care of high-profile guests, corporate groups or movie producers would "buy the house," renting out the entire hotel for days at a time. And as word of our success spread, the opportunities and events began to be even bigger and better. We got the chance to do the wrap party for the cast and crew of *Godfather III*, serving folks like

George Hamilton and Al Pacino. And we were even invited to cook for a polo match at Windsor. We worked with Chef Anton Mosimann and Chef Paul Bocuse to do a luncheon for Prince Charles and Princess Diana following a match in which Prince Charles played. Life didn't get much better than that.

And then we got the news that Gale's father had been diagnosed with prostate cancer. We were torn but finally decided to end our time in England. The theory was that England would always be there, but Gale's dad might not be. We decided that family came first. We gave Bob our notice and headed home a few weeks later.

Once we arrived in Chicago, we were shocked to find that while her dad was fine, Gale's mom had been admitted to the hospital for dizziness and numbness. Shortly after we arrived, she was discharged with no real idea of what had caused her dizziness. We decided to unpack and head out to Rochester for Christmas and New Year's. It was great to see my folks again, and they were relieved to know we were back in the United States for good.

When we flew back to Chicago, Gale's parents picked us up at the airport and her mom reported that she was feeling "110 percent better."

That night, she died of an aortic aneurysm. And for the first time since I'd met her, Gale was unable to find the bright spot in any of this. She barely spoke and barely ate, trying desperately to reconcile the fact that her mom was gone.

CAMPAGNA-STYLE PICKLED MACKEREL

I never liked pickled fish until I went to Europe. There I sampled it at its finest, and once I learned the traditions behind it, I was inspired to use pickled fishes in different applications and with different garnitures. Grilled vegetables complement the fish wonderfully.

Prepare this dish one day in advance. — *SERVES 4*

For the mackerel

4 fresh mackerel, 10 to 11 oz. each; with heads off (but not skinned);
    cleaned and butterflied
¼ c. olive oil
Kosher salt and freshly ground pepper
1 lemon, juiced
1 bay leaf
½ to 1 c. white wine

For the pickling mixture

¼ c. fresh mint, julienned
¼ c. flat-leaf parsley, chopped
1 Tbs. shallots, minced
2 garlic cloves, minced
½ c. sherry vinegar
4 Tbs. olive oil, plus enough to season the fish
Kosher salt and freshly ground pepper

For garnish

1 Tbs. orange zest
Freshly squeezed lemon juice
1 Tbs. fresh mint, julienned
½ tsp. black peppercorns

1. Preheat oven to 400°F.
2. Lay mackerel in a large baking dish, skin side down, and season with the olive oil, salt, pepper, lemon juice, bay leaf, and white wine. (Use enough wine to almost cover the fish.)
3. Bake the mackerel in the preheated oven for 10 to 12 minutes.
4. Remove fish from baking dish, and gently remove skin from the fish. Lay mackerel on a platter to cool. When it is completely cooled, remove any bones that remain. Strain the juices from the baking pan and set aside to use in the pickling mixture.

TO MAKE PICKLING MIXTURE

1. Mix the mint, parsley, shallots, and garlic together in a bowl. Pour in the vinegar, whisk in the olive oil, and season with salt and pepper. Stir in the juice from the baking pan.
2. Lay two-inch chunks of the mackerel in shallow serving platter. Pour the pickling mixture over the top. Cover the platter and refrigerate for 24 hours to pickle the mackerel.
3. To serve, lay the chunks of mackerel out on a plate and drizzle with olive oil. Garnish with orange zest, lemon juice, mint, and peppercorns.

——— 16 ———
TRIO

My God shall supply all your need
according to His riches in glory by Christ Jesus.
PHILIPPIANS 4:19

For the first few months after returning to Chicago, Gale and I both felt a little like fish out of water. Not only was Gale still reeling from her mom's death, but we had both come to relish our European lifestyle and had loved being immersed in European culture. Even the ingredients and recipes we had used overseas had become second nature. Additionally, we had both earned all kinds of press and credibility while we were overseas, but weaving ourselves back into the American cooking community was tougher than we'd expected.

Word of our European success had followed us, and we were both pretty well known by now. But at the same time, it seemed like we had taken a step backward in returning to Chicago.

Regardless of how much acclaim we had earned, we still had bills to pay, so we needed to find jobs. But where? After running our own kitchen, could we really go back to working for someone else? Rich graciously found a spot for me as executive chef at Avanzare, and I was thrilled to be back under the Lettuce umbrella. But even so, I missed working with Gale and multicourse, high-end dining.

In the years since we had left, Charlie Trotter had really taken

Chicago—and the whole country—by storm and was at the peak of his success. Now that Gale had a world-class reputation, he offered her the executive pastry chef position as soon as he heard she was available. Our hours were just as brutal as in England; the big difference was that we now had an hour commute from our home in Buffalo Grove.

I didn't want Gale making that drive alone after a long shift. Afraid she might fall asleep on the road, I often talked to her on the phone during her drive home—even though cell phone minutes were extremely costly at that time.

We managed to keep up this pace for about six months, but in the meantime we always had an ear to the ground, listening for any new opportunities that would allow us to work together again and move our careers to the next level—either a partnership or the opportunity to open our own place. One afternoon, I got a call from Henry Adaniya, manager of the high-profile restaurant Ambria and a colleague from Lettuce. He also used to be a manager at Café Provencal in Evanston.

Café Provencal's owner had been Chef Leslee Reis, one of the few female chefs in the Chicago area at the time. Leslee had recently passed away, and her husband was putting the building on the market. Henry wanted to buy it.

"If you and Gale agree to be my chef and pastry chef, I'll make you partners," he said. "We can do this. I know we can. We would make a good team—a trio. The city needs another fine-dining restaurant and more competition."

Our own place! With its cozy interior and setting across from an old stately church, the building almost made us feel as if we were back in a small English town. Gale and I immediately put our heads together to see what kind of cash we could come up with. Thankfully, we had been pretty frugal during our time in England. With few expenses, we'd managed to put quite a bit away. Between the three of us, plus some outside investors, we raised about $350,000—not a huge amount, but enough to get us started at least.

We knew we wouldn't be able to take much of a paycheck—about $25,000 a year each—and that we'd have to do quite a bit of the work ourselves, but the chance to open our own place seemed well worth the sacrifice. This was our chance to be partners and make a dream come true.

Before we made our final decision, I went to Rich Melman.

"We have this great opportunity, but I won't go if you need me to stay," I said. "I really want to do high-end fine dining, and I'd love to do it with Lettuce."

Unfortunately, Rich wasn't ready to go in that direction quite yet since his time and energy were currently being consumed by Maggiano's and the Corner Bakery, two new concepts he was developing. He even invited us to be part of those, but we decided to do Trio instead. With Rich's blessing, I called Henry.

"We're in," I said.

We decided that Henry and I would work on getting the place in shape over the summer, while Gale continued to work at Trotter's. That provided us with a little steady income until we opened Trio. We told very few people what we were doing, trying to keep things off the radar until we were ready to break the news to the industry and the press.

We started with our dream file, all the ideas Gale and I had gathered over the past ten years of our careers and travels, and although we didn't have enough cash to implement all of our ideas, we at least were able to cast a vision using our notes and drawings.

If we hoped to have our new place open by the fall, we had a lot of work to do in less than six months. We had to clean, gut, and paint the interior; install used equipment; put together a menu; hire and train a staff; and do some practice parties. Though popular, the place had not been renovated in over fifteen years, so it was a mess.

I didn't mind the physical labor one bit; we fixed whatever needed to be fixed, and we loved every minute of it. We took the place down to the studs and put up all new drywall and wall paneling. We were committed to doing the job right.

In order to cut costs, Henry acted as the general contractor and hired plumbers or electricians as we needed them. I took over the kitchen. I started by hiring a couple of chefs to help me get the place in shape. I envisioned a bright, clean, European-style kitchen with a quaint, living room–like dining room. I wanted it to be the kind of place people talked about, took tours of, and photographed.

With that in mind, we set up a chef's table for special reservations, one of the first of its kind in Chicago. This table was set up in the middle of the kitchen on a pedestal. Four people could dine on a meal made specially for them while getting exclusive attention and observing Trio's nightly service.

Our goal was to make the restaurant feel like somebody's home, like some of the restaurants we had dined in outside of Paris and in the English countryside. We refurbished the fireplace in the dining room and tried to create an understated elegance with the decor.

Meanwhile, I worked hard to make sure that the food was anything but understated. We were going for four stars, competing with places like Trotter's, Everest, Ambria, and Le Francais, the hottest restaurants in the early 1990s. We knew how important it was to come out of the gate feeling professional, confident, competitive, and upscale—and looking that way too.

We also knew that in order to rank well in all the guidebooks, such as Mobil, Zagat, and AAA, we needed to have certain items like Riedel glassware, multiple-course tasting menus, and a deep wine list that included some older vintages. We needed beautiful uniforms for the waiters; great after-dinner and cheese carts; an extensive dessert menu that included chocolates and petits fours; giveaway bags containing truffles or chocolates; and an outstanding à la carte menu.

Being the new kids on the block, we tried to make our name known by adding personal touches wherever we could. We decided we would include multiple amuse-bouche with every meal. We would also offer customized menus, which meant that we would stop by each table to discuss the diners' likes and dislikes and then come up with a meal just for them. We'd then create and print out a copy of their personalized menu, which Gale and I would sign and give them on their way out of the restaurant. We also provided valet service and hired a well-trained staff who knew what it meant to work fine dining.

In order to earn a four-star rating, our meals had better be worth the price we would need to charge, so every night Gale and I worked on developing out-of-this-world menus with very interesting plate presentations.

But just like any difficult project, you never know what you're getting into until it's too late. One afternoon while we were working on some of the pipes in the kitchen, the plumber noticed a soft spot in the middle of the kitchen floor. Before he had time to stop what he was doing, the whole floor began to give way beneath him, caving in and dropping him all the way down to the basement level. Thankfully, he wasn't hurt, but the accident put us twenty-five thousand dollars and a week behind while carpenters stabilized the floor and cleaned up the mess. We had planned to put a new floor in the kitchen; now the money we had budgeted for that was spent fixing the floor instead.

I refused to be discouraged. I went out and bought five gallons of lavender paint. After using it to paint the entire floor, we splattered all kinds of wild colors on top of that. Contrasted with the stark, white walls, it ended up looking pretty art deco. I loved it! We installed ceiling fans to give the kitchen a homey feel, and we polished the used equipment until it looked brand new.

We asked Henry to unboard a window in order to bring in more natural light, and then we added white blinds to dress it up. We loved the light in the room, which helped give it the look and feel of a home kitchen.

When it came time to choose the china, we realized we didn't have enough money to buy what we really wanted, and we didn't want to settle for second best. One afternoon we had to make a run over to Builders Square to pick up some supplies for the bathrooms. As we were trying to decide which tiles to buy for the floor, I looked down at the two I held in my hand. The colors were beautiful and the surfaces perfectly smooth. A thought occurred to me: *What if we used nontraditional surfaces to serve on?* These tiles were every bit as unique and beautiful as the china we'd been looking at earlier that week. I could buy tiles for three or four dollars apiece and use them as china—much better than the twenty-five or even fifty dollars per plate I would have to spend if we bought Limoges porcelain or fine china from Wedgwood.

I loaded up my cart with stacks of twelve-by-twelve-inch granite, marble, and ceramic tiles in all different colors, as well as four-by-four-inch tiles. Then I went back and found a medicine cabinet that used strips of long mirrors for the shelves. I bought the medicine cabinet, took out the shelves, and threw the rest of it away.

And then I started cooking. Using all the techniques I had learned over the past ten years, I began to create beautiful dishes that were as pleasing to the eye as they were to the palate. My inspiration was always the arts; I thought about Dali's and Pollock's paintings and tried to recreate them on my plates à la Tramonto.

Almost by accident, I had created a look and a style that was all our own. Once we got the menu figured out, we started talking about a name for our new venture. After a little brainstorming, we came up with "Trio," a name with multiple meanings. In addition to symbolizing our three-way partnership, it also reflected the fact that our food was French-, Italian-, and Asian-inspired.

Henry, Gale, and I had put everything we had into this; now the only thing we had left was our own sweat equity—and lots of it. We started hiring staff and began to conceptualize the service and build on our unique identity, thinking about who we wanted to be.

We all agreed to take it one day at a time, one guest at a time, and work through all of our operational issues as they surfaced. We began with a couple of tastings and practice parties, and then had a soft opening.

I had hired a sous-chef, Shawn McClain, to help with the opening. Our team was solid, and we felt very confident going into the opening. By now, the food community and the critics knew who we were, and they expected perfection right out of the gate. Because of our reputation, we figured they weren't going to give us a lot of time to get our act together, and we were right. We hadn't even been open three months before Phil Vettel, food writer from the *Chicago Tribune*, came in to review Trio.

After work that night, Henry, Gale, and I drove down to the *Tribune* building and waited for the paper to come out at 3:00 a.m. We knew the implications Phil's review would have on the rest of our journey at Trio and our future careers. His comments could mean the start of something big—or they could force us to revise what we were doing or even shut us down before we really got started.

When the paper landed, we quickly grabbed copies and huddled with our coffee on the steps in the snow and freezing cold to read the review.

"I've seen the future of fine dining, and its name is Trio. . . . Trio's food, in terms of sheer excitement, ranks among that of such masters of the unexpected as Jean Joho [chef/proprietor of Everest] and Charlie Trotter."*

Jackpot! The review had put us in exactly the company we had hoped in one sentence. Not only did we achieve the concept we were going for, we managed to rank right up there with the best of the best.

Flowers and messages of congratulations began to pour in from friends, family, vendors, and other chefs in town. By midafternoon, our phone was ringing off the hook, and by the time we opened our doors for dinner, our reservation book was filled three weeks out. The exclusive chef's table in the kitchen was reserved five weeks out. That was just the beginning. Over the next week, we booked the next three months solid.

After our final course went out that night, I stood in the doorway of the dining room and looked around. The place was filled. Everyone was smiling and eating and laughing, clearly enjoying themselves. *That's what it's all about,* I thought.

Later, I congratulated our staff and told them, "Now the work really starts." All the labor we'd poured into the opening and training would be nothing compared to the work ahead of us as we proved that the review had been on target. In fact, the restaurant rode on the reputation created by that review for the next two years, so we focused on maintaining our high standards.

Following that first *Tribune* review, the *Sun-Times* did another four-star review. *Chicago* magazine came out to do a feature on us, ranking us among the top ten best fine-dining restaurants in the city. Now our reputation moved beyond the local level, and we started to earn national recognition. Within months, we got a call from the James Beard Foundation. We had been nominated for the best new restaurant award!

The Zagat guide ranked us among the top three restaurants in the city of Chicago, and the reviews continued: *Esquire, Food & Wine, Gourmet.* Everyone said the same thing: "Great food, great service,

---

*Phil Vettel, "Trio's Triple Threat: Artistry, Gastronomy, Comfort," *Chicago Tribune,* 4 February 1994.

great restaurant, great wine list." We made the cover of *Food Arts* and *Chicago* magazine. Gale and I were named as two of the top ten new best chefs in America by *Food & Wine* magazine, which earned us an invitation to the Food & Wine Classic in Aspen, where Julia Child herself presented our award.

The night before the awards presentation, we sat around a fireplace at the Hotel Jerome in Aspen, talking with Julia Child and three or four other chefs. She had a great sense of humor and showed genuine interest in us, graciously answering our questions. Her kindness extended to other people as well. She welcomed every fan who approached her for an autograph or photo and never appeared to be flustered.

I couldn't help but think about how far we had come. Who would have thought that I, a kid from upstate New York who got his start at Wendy's Old Fashioned Hamburgers, would one day share the stage with Julia Child? Interestingly, Julia and I hit it off right from the start. For whatever reason, she just seemed to take to me, and of course, I to her.

Our life was a whirlwind, and every day we simply tried to keep up with the craziness. We were suddenly going 100 miles per hour, never really getting the chance to stop and reflect on what was happening. One afternoon, I happened to be standing in the dining room when the phone rang. I picked it up.

"Thank you for calling Trio. May I help you?"

"Hey, Rick, it's Eileen."

Eileen! Eileen and I hadn't talked much since Bella Luna. It was great to hear her voice again!

"I saw the article about you and Gale in *Food & Wine*, and I just wanted to call and say congratulations! You've really done well for yourself and I'm so proud to say I knew you when."

We talked for a few more minutes, catching up on what we were both doing. Eileen was still in Michigan. She had had a baby, a son named Sean.

"Wow," I said. "Congratulations to you, too. You will make an awesome mother."

And then I paused.

"Hey, Eileen, I'm really sorry for the way I treated you back at Bella Luna. I was a real jerk; I know that. I'm working on it."

"Hey, Rick, it's okay. Water under the bridge."

I smiled as a weight I hadn't even realized I'd been carrying slipped off my shoulders. Even though Eileen and I hadn't talked for years and weren't a part of each other's daily life, she was still such an important part of who I was.

Though I was feeling great about Trio's success, I couldn't seem to let up. About this time Rich Melman advised me to make sure Gale and I took some time to enjoy what we were doing and relax a little. He told me we'd regret it if we didn't.

I heard what he was saying, but I wasn't sure I could do that quite yet. While Trio was clearly doing well, there was always more work to be done, more improvements to be made. Sure, we were earning great reviews, but if we weren't careful, we could easily lose it all.

The very idea of taking a break was terrifying to me. Just the thought of stepping out for even a moment made my heart race and my palms sweat. I couldn't stop now.

CHILLED ROASTED RED AND GOLD BABY BEET SALAD WITH HORSERADISH FOAM

While at Trio, I did a lot of experimenting with different flavor combinations and techniques. During this time, the culinary world was especially interested in the science of food and molecular cuisine.

I love beets, always have, and this cheerful, colorful dish is all about the beets. For this recipe, I suggest baby red and gold beets and large gold beets, but if you prefer a slightly different combination, go for it. Use beets that are in season. Horseradish and beets, a classic duo in my world, are paired here, although I've made the horseradish a foam here, for two reasons. First, it lightens the horseradish; second, at the time I was developing this recipe, I was experimenting with molecular cuisine. — *SERVES 6*

   10 baby red beets
   10 baby gold beets
   4 large gold beets
   ½ c. extra-virgin olive oil, divided in half
   1 Tbs. finely chopped fresh tarragon
   Kosher salt and freshly ground black pepper
   ¼ c. fresh orange juice
   Horseradish foam (recipe follows)
   ¼ c. micro chervil or other micro herb, for garnish
   Cracked black pepper, for garnish

1. Preheat oven to 350°F.
2. In a large mixing bowl, toss the beets, ¼ c. of the oil, and tarragon; season to taste with salt and pepper. Transfer the beets to a shallow roasting pan and roast for about one hour, or until tender. Immediately peel the beets by rubbing the skin off with paper towels. Cut the baby red and baby gold beets into quarters and set aside.
3. Coarsely chop the large gold beets and transfer to the bowl of a food processor fitted with a metal blade or a blender. Pulse until the beets are finely chopped but not pureed. They should have some texture. Scrape the beets into a bowl and stir in the orange juice and the remaining ¼ cup of oil.
4. To serve, place a 1½-inch ring mold in the center of a glass plate. Fill the mold halfway with the finely chopped large gold beets and then add enough baby beets to fill it all the way. Carefully remove the mold. Top with micro chervil salad. Shake the horseradish foam vigorously and spray the foam next to the beets. Sprinkle with cracked black pepper and drizzle with extra-virgin olive oil. Repeat to make 5 more servings.

Horseradish Foam (makes 2 cups)
2 c. heavy cream
½ c. grated fresh horseradish
Kosher salt and freshly ground white pepper
1 sheet gelatin
iSi Gourmet Whip canister
2 iSi N20 cream chargers

1. Put the cream and horseradish in a medium saucepan. Season to taste with salt and white pepper. Bring to a boil over medium-high heat. Remove cream mixture from the heat and allow to steep for 20 minutes.
2. Meanwhile, fill a large bowl with cool water. Gently drop the gelatin sheet in the water. Let it soften and bloom for about 5 minutes.
3. Using your hands, lift the gelatin sheet from the water and squeeze it gently between your fingers to remove excess water. Transfer the sheet to the cream mixture and stir gently until gelatin is dissolved. Let cream mixture cool slightly, and then strain it through a chinois or other fine-mesh sieve into a bowl.
4. Pour cream mixture into a chilled iSi Gourmet Whip canister. Charge the whipper with 1 or 2 N20 cream charges. Chill the foam for at least one hour and serve.

17

BRASSERIE T

He who has begun a good work in you
will complete it until the day of Jesus Christ.

PHILIPPIANS 1:6

The success of Trio had propelled us to the next level of culinary accomplishment, and with the reviews and awards came new opportunities. Every week we were invited to showcase our talents at special events all around the country: the Masters of Food & Wine, Kohler Food & Wine Experience, James Beard dinners, even cooking at the Super Bowl and the Los Angeles benefit for Meals On Wheels.

When Julia Child asked Gale to film the season finale of *Baking with Julia*, I was invited along. Julia would interview me for the show; then I would watch the taping of Gale's segment. When we arrived in front of Julia's Boston home, film crews were already hard at work.

As we entered the large Victorian home, we were greeted by the wonderful smells of fresh-baked breads and pastries. Black-and-white photographs filled the walls: Julia and her husband, Paul, on their many travels through Europe, as well as Julia with diplomats, presidents, popes, celebrities, and chefs from all over the world.

Julia's assistant, Stephanie, led us upstairs to the office, where Julia was on the telephone while working at the computer. She motioned to us to have a seat, and then quickly finished up her call.

She stood up to greet us and give us hugs. "Hello, dearies," she said in true Julia fashion. "I apologize for that. But when the White House calls, one must take the call."

We caught up a little and then she sent us down to the basement prep kitchen to get ready for the show. The taping went off without a hitch, and since this was to be the last segment in her series, Julia wanted to celebrate with a dinner and wrap-up party later that night for the crew and producers. As we were cleaning up, she began to assign tasks for the meal.

"Rick, have you ever cooked buffalo hump before?"

"No, I haven't."

"Well, someone sent me a buffalo hump. Would you mind cooking it up?" she asked. "It's in the back cooler."

Buffalo hump? Not wanting to disappoint Julia, I nodded and then headed for the kitchen. What did I get myself into?

I pulled the box out of the refrigerator and was relieved to find that the buffalo looked a lot like a beef steamship round. I decided to treat it in the same way I'd treat a piece of beef, studding it with garlic, rubbing it with olive oil, rosemary, salt, and pepper, and then searing it on top of the stove. Next I put it in a large roasting pan along with some vegetables. After I put it in the oven to slow roast, Gale and I headed for the hotel to freshen up.

When we returned for dinner later that evening, Julia had laid out a beautiful buffet: salads, side dishes, and desserts lined the butcher block island in the kitchen. In the center of the table lay a huge turkey.

My stomach lurched. *Oh no! The buffalo hump didn't turn out and Julia had to cover for me with this turkey.* I was so embarrassed. What was I thinking, trying to pretend like I knew what I was doing? I had never cooked buffalo before, let alone a whole buffalo *hump*.

I slid over toward Julia.

"I'm so sorry about the buffalo hump," I whispered. "Did it not turn out?"

"Oh no, dearie," she said. "It's just resting in the back. In fact, I think it's time for you to go get it and bring it out to slice. It's beautiful."

"So what's up with the turkey?"

"Oh, there are some non-beefeaters here."

In the kitchen, the buffalo looked just perfect. Relieved, I sliced it up, made a little sauce with the pan drippings, and put it on a serving platter. As I carried it into the dining room, I tried to act as if buffalo hump was just a part of my everyday repertoire—no big deal.

But always the smart one, Julia had a different plan. At the end of the meal, she stood to her feet and raised her glass.

"I would like to propose a toast," she said. "I want to thank you all for helping me wrap up this season of programming in such grand fashion. And I especially want to thank Rick for the best hump I have ever had."

After a few long seconds of silence, the room exploded in laughter, and both Julia and I turned about as red as the beet salad on our plates. I still love and miss her. Her humor was always spot on, and her zest for life was contagious.

Experiences like this made all the hard work of being a chef worthwhile. And thankfully, all the extra effort we had devoted to Trio was paying off. The place was humming along quite nicely and even turning a pretty decent profit for such a young venture.

I loved doing fine dining, but I also missed making some of the brasserie-style dishes we'd been able to do in England. Once in a while, I tried to sneak something more casual onto the menu, but Gale was always quick to remind me that that was a whole other restaurant. After talking about it, we decided to try our hand at a second, brasserie-style concept. But when we talked to Henry about it, he was surprisingly unenthusiastic.

"I'm just not ready to take that kind of financial risk right now," he said. "It's fine if you guys want to do it, but you'll have to raise the capital yourselves. I just don't have anything extra to put into it." Henry was a native of Hawaii, and he dreamed of moving back there and opening his own hot dog stand. (In fact, Hank's Haute Dogs opened in Honolulu in 2007.) Though he wouldn't be investing financially, we still counted on his business expertise and partnership as we looked to expand to a new restaurant.

Gale and I didn't have any spare cash either. But over the years, we'd both been approached by people—well-known business leaders, celebrities, and community members in and around the city—who had seen our success and were willing to get behind us financially. We made a list of everyone we could think of who might want to partner with us, and within a few months we were able to pull together a strong team of people who shared our vision for Brasserie T.

Starting a business from the ground up was a whole new world for us, and we basically had to go back to Business 101—though neither one of us had ever taken a business course. We talked to Rich Melman, and we read everything we could get our hands on about putting together a business plan, setting projections, and creating budgets. We set up a corporation and sold $25,000 to $100,000 blocks of Brasserie T, with the understanding that once the restaurant got on its feet, we would pay back the investors a little at a time until their initial outlay was taken care of. After that, the profit percentages would begin to shift more our way.

All told, we raised around a million dollars for our opening, quite a bit more than we had started with for Trio. But we had both done enough openings by this time to know not to get too excited. Even though a million dollars seemed like a lot of money, it wasn't going to stretch very far since we were remodeling the kitchens and dining room and installing high-ticket items like wood-burning ovens and grills. Visions of crumbling concrete floors flashed through my mind, reminding us to be as fiscally responsible as we knew how.

The next step was to find a location. We started scouring the city in hopes of finding just the right site: something warm and inviting but contemporary at the same time. More than once, we thought we had found the perfect place, but whenever we'd bring Henry through, he'd manage to find ten or twenty or fifty things wrong with it.

Finally after several months, we found a great little building up in Northfield, just fifteen minutes from Trio. Though we really wanted to do something in the city, we figured Henry would be more comfortable in the suburbs. And when we gave him the tour, he found very little to criticize. On top of that, the landlord offered to contribute another $500,000 to the demolition and build-out.

I knew we were pushing Henry outside of his comfort zone, but I hoped that once we got going and he saw the results, we could mend the cracks in our relationship. With two solid concepts under our belts, the three of us would be positioned to take the Chicago restaurant scene by storm. Now was the time for us to make a name for ourselves, to create a brand and drive it forward into the future.

On the day that we were scheduled to finalize the loan and the lease, though, Henry pulled me aside.

"Rick, my heart is just not in this. I can't sign those papers," he said. "This is not what I want to be doing at this time in my life. I'm really sorry. I'm out."

I was very disappointed. Henry knew so much more about business than I did, and we had really been counting on his insights to help get this thing off the ground. But Henry was content to pour all of his energy into Trio; he wanted to be a one-restaurant guy with a one-restaurant chef. Gale and I, on the other hand, had envisioned Trio as the foundation for a company that would expand, multiply, and grow. We also wanted to have a family, which meant our business needed to grow. Now we had no choice but to turn our trio into a duo—at least where the brasserie was concerned.

For the next six months, Shawn and Henry kept things going at Trio, while we remodeled the kitchen and dining rooms at Brasserie T, attended village board meetings, petitioned for zoning approvals, and applied for liquor licenses. We were constantly running, answering questions, and putting out fires.

After once again working our tails off seven days a week to get things going, Brasserie T opened to great reviews and did strong business right from the start. We had installed a beautiful wood-burning oven in the center of the dining room, with a chef's counter that ran all the way around. We hired a general manager, Mohammad, and a chef de cuisine, Mark, and together we served up typical brasserie fare with Italian-American flair. Our menu included burgers and sandwiches, roast chicken, grilled pork chops with braised cabbage. We did braised lamb shanks and pizzas out of the wood oven and osso buco, bringing in some of my Italian heritage. The kitchen was large enough to accommodate banquets and parties, and we even did a little catering on the side.

We had known from the start we wouldn't be able to draw a salary for a while, but we weren't too worried initially. Things had started on the right track, and we hoped to pay things back fairly quickly.

As time went on, however, we weren't paying back the investors as quickly as I would have liked. Although things were still going well overall, our cash flow was tight. Whenever I thought we might be able to get a little ahead on things, something inevitably came up: a piece of equipment needed to be replaced, a compressor on the walk-in cooler would go out, the computers crashed. We always managed to pay the bills, but it felt to me that we were still scrounging for every penny and every award. I had hoped by this stage we might at least be able to breathe a little easier.

By now, people were pressuring us to do a cookbook. All the top chefs were doing them, and we knew we'd better think about it if we wanted to keep up with the times—chefs were going multimedia, with multiple restaurants, TV shows, and cookbooks. I talked with Bobby Flay, a friend from my days in New York. He was doing a lot of work for Food Network, and his career was beginning to explode. He had recently put out a great cookbook as well, and I asked him how he did it.

"A little bit at a time, man," he said. "You can do it. You know all that stuff because you do it every day. Now you just need to get it down in book form. Get yourself a good agent, a good writer, and a good publisher, and you're set."

Bobby connected me with his book agent in New York, Jane Dystel, and Gale and I made an appointment to see her. We flew to New York, and when I showed her all of our press clippings, I explained that I would really like to do a fine-dining cookbook, much like Daniel Boulud's, Jean-Georges Vongerichten's, or Charlie Trotter's.

Jane took it all in and then she looked up.

"Well, this is all good stuff, but to be honest with you, I don't think I can sell a fine-cooking book to a publisher just yet. You guys are just too new and too young. You may be celebrities in the Midwest, but I don't think your national celebrity has taken hold yet. I'm actually much more interested in this article here on your brasserie cooking. Do this simpler book first."

Explaining that modern readers were looking for something they could tackle themselves, she sent us home to bang out a second proposal. Though I was disappointed that I couldn't do a fine-dining book around Trio, I was happy to be on the way to a book deal for our first book, *American Brasserie*.

Sometime into the second year, we decided to open the Vanilla Bean Bakery. We had done a lot of research on bakeries; we wanted to do something similar to the Corner Bakery but in a smaller, single unit. In addition to showcasing Gale's fabulous creations, we saw the bakery as a good investment since it would allow us to become our own vendor, providing all of the brasserie's bread, pastries, soups, and desserts. We also hoped that other local restaurants would begin to buy from us. But unfortunately, just as we got the Vanilla Bean running, business at Brasserie T suddenly began to slow down. Thankfully, we had just signed a second book deal, *Butter Sugar Flour Eggs*, and we figured that would help us get over the financial slump.

Yet the challenges continued. We were used to working with professional waitstaff, but the pool we had to draw from in the suburbs wasn't nearly as large or as qualified as what we had in the city. Brasserie T's front-of-the-house crew was mostly made up of college kids and part-timers who just wanted to make a couple of bucks but were definitely not in it for the long haul.

The people in Chicago's North Shore were wealthy and well-traveled, and they expected a lot when they went out for a meal. They were not afraid to complain when service didn't meet their expectations. Nearly every day I was dealing with either customers complaining or creditors screaming.

As the customers continued to dwindle, so did the cash flow. We had made the mistake of tying the bakery's finances to Brasserie T's rather than securing a second set of investors, and the two businesses began to be a drain on one another. I knew we were in trouble when we had to take out a line of credit just to make our payroll one week. With a staff of about fifty people, I felt very responsible to them. I couldn't stand the thought that I might be letting them—and their families—down.

I was putting more time than ever into the restaurant and bakery, trying to muscle out some kind of solution to our financial problems. It frustrated me to no end to see our dreams sinking fast and yet not be able to find the rope that would pull us out of the deep end. By this time, I was an obsessed workaholic, trying everything I could think of to keep my head above water.

Since our personal and professional lives were so intertwined, it was tough for me to disconnect. If money was tight at the restaurant, money was tight at home. If stress was high at the restaurant, stress was even higher at home. Gale was much better than I was at separating the two parts of our lives. She understood that sometimes what was best for our careers might not be the best thing for our relationship. When we got home at the end of a very long day, she could stop being Gale-the-Chef and start being just Gale.

I, on the other hand, had no idea how to balance my life with my career. My life *was* my career. And my career was my life. For whatever reason, I felt compelled to drive 150 miles per hour into the same brick wall every day, then back up and do it again the next day, and the next and the next.

No one seemed to notice except Gale. But when she tried to encourage me to slow down, I felt like she was trying to hold me back, so I fought even harder. I took out my frustrations on her, picking at every little thing she did. Like my mom, I was a screamer, and as much as I wanted to just hold Gale and love her, I often found myself going off on her instead—usually over something stupid like the shoes she left on the floor, the dishes she hadn't put in the sink, or the mess she left in the bathroom.

And then we got news that stopped me in my tracks. I was on a flight back from New York after filming *Ready . . . Set . . . Cook* with Gale for the Food Network. The show was a competition between the two of us—a Valentine's special pitting husband and wife against each other. I lost, of course.

I was still licking my wounds over the sting of defeat when, as the plane was taking off, Gale casually leaned over and announced she was pregnant.

Wow. This was huge. Though we had been talking about having kids for a long time, I was totally unprepared for the reality of it. On the one hand, I was thrilled with the idea of having a child of my own, but I had plenty of doubts about me. What did I know about being a parent? My own father hadn't been around much when I was a kid, and my relationship with my mom wasn't very strong—and look at all the trouble I had gotten into as a result. Plus, I could hardly keep up with my life as it was; how was I going to fit parenting into the mix?

I was speechless all the way home. As much as I wanted to be happy, the only emotion I was able to really feel was fear. Deep, soul-wrenching fear.

Gale, on the other hand, was characteristically optimistic. Convinced that we could work things out, she suggested we go to marriage counseling and try to get back on track. Figuring things couldn't get much worse, I agreed. But the counselor was tough. As soon as she heard our story, she seemed to really narrow her focus to me, pointing out all of my flaws and really wanting to dig deep into my past. As much as I wanted to save my marriage, the last thing I wanted to do was dig up all the childhood issues I had buried so long ago.

Struggling to make sense of all that was happening—the success of our restaurants and all the awards—against the pain of my marriage and this new baby, I felt more alone than ever. Why was that?

One night after a long, frustrating shift, I picked up the phone and called Eileen.

"Hey, Eileen, it's Rick," I said.

"Rick! It's so nice to hear from you! It's been too long."

She filled me in on her life. I learned that her difficult marriage had ended in divorce, and she was now raising two sons, Sean and Brian, on her own while working as the events coordinator at the Michigan Union on the University of Michigan's campus.

"What's going on with you and Gale?" she asked.

I told her that we were expecting, and she was excited for us.

"That's fantastic news!" she said. "You are going to love being a parent. It's the best feeling in the world."

I wasn't so sure. And then I spent the next hour pouring out my concerns. Eileen knew my past, what it had been like growing up in my family, and how hard I had worked to get by.

"Even though things seem to be going well, I am just scared to death," I told her. "What if I mess this up?"

"You won't," she said confidently. "And you know why I know that? Because you care so much. I watched you work your way up from a prep cook at Wendy's to an award-winning chef. You didn't have anyone help-ing you, and still you managed to do it. You will do the same thing when this baby comes. As long as you have love to give, you'll be fine."

Her words were comforting and encouraging. If she thought I could do this, maybe I could. But as much as I wanted to believe her, the negative voices in my head continued to remind me of all I had going against me:

Your mom was a mess and your dad went to prison. What do you know about being a father?

You don't even have a high school diploma. What are you going to do when this kid needs homework help?

You had a drug problem and have a bad temper. You barely have time to fix your marriage; how are you going to squeeze this into your schedule?

As Gale neared her delivery date, I felt myself growing more and more distant. We continued to go to counseling, but I put little to no effort into our sessions. Sometimes I didn't even take off my coat while we sat in the tiny office. I started going in to the restaurant even earlier than before and staying even later. Gale really wanted me to join her for doctor appointments, but I never felt like I could afford to leave the brasserie. If Gale was going to spend all her time decorating the nursery and buying baby clothes, I would have to do the hard work of keeping a roof over our heads.

We were in a management meeting one afternoon when Gale's water broke. Dropping everything, we rushed home to Buffalo Grove, packed her bag, and headed for the hospital.

Never one to panic, however, Gale wanted to run through a drive-through and stop at the video store on our way. I worried that we wouldn't make it in time, but once we checked in, the doctor informed us that we still had a long way to go before the baby arrived.

"It could be hours," he said. "I recommend that you settle in and get comfortable."

He was right, and as the sun began to set outside the window, Gale suggested that I run back home to check on the dogs.

"It's going to be a while," she said. "Why don't you stop at work and make sure everything is okay there and then go let the dogs out? I'll be fine."

I stopped by the restaurant and let everyone know what was going on, then ran home to grab a bite to eat. I sat down on the living room floor and flipped on the television. A wave of exhaustion swept over me, as was often the case whenever I stopped moving. Leaning my head back against the couch, I figured I would take a quick power nap to help me get through the next few hours.

I woke with a start to the sound of the phone ringing. And ringing. And ringing. And ringing.

"Mr. Tramonto?" a nurse said. "Where are you? Your baby is about to be born, and your wife needs you *now*."

I rushed out the door, still wearing my stained chef's coat. Bleary-eyed from sleep and worried I might miss my baby's birth, I barely noticed the scenery flashing past my window as I raced toward the hospital. Hurrying up the stairs and into the delivery room, I broke through the doors just ten minutes before my tiny son entered the world.

I couldn't believe how small he was. Worn-out but glowing, Gale looked up at me and beamed.

"It's our baby, Rick! Our son! Can you believe it?" I couldn't. The doctor handed the tiny bundle to me and I immediately felt uncomfortable. Holding him stiffly and awkwardly, I wasn't sure what to do. As an only child and the youngest cousin in our extended family, I felt completely out of my element. Part of me desperately wanted to give in to the love that was threatening to burst out of my heart, but another part of me held back.

I handed him back to Gale and released the breath I hadn't even realized I was holding.

"Hello, little one," she said, smiling down at him with such unmasked love and adoration that I couldn't help but grin myself.

Our son went without a name for a couple of days. We had agreed that Gale would get to choose his first name if the baby would take my last name. She was still undecided on what to call him when I began packing the car for our trip home only to be told we couldn't leave until he was named. We finally agreed to name him Giorgio Tramonto—Gio for short—adding an Italian twist to George, after Gale's grandpa.

For the first few months after we brought Gio home, things seemed

202 || SCARS OF A CHEF

to be getting better for Gale and me. Gio was such a good baby that I couldn't help but soften when I was around him. I loved this little guy more than I had ever loved anyone; I vowed to be the very best dad and husband I could be. No matter what.

One afternoon, Eileen called me at the restaurant.

"I'm in town, and I thought I'd stop in for a quick visit."

We hadn't seen Eileen since Bella Luna, so I called Gale and asked her to bring Gio down. We were both thrilled to reconnect with Eileen, especially now that we also had a child of our own.

As we sat together in a booth, all staring at this beautiful little boy, I couldn't help but laugh.

"Did you ever think all those years ago at Wendy's Old Fashioned Hamburgers that we'd one day have our own kids?" I asked.

Eileen nodded. "Yeah," she said. "I did. I'm glad things are going so well for both of you."

I didn't have the heart to tell her that things aren't always as rosy as they appear. Gale and I were still meeting with a marriage counselor, although it seemed like we weren't really getting anywhere. One day, after a particularly grueling session, we came out of the counselor's office, both of us fuming at each other. Gale was furious that I wasn't engaging in the process.

"How could you just sit there and pout like that?" she asked. "Don't you care at all about our marriage and our future and our family?"

"Of course I care," I snapped. "And I wasn't pouting. But you'd be ticked too if the counselor was always pointing out all of *your* flaws. Obviously, you both think this whole thing is my fault. I'm sick of always feeling like the bad guy."

I slid into the car, slamming the door hard behind me. Gale stood outside, trying to regain her composure before continuing the conversation. I started the car and waited, checking my phone for messages.

Fifteen messages! Oh brother. The creditors were getting more demanding every day. I put the phone down, not wanting to think about my financial failures on top of everything else right now.

Gale continued to stand outside the car. *She probably wants me to come out there and apologize,* I thought. *No way. I can sit here all day.*

Trying to look like I didn't care, I flipped open my phone and dialed the voice mail. The first message wasn't from a creditor; it was our general manager, Mohammad: "I'm not sure where you guys are, but I wanted to let you know we had a little problem at the restaurant. A spark went up through the wood-burning grill and there was some smoke on the roof, but I think we've got it under control. Everything seems to be okay, but call me back as soon as you can."

Wow! Thank goodness he caught it in time. That could have been bad.

I hit the delete button and listened to the next message, this time from my chef, Steven.

"Hey, Chef, just to let you know, the spark on the roof ignited, and we decided to call the fire department and evacuate. I'll let you know what they find out."

I played the next thirteen messages as Steven continued to describe the chain of events that followed. Finally, I got to the last one.

"Hey Chef, we are standing out front and the place is on fire. You'd better get down here right away. It's really bad."

I motioned for Gale to get into the car. She waved me off, her own cell phone to her ear. Obviously, she was listening to the same messages I was. We raced up to the North Shore, praying desperately that the fire department had been able to save the building. But by the time we got there, the place was trashed. Charred timbers hung wildly in every room and water dripped on our heads as we made our way through broken glass and ravaged furniture. In order to stop the blaze, firefighters had hacked through the walls with their axes and torn off the roof. Anything that was left of the building was completely water soaked.

We had no choice but to close Brasserie T and let our staff go until we got the insurance money and put things back in order.

We spent the next few months ripping out waterlogged carpeting, tearing out moldy drywall, bringing in a company to de-smoke the building, and trying to salvage what little we could. Most everything was smoke damaged and just not worth saving. Forced to start almost from scratch, we basically had to remodel the brasserie—but this time with very little time and no money.

We called back a skeleton crew and reopened just a month after the fire. Unfortunately, we just didn't have enough cash or insurance money to push us over the initial hump. And although the bakery was not affected, it was in no financial shape to support both businesses. Hoping to relieve the leaking flow of funds, we decided to close the Vanilla Bean. This allowed us to settle some of our debt, but it basically drained every last penny we had.

Looking ahead, I figured we might be able to stay afloat for only another six months—if we were lucky. I talked with Rich Melman, and he agreed that we had to make some big decisions.

"Until you get some failures under your belt, you'll never be a true success. You have to learn how to mourn your loss and see it as a negative but necessary experience. Believe me, I know. I've had to close or reconceptualize plenty of restaurants. Sometimes you just have to know when to cut your losses. Now seems to be that time."

Rich then explained that he had recently been thinking about reconceptualizing Avanzare. The place had been open for fifteen years and was still doing pretty well, but it was time for a fresh idea. "What would you think about fine dining there?" Rich asked.

"Yeah, I would definitely love to do that," I said. "And you know how much I love the Avanzare space. It feels like home to me."

If I took this new opportunity with Rich, I would be a chef partner for the first time and would also be able to work in a handful of restaurants and try my hand at various concepts.

The possibility of working with Rich definitely pulled at me and distracted me from our current problems, but it also disturbed me. I felt like such a failure. My marriage and my business were both spiraling out of control. How could I even think about doing something new, especially with Rich, someone I loved and respected? I had let so many people down over the past few years: Gale, Henry, our investors, our staff, myself. I couldn't stand the thought of letting Rich down too.

I explained that as much as I wanted to do fine dining with him, I was in over my head at the brasserie. An experienced restaurateur, Rich was unfazed. He brought a team from Lettuce into Brasserie T to do an evaluation. After assessing the traffic flow and our books, they concluded that it really wasn't worth keeping the place open. Next, we consulted with Lettuce corporate attorneys. They recommended that we file Chapter 11 to get out from under our debt. I understood what they were saying, but I really struggled with this. If we did file bank-ruptcy, who would get burned in the end? Vendors, investors, staff—I couldn't imagine doing that to so many people who had trusted us and believed in us.

Rich was empathetic. "What other options do you have?"

"I looked at getting a bank loan or finding new investors but have come up empty."

In the end, Lettuce attorneys stepped in and helped negotiate us out of our lease and other obligations. As thankful as I was to have so many experts helping me to navigate these uncharted waters, I hated every minute of it. I came to work feeling nauseous each day. To me, these weren't routine business transactions. This was my name, the restaurant into which I'd poured a lot of time, and I knew the people who had put up the money. I had given everything I had to this place, sacrificing everything: relationships, health, financial security. But in the end, it just wasn't enough. I had no choice but to start to close up and finally admit defeat. My grief lingered for a long time. I learned—not for the last time—that when your restaurant closes, it feels like a death that must be mourned.

To add more salt to the wound, I got a call from my dad one afternoon. Just a few weeks before, he and my mom had visited over the holidays to see Gio. Mom was tired and not feeling well during the trip. Now my dad was calling to tell me she had just been diag-nosed with stage IV stomach cancer. She was expected to make it only another twelve weeks. I was devastated. The year had been full of losses—our marriage, our restaurant, and now my mom. I went home for one last visit, spending some good quality time with her. And then I said my good-byes. I just didn't have it in me to deal with this right now.

When Mom passed away a few weeks later, Gale and Gio and I returned to Rochester for the funeral; as always, the Italian food crew was ready and waiting when we arrived. Within minutes of dropping my bags inside the door, I was enveloped in the warmth of family and food and friends. I still ached over losing my mom, but being home was definitely good for the soul.

Eileen, who was in town visiting her family when my mom died, came to her funeral because she had spent so much time with my family during our teen years. Afterward, she and I, along with a few other friends, went down to Wendy's Old Fashioned Hamburgers and ordered burgers and Frostys. After our other friends left, Eileen and I continued to talk. I told her about the grief I was feeling, not only over my mom's death, but also over the closing of Brasserie T and my marital problems. Eileen was fond of both me and Gale, and she told me she was sad to hear we were struggling.

We said good-bye and promised to do better at keeping in touch, and then I went home to be with my dad for a few hours before I had to leave again. He seemed to be handling my mom's death as well as could be expected, but I could tell the grief was taking its toll on him. I hated to leave him, but my aunts and uncles promised to check in on him every couple of days, and I knew they would keep him from getting lonely and wouldn't let him go hungry.

FRIED POLENTA SQUARES

This was a favorite of diners at Brasserie T, which brought together French, Italian, and American cuisine. The polenta mixture is prepared and refrigerated overnight so it can set up. After being cut into squares the following day, they're lightly floured and fried. — *SERVES 4*

1 c. heavy cream
½ c. chicken stock
2 c. water
Kosher salt, to taste
1 c. polenta or cornmeal
½ c. Parmesan cheese
4 oz. extra-virgin olive oil
Freshly ground black pepper, to taste

1. Put the heavy cream, chicken stock, and water into a large pot. Bring liquid to a boil and then add salt.
2. Bring the liquid back to a boil; add polenta. Cook for 10 minutes.
3. Add Parmesan cheese, olive oil, and black pepper.
4. Spread out the mixture in a lightly buttered lined cake pan or sheet tray. Spread out with spatula and cover; place in the refrigerator overnight.
5. Once the polenta is set, cut into squares. Lightly toss in all-purpose flour and shake off excess. Fry them in olive oil in a sauté pan until they are golden brown. Flip and repeat.
6. Serve hot or at room temperature.

PART V

THE REAL WORLD

Late 1990s through 2010

18

TRU

I can do all things through Christ who strengthens me.

PHILIPPIANS 4:13

Richard Melman was all about reinvention. Never content to stick with the status quo, he was always looking for ways to improve upon his concepts, even if it meant starting over. Avanzare had been extremely popular over its fifteen-year stretch, but Rich was ready to make a change, and he wanted Gale and me to help him do it. Located right off Michigan Avenue on St. Clair in Streeterville, Avanzare offered a great space for a new world-class, fine-dining restaurant.

But as excited as I was about the possibilities of going back downtown and building on my reputation, I was also burned out and still reeling from the failure of Brasserie T, my crumbling marriage, and my mom's death. I felt like the rug had been ripped out from under me, and my soul was pretty tired, just as it had been so many years ago when my dad went to prison. I never wanted to be that vulnerable or put myself on the line like that again. The feeling of abandonment and my sense of failure were just too much. Somewhere along the way, I had lost my passion for the whole thing.

I clearly didn't have the temperament or training to deal with the financial aspects of doing business, and this time around I wanted nothing to do with the money part of it. I just wanted to do what I did best: focus on the concept and the food. It was such a relief to let Lettuce Entertain You handle things like HR, payroll, benefits, leases, taxes, infrastructure, and resources so I could focus on the cuisine and creative design and operations.

On the other hand, I knew I needed to be a partner. I needed to feel some sense of ownership. If we were going to do fine dining in Chicago, I knew we would have to really step it up a notch, making this restaurant bigger and better than anything we had done at Trio or Stapleford Park.

Rich and I set off on a whirlwind tour of as many high-end restaurants as we could get to, analyzing, studying, and dissecting everything from menu to service to decor. We took notes on the food, the tablecloths, the amenities, and even the valet services, coming up with a huge list of everything we would need.

I showed Rich the dream file Gale and I had been putting together for the past ten years, and he was blown away.

"This is great stuff," he said. "How much of this would you like to implement at the new restaurant?"

"As much as we can afford," I joked. "Though I think we need all or most of it."

He started in with his Rich-isms. "Okay then, let's make this happen. Let's be the best of the best. Remember, we don't want to be the biggest, we just want to be the best. Ricky, it's not about one thing but about a hundred different things."

Before he went on, I stopped him. "Hey, Rich, are you sure you want to spend this much time and money? I've got some things in here that are really over the top: Armani suits for the waiters, Sheffield silverware, custom Limoges porcelain, Riedel glassware, Frette linens, cheese carts, purse stools—real luxury items."

Rich pulled out a piece of paper and started to calculate some rough costs on paper. He figured the cost of our dream restaurant would be somewhere in the $4 million range.

"It's a lot of money, but I really think we can do this, Ricky," he said. "I've got all the confidence in the world in you and know you'll work your tail off to get the restaurant on the map. I know you are serious, and I also know you have what it takes to compete in this venue. Let's do it." I was overwhelmed. No one had ever given me the chance to build my dream like this with an international stage to play on. It was the best gift I could ever imagine, and I couldn't wait to get started.

Once Avanzare closed and was gutted down to the studs and cement, we spent a couple of weeks just sitting in the empty space looking around. We thought about what we wanted it to look like and what mood we wanted to convey.

In the back of my mind, I kept going back to the meals Gale and I had shared at Pierre Gagnaire's on our honeymoon. Everything about Restaurant Pierre Gagnaire reflected Gagnaire's personality and style. The food was daring and progressive, and the dining room was filled with contemporary artwork and avant-garde design. Just as Gagnaire had instilled a bit of himself into every aspect of his restaurant, I wanted our new restaurant to be a reflection of our dream.

Thankfully, Rich gave us permission and the ability to think outside the box. He had the wherewithal and guts to take the risk to make it happen and let us really make the restaurant our own. If we wanted to move the entrance, we could. If we wanted to make the restaurant blue and black, we could. If we wanted to hang an Andy Warhol painting, we could. No idea was a bad idea, and nothing was impossible. Everything was up for discussion. Rich provided us with a blank canvas upon which to paint our dream. And we did—and then some. We were always thankful to Rich for that.

We decided to call the restaurant Tru, which had multiple levels of meaning. First, it was a play on the idea of being true to our craft. It was also a combination of Tramonto Unlimited, reflecting the idea that we were unlimited in our creativity, imagination, and potential.

Just about this time, Gale got an offer to do her own television program on the Food Network. *Sweet Dreams* would be the first all-dessert show produced by the network, giving her the opportunity to show off her amazing talents in the pastry kitchen. She would need to be in New York for about six weeks at a time to tape a full season of episodes. I knew this was all part of the grand plan to solidify our credibility in the culinary community.

As we began to work through the details of getting Tru open, my career began to get back on track. To those on the outside, it looked like I had it all, as if Brasserie T's closing had all been part of the plan. In the eyes of the media and our fans and customers, I was still a rising star, an acclaimed chef with the world at his feet.

But I knew better. On the inside, I was falling apart. The smile on my face was only a mask to hide my ever-hardening heart. I knew it and Gale knew it. She was tired of my dark moods and stubborn ways. Even though we were always in perfect agreement in the kitchen and the restaurant, in real life we disagreed about almost everything: how to live life, how to raise Gio, how to treat each other, how to spend our free time. Our beliefs were just too different. We simply didn't know how to be together if it wasn't somehow connected to food or work.

She wanted me to consider antidepressants, but the idea of going on any kind of drugs—even a prescription medication under a doctor's supervision—scared me to death. It had been years since I had overcome my addictions. I wasn't ready to risk getting hooked again.

After many months of trying to work through our issues, we finally just looked at each other one day and admitted that we needed to separate. The timing couldn't have been worse. We were right in the middle of building Tru from the ground up. We had recently put together a fantastic team of professionals who would become the heart of the business, and we couldn't let them think there were any cracks in the foundation. We agreed that though we couldn't continue to live together, we needed to keep our problems to ourselves, at least until Tru was running smoothly.

After finding a little two-bedroom apartment in Buffalo Grove, I packed up a few things, mostly chef whites and cookbooks, and got ready to move out. As I piled my suitcases into the back of my car, my heart was heavy in my chest. I thought about my own dad and how I had felt as I watched him being led from the courtroom so many years ago. And now, here I was leaving Gio. I promised myself that I would never abandon him. If not for my son, I almost certainly would have left Chicago at that point and moved back to New York City.

Practically speaking, I was also pretty worried about how I was going to handle things without Gale. She had always taken care of our insurance, mortgages, finances. She knew who to call when an appliance broke or the bank statement was off. My parents had never taught me any of that stuff, not even how to balance my checkbook. I was too busy getting high, making a paycheck, or simply staying out of jail.

It seemed like Gale could blast through this life stuff with her eyes closed; I just knew how to make a great steak or bowl of pasta.

It didn't take me long to settle in to the apartment, since I didn't have much. The first night in my new apartment, I sat on the single chair in the middle of my empty living room and couldn't believe my life had come to this. What would people think if they could see me now: the celebrity chef, owner of what would soon be one of Chicago's biggest restaurants, sitting on a lawn chair in a dark apartment all alone? I pictured Gio, who was a preschooler by now, and wondered what he was doing. I already missed him so much it hurt.

During that dark time, I'd often sit in my little apartment and contemplate immersing myself in the drug world again just to dull the pain. I knew if I did, however, it would be the death of me. I couldn't bear to do that to Gio.

The ache of loneliness was really nothing new. It was the same emptiness I had felt as a kid, especially after one of my parents' horrible fights. It was the same emptiness I had tried to cover up during the long nights after my dad went to prison. It was the same pain that drove me so hard toward drugs and success and accomplishment and that fueled my fear of failure.

But now, without Gale to preoccupy my heart or drugs to numb my emotions, the pain was impossible to ignore. I allowed myself a good cry, and then I was done. The only thing I had left now was my career. I couldn't afford to mess that up.

Before Gale and I gave up completely, I did agree to give counseling one last shot, but after the first week, I knew it just wasn't going to work. This was Gale's deal; it still felt like she and the therapist were working against me, trying to change *me*. Everyone was telling me what was wrong with *me* and what *I* needed to change. I felt attacked and belittled, so I began to stonewall, just as I had in the past.

As we left the therapist's office one afternoon, I was so overcome with sadness, despair, and emptiness that I could barely hold back the tears. I couldn't see any good in life, and I knew I didn't want to feel

214 || SCARS OF A CHEF

this way anymore. I got in my car and pulled out onto the Kennedy Expressway. As I drove toward Buffalo Grove, I thought about how easy it would be just to swerve off to the right and ram head-on into the concrete retaining wall. With my luck, though, I would end up only hurting myself or someone else, not to mention Gio.

In fact, Gio was the one bright spot in my life. I remembered the good times I had had with him, even at my apartment. I loved the time we spent feeding the ducks in the pond behind my building or playing with a plastic bowling set in my hallway. I didn't even mind coloring with him while we watched our favorite TV show *Clifford the Big Red Dog*.

I reached down and flipped on the radio, hoping to drown out the negative voices and darkness in my head.

A warm voice came through the speakers.

"Are you tired and worn out and feel like you just can't take another step?"

Yes. That's exactly how I felt.

"Is your life such a mess that you can't imagine how you will ever untangle it?"

This guy was talking directly to me.

"It's time for you to sit at the feet of Jesus and let him take over."

Huh?

An announcer came on next, introducing the speaker as Pastor Gregory Dickow of Life Changers International Church, which was meeting in Barrington, Illinois, then. As I continued my commute toward home, the speaker began to tell a story about two sisters, Mary and Martha, who had welcomed Jesus himself into their home. He read from Luke 10:

As Jesus and the disciples continued on their way to Jerusalem, they came to a certain village where a woman named Martha welcomed him into her home. Her sister, Mary, sat at the Lord's feet, listening to what he taught. But Martha was distracted by the big dinner she was preparing. She came to Jesus and said, "Lord, doesn't it seem unfair to you that my sister just sits here while I do all the work? Tell her to come and help me."

Wow, I could certainly relate to Martha's feelings of frustration. But then the speaker continued:

But the Lord said to her, "My dear Martha, you are worried and upset over all these details! There is only one thing worth being concerned about. Mary has discovered it, and it will not be taken away from her." (NLT)

Mary had discovered the *one thing* worth being concerned about, and it was a relationship with God. Wow. This was heavy. Like Martha, I had spent my life worrying about so many things, but never the most important thing: knowing Jesus Christ. Focusing on things that weren't worth my time, I had left God completely out of the picture.

Pastor Dickow closed his message with this: "Are you chasing after things that won't last? Are you ready to lay it all down and sit at the feet of Jesus, to focus on the one and only thing worth being concerned about?"

I was.

"If you are ready to turn your life over to him and get right with God, pray this prayer with me."

With tears streaming down my cheeks, I repeated the words aloud:

"Heavenly Father, I invite Jesus Christ into my life as Lord and Savior. I believe that he died for my sins and his blood was shed so I could be forgiven. I believe that he has risen from the dead, and from this moment forward I receive his forgiveness of sins.

"Take out my old heart and give me a new spirit and new life. I will follow you, with your help and your grace, all the days of my life. Amen."

With that final amen, a sense of peace washed over me like nothing I had ever felt before. It was stronger and more powerful than any drug, and I knew my life would never be the same.

I pulled my car off the interstate at the next exit and started heading toward Barrington, driving until I found the Life Changers campus. I wasn't sure where I was going or what my purpose was, but I felt compelled to go in. Still shaking, I jumped from the car and wondered if I was at the right place. The building didn't look like any church I had ever seen: no steeples, no stained glass.

Entering the foyer, I wandered around a bit until I finally found an office. An older woman was seated behind a desk. She looked up at me and smiled as I entered.

"Hello," she said, warmly. "Can I help you?"

"I hope so. I just heard a message on the radio from this church, something about sitting at the feet of Jesus. Can I get a copy of that somehow?"

The woman looked perplexed.

"I'm not exactly sure which message you are talking about, but let me see what we can find for you."

She led me to another section of the building that housed a small bookstore. There, she pulled numerous cassette recordings off the shelf and handed them to me.

"I'm not sure if this is what you were looking for, but it will definitely get you started," she said. "Are you a member here?"

I shook my head no. "I've never been here before. I just really liked the message I heard."

She handed me a handful of brochures and pamphlets about the church, including a schedule of service times and class offerings.

"We'd love to have you join us this weekend for worship," she said, smiling again.

My heart felt strangely happy, and I nodded.

"I work a lot, but I will definitely try to be here."

As I was leaving, I noticed a shelf of Bibles.

"Can I get one of those too?"

"Yes, sir," she said, adding a black leatherbound Bible to my stack.

I went back to my car and pushed the first tape into the cassette player. She had found the exact message I had just heard! I listened to the whole thing again, not even bothering to head back toward the city. This was what I had been missing my whole life.

"God, I've made such a mess of things," I said aloud. "I can't believe that you would love someone like me, but I'm so glad that you do and I'm so grateful that you're the God of the second chance. Please forgive me for thinking I can do this all by myself and living life like an island—all alone. I need you to step in and save me. Please save me."

I went home and called in to work to let them know I wouldn't be in that day. Everyone was shocked. I never called in sick unless I was having surgery or going to a funeral; though in a way, I *was* going to a kind of funeral—my own. I told them I would be taking the entire weekend off. After hanging up, I settled in with Pastor Greg's tapes and my Bible. I spent the next forty-eight hours listening to Pastor Greg's messages, poring over the material, and reading my Bible. I also spent lots of time praying, asking God for the wisdom to change my life and to set me on the right course.

On Sunday, I was back at the church for the 8:00 a.m. service. I sat up front in the first row so I could be sure I wouldn't miss a word of the message, and then when it was over, I couldn't leave. I sat through the 10:00 a.m. service as well, soaking up everything I could and just letting God's Word wash over me. This was the real deal, and I couldn't get enough of God's Word and truth.

I was so excited about my newfound relationship with Christ that I couldn't wait to tell Gale. If Jesus could save me, surely he could save our marriage. After much cajoling, I finally talked her into coming to a Sunday night service at Life Changers with me. I hoped we could find some common ground to work things out. This might be exactly what we needed.

We sat through the service, and Gale listened closely. As the invitation began, I sneaked a glimpse her way. She was crying! I couldn't believe it. The sermon must have moved her; this was the breakthrough I had been hoping for!

Gale was such an intellectual person; she rarely broke down or allowed her emotions to get the better of her. I was thrilled as we walked to the parking lot through the pouring rain. Already envisioning a brand-new future together, I turned to her.

"So . . . I noticed you were crying. What did you think?"

"Oh Rick, I wasn't crying because of the service. I was crying because for the first time since we separated, I realized this is really over. I am never going to believe this stuff. You should be with one of those Christian girls up in the choir instead of me. This is over."

I was stunned. I dropped her off and went back to my little dark apartment with no furniture. And then I sat on the floor and began to cry myself as waves of sadness and remorse washed over me. I was completely alone now.

I had no one to reach out to, no way to fill the gaping hole in my heart. I had tried everything: alcohol, food, drugs, sex. Nothing could ever take away my pain and fill my soul.

As I sat in the middle of the room with my head in my hands, I thought back to what Pastor Greg had taught on that night. I heard a voice in my head: *I'm with you. I will never turn my back on you. I will never abandon you. I will never leave you or forsake you. And I will satisfy.*

My marriage was over, of that I was convinced. But I was going to be okay because I was not alone. Jesus was with me.

I called Gale and told her I was ready to move forward with the divorce. We were parents to Gio first and foremost. Second, we were business and culinary partners, and we had always gotten along on a professional level. So in one sense, the divorce felt like another business transaction. We just did what we had to do. We each hired an attorney and got the ball rolling, but after only a few weeks, things were worse than when we started. The lawyers always seemed to be creating division and stress where there hadn't been a problem in the first place. They wanted us to be angry with each other and to fight to the death for our rights. But Gale and I knew that life was too short for that, and we could work this out on our own. Finally one afternoon after a particularly painful meeting, Gale called me.

"Rick, I'm sorry things are going the way they are with the lawyers," she said. "I never wanted this to get so out of hand, and this is getting really expensive."

"I completely agree," I replied. "I wish we could work this out without them."

"Why can't we?" Gale asked. "We've always managed to get along just fine, even when we *weren't* getting along. Let's you and me just sit down and do this."

We met the next day for lunch at Corner Bakery and made a pact: we would not leave until we had resolved every last detail of the divorce. Over tuna fish sandwiches and bowls of tomato soup, we worked out an agreement. With our mantra of "what's best for Gio?" we sat together and went through all the finances and the house and the visitation and even the dog. We tried to be as fair as possible in drawing the lines, splitting everything fifty-fifty. Gale had her Food Network deal, and I had my cookbook deal. She wanted to keep the house, so she agreed to buy me out. I agreed to buy a place close enough that sharing full custody of Gio would be easy. Within three hours, we had worked out every detail.

As I sat across the table from Gale, with our whole life spread out before us, I couldn't help but think about how much I respected her. I had grown up with Gale, and together we made a powerful team. Over the years we had developed such a comfortable working relationship, and we had learned how to balance each other really well. We shared the same history, and we spoke the same language. I couldn't have asked for a better teammate.

Unfortunately, the seeds we had been planting were mainly professional seeds. I wanted to cook with Gale before I wanted to live with her. If only I had worked as hard on our marriage as I had on my career, we probably wouldn't be dealing with all this baggage now. For that, I felt deep regret.

We wrapped up all the final details, and I reached out to take her hand.

"Well, we may not have had the best marriage in the world, but I promise you, we will have the best divorce in the world. When we walk into Tru on Monday, no one will ever know that anything has changed between us. We are still the dream team, and Tru is going to be the best we can possibly make it."

And I was right. The next week we were right back at it, working with our team at Tru. Other than our lawyers and our families, Rich was the only person we confided in.

"Are you guys going to be able to do this?" he asked. "We've already signed the deal, and we're right in the middle of construction mode. You're supposed to be going to France next week to look at china. I'm concerned."

We assured him we could do it. Gale and I knew how to do the business thing together; that was the one area of our lives we knew how to do well. In addition, we had put together an amazing team—they were truly the best of the best—and we trusted them completely.

We brought in a managing partner, Scott, someone I had worked with at Avanzare. I wanted him on the project from the start so that he could participate in every stage of planning and development. He would also oversee the construction projects and help with staff training. Next we brought in a woman who had worked with us for many years at Trio as our dining room captain. She helped me put together a dream team of servers, people who understood this industry and were committed to Tru for the long haul. Finally, we hired a top-notch sommelier. We needed to make a statement with our wine program, so our sommelier had to be the best.

As we got the ball rolling, Rich was extremely generous with his time, wisdom, and resources. And he gave us carte blanche to do what we wanted to do. He knew when to share his opinions and when to step back and let us make decisions for ourselves.

"This is *your* restaurant, your vision, your dream," he said. "I know you have a very clear idea of what this can and should be. You have my blessing: now make it happen."

For a chef, that kind of freedom was rare—almost unheard of. More often than not, the financial side of the business outweighed the creative side, forcing a chef to stifle his vision and dreams. This was not the case for us at Tru. Rich often pointed out that there needs to be a great balance between the art of a restaurant (the food, service, beverages, and artwork) and the science (the business side, systems, and operations).

Because first impressions are so important, we commissioned Atlanta-based designer Bill Johnson to help us design the space. In order to really bring out the artistry of our food, we decided on an all-white decor, with accents of blue, my favorite color. Gale and Rich worked closely with some of the best art dealers in the world to bring in first-class artwork and create an art museum feel throughout.

And then we moved on to my favorite part of the project: creating our custom kitchen. We combined the best of all that we had seen— French island ranges, custom knife drawers, portioned vegetable bins, copper cookware, invisible garbage drops, granite countertops, a separate pastry kitchen, a chef's table—and came up with a gorgeous workspace we felt really good about.

We were excited to get Tru off the ground, but we wanted to do it right so we took our time, spending a lot of time in Lettuce's test kitchens, being very methodical about every decision we made. While the construction crews got started, our team was hard at work deciding on linens, china patterns, artwork, glassware, and menu covers. The research and review process was ongoing and relentless, often keeping us there late into the night to taste one more round of caviar or go over one more press release.

And all the while, no one except Rich had any idea that Gale and I were divorced. Every day, we made sure to arrive at the restaurant at the same time in the morning so the staff would see us coming in together. Everyone had put so much into the restaurant already; we didn't want them to worry or lose their focus. If they thought our marriage was deteriorating, they would surely begin to question the stability of the professional partnership and maybe even start looking for other positions. We had worked so hard to put together the perfect staff; we couldn't afford to lose any of them now.

My heart still ached for the failure of my marriage. Occasionally, Eileen and I would talk by phone. Having gone through a divorce herself, she could relate to the grief and loneliness that sometimes welled up inside me as my marriage ended. She also was a great sounding board when I needed some advice on handling the challenges of single parenting.

My greatest source of strength, however, came from the Lord. I was learning to lean heavily on him. I attended church every chance I could, sometimes even going to three or four services a week.

I really liked the things that Pastor Greg was teaching from the Bible and couldn't get enough of God's messages. I loved the praise and worship. This was different from anything I had ever heard before. Life Changers was just that: life changing.

I was growing in my faith by leaps and bounds, filling my heart and renewing my mind with the Word of God every chance I could. After so many years of trying to satisfy the hunger in my soul, I had finally found the Bread of Life and the Source of living water. God alone—not food, not drugs, not sex, not romance, not success—was the only thing that completely filled the void and made me whole.

As we neared Tru's opening, we sat down with Rich and the team and came up with a list of things we'd like to achieve over a five- and ten-year period. The top ten list included things like:

1. Receive a four-star review by the *Chicago Tribune*, *Sun-Times*, and *Chicago* magazine
2. Rank in Zagat's top five restaurants
3. Earn a James Beard award for service, pastry, and best chef of the Midwest
4. Be asked to become a member of Relais & Châteaux
5. Achieve *Wine Spectator*'s Grand Award
6. Release a Tru cookbook
7. Win the Ivy award from *Restaurants & Institutions* magazine
8. Get into The Michelin Guide
9. Get into the Mobil Guide
10. Get into the AAA Guide

This list was a great motivator. We posted it in the office so we could look at it every day. We needed to know how the industry and the critics were looking at us, and with a list like this, we could easily chart our progress.

The menu itself was a huge undertaking. We planned to run a three-course prix fixe menu, a six-course vegetarian menu, an eight-course grand menu, a ten-course chef's menu, and a twelve-course kitchen table menu—none of which included any of the same dishes. Needless to say, the *mise en place* and prep lists were daunting—but I knew we had the team to do it. We were in the big leagues now, and I planned to be a worthy competitor.

Playing off the art museum theme, we decided to present the menu as a series of "collections"—the Chef Tramonto Collection, the Market Collection, the Ocean Collection, the Vegetable Collection. Each tasting would give our guests the opportunity to try a variety of items and flavor profiles. For instance, when a table of six ordered the chef's menu, each person got something different at every course.

That meant we would provide six different soups, six different amuse-bouche, six different hot appetizers, six different cold appetizers, six foie gras presentations, six different fish courses, six different meats, and twenty or more different cheeses from our cheese cart. A parade of desserts that included several courses followed by a spectacular petits fours cart with numerous types of chocolates and candies rounded out the meal. Our Tramonto Tasting Collections were truly unique, and I hoped they would be an integral part of the restaurant's success.

Once we signed off on the menu, we turned our attention to the serving pieces. This time around, we didn't have to go to Home Depot; we had the budget to buy what we wanted: fine china and porcelain made by Rosenthal, Versace, and Limoge. Even so, we had worked hard to create a signature look at Trio, and we wanted Tru to reflect that same image. So instead of pulling the mirrored shelving out of medicine cabinets, we hired glassblowers to create the face plates that were placed at each table setting before diners were seated, as well as the piece I would use in my caviar staircase. We simply built off the basic concepts we had developed years ago and infused them with the luxury required to be a world-class competitor.

With everything in place—menus, wine lists, service manuals—we began doing practice runs. My number-one priority was for Tru customers to experience fine dining like never before. In the kitchen, we did tastings and mock services over and over again until we felt we had hit our stride. In the front of the house, the staff trainers focused on creating a culture where the customers felt cherished. This meant that from the moment a guest pulled up to our front door, he or she was treated like a VIP. Our servers were taught not only to meet the needs of our customers, but also to anticipate those needs and to go above and beyond at every opportunity.

As we began to count down the hours toward our soft opening, I still wasn't sure we were quite ready. Just as passionate about this project as we were, Rich was more than willing to delay the opening for a week, an incredible financial commitment on his part. Although it wasn't in the budget, he understood the importance of getting the opening right. If people were going to spend two hundred dollars a meal, we wanted them to be blown away by the experience.

As a result, we created what we termed our "blow-away sheet." Every person who came in contact with customers or touched the table had this sheet, and after each service, we asked the staff to rate themselves based on their level of service.

We used our extra week as a dress rehearsal of sorts. Every day, we went through the motions of service just as if we were actually open for business. Each evening ran like clockwork. We started with a pre-shift staff meal at 3:30. Then at 4:00, we held our staff meeting, almost like a pregame huddle. Gale would go over the cheese carts and desserts for that night, and I would go over the tasting menus and multiple amuse-bouche. I'd talk about any problems from the night before and what adjustments we needed to make. We'd open the doors promptly at 5:00. Game on.

When we finally made it to opening night, everything felt right. That extra week had made all the difference in the world. Gale and I both felt quite a bit of pressure to succeed. At that time, no chef in Chicago had ever managed to do two four-star restaurants back-to-back, but that was our goal. To this day, the only other Chicago chef who has pulled this off is Grant Achatz, who became executive chef at Trio in 2001 and then opened Alinea in 2005 in Lincoln Park.

From the beginning, we spent a lot of time looking at each and every reservation. We made sure everyone on the staff was aware of dietary restrictions, celebrations, and special guests. Everybody was a VIP, but if a customer was a celebrity or from the press or culinary industry, the kitchen knew to prepare an extra course to complement his or her meal. We knew from experience that though they wanted to be treated like everyone else, true celebrities inevitably required extra attention. Privacy and security were extremely important to those who lived their lives on the public stage, so we built concealed entrances into the back of the building. A limousine could drive into the alley and let off passengers through the loading dock area. The guests could then get into the kitchen and private dining areas without anyone ever noticing.

Only eight weeks into service, we received our first review: four stars from the *Chicago Tribune*! After that, the media attention really picked up, and with it, our notoriety. Tru and the Tramonto/Gand brand gained momentum like a snowball racing down a ski slope. Every interview led to four more; every article opened doors to television appearances, charity requests, countless food and wine festivals, VIP events, and more books.

Just six months into Tru's opening, we found ourselves once again caught up in a whirlwind of attention and awards. On top of that, the reviews quickly turned into reservations. We had started out doing thirty to forty covers a night, but within weeks, our reservations had nearly tripled that number. With multi-course tasting menus, with ten-course menus, you do the math: that's a lot of plates.

As we moved toward our goals, the local reviews became national reviews, and the restaurant and staff began earning more major national and international awards. Our dining room was reaching capacity every night of the week, and our reservation book was filled six to eight weeks out.

When Jane called with an opportunity to do a two-book deal—my first solo book, an amuse-bouche book, and then a Tru cookbook—I realized that I had achieved almost every goal on our original magic list. Everything was going according to plan, yet I wondered if I should think about moving back to New York to be closer to my family—or what was left of it. My mom and all of my grandparents had died, and I had no siblings. In addition to being able to take care of my dad, moving home would also be good for me personally. At least in Rochester I would have some support: someone to help me move my couch or to eat spaghetti with during a football game. With the right team, I knew I could do this Tramonto cuisine stuff anywhere.

I talked to Rich about it, but he encouraged me to stay put.

"You've done great work here in Chicago," he said. "The press loves you, and you have established a great customer base and notoriety here. You need to get some of your own things and take some time for yourself. Spend the next six or eight months focusing on Tru and Gio. Be the father Gio deserves. Give yourself some time and then step back and assess the situation. If you still feel the same way, you can leave."

Rich was smart. He knew that Tru was going to be successful—really successful, as in globally successful—and that it would change my life forever. He had already invested millions of dollars in the place, and he wanted to protect his investment. It would have been real easy for me to just pack it up and split. I was good at starting over. I had done it more than once; I could do it again. But Rich knew my weaknesses were Gio and Tru. I didn't want to be an absentee father, and I would not have torn four-year-old Gio from his mom at this time in his life.

Rich also knew that if he could get me to begin thinking long-term, I'd have even more reason to stay. Now it was time to turn our focus toward longevity. Very few restaurants survive past the first two years, and those that do get tired by year five. Rich's voice continued to ring in my head—*we don't want to be the biggest, we just want to be the best*—and I knew beyond a shadow of a doubt that he was right.

I decided to take Rich's advice and start looking for a house of my own. I needed to find a town close enough to Gale's to make it easy for each of us to drop off and pick up Gio. I also wanted to be relatively close to the city and the airport. One afternoon, I happened upon a new subdivision set on a golf course. Though there was nothing about the area that drew me—I was not a golfer, and the homes in this neighborhood were all much larger than anything I would ever need—I still felt a strange pull to check it out.

Granted, I was thinking about Gio, and I knew the town had great schools and would be a safe and comfortable place for a child to grow up. I talked to the developer and toured one of the models. As I moved from room to room, dueling voices battled in my head: *What in the world are you doing here? You don't need a four-bedroom house in Vernon Hills! Get something small and simple, something close to work.*

The realtor continued her pitch. She even suggested the home would be perfect if I remarried. Though I kept my mouth shut, I was thinking, *That's the furthest thing from my mind, lady.*

Yet another voice called to me from inside: *Trust me. I am the God of the second chance. My ways are not your ways.*

Though I had been walking with the Lord for only a short time now, I knew enough to listen when he spoke. Even so, I felt a bit like Noah, who built an ark even though there was no sign of a flood. The idea of building a six-thousand-square-foot, four-bedroom home made no sense at all for a single guy like me. Still, I found myself drawn back to the homesite again and again. Finally I couldn't ignore the promptings any longer. I met with the builder and signed the papers to start construction. I sure hoped God knew what he was doing.

FOIE GRAS FOAM WITH PORT WINE REDUCTION

At Tru, we went through about 40 lobes of fois gras a week, leaving us with a lot of end pieces and scraps to use up. When I started to experiment with foie gras foams, I discovered they made a great one-bite amuse-bouche. When squirted on chips or tiny toasts, foie gras foam makes a delicious hors d'oeuvre. There's so much fat in the foie gras, you don't need much else in the mixture to make a foam. — *SERVES 6*

1½ c. half-and-half
1 c. heavy cream
8 oz. duck foie gras, cut into small pieces
3 sheets gelatin
Kosher salt and freshly ground white pepper
1½ c. port wine
¾ c. granulated sugar
iSi Gourmet Whip canister
2 iSi N20 cream chargers

1. Put the half-and-half and heavy cream in a large saucepan and bring the mixture to a simmer over medium-high heat. Add the foie gras to the simmering cream mixture; whisk until the foie gras melts and is incorporated into the cream. (Some small pieces won't dissolve.) Remove from heat.
2. Meanwhile, fill a large mixing bowl with cold water. Gently drop the gelatin sheets in the water until all are submerged. Let the gelatin soften and bloom for about 5 minutes.
3. Using your hands, lift the gelatin sheets from the water and squeeze them gently between your fingers to remove excess water. Transfer the sheets to the hot cream and stir gently until the gelatin is dissolved. Season to taste with salt and white pepper. Strain through a chinois or fine-mesh sieve into a large bowl. Set aside to cool to room temperature.
4. Pour cream mixture into a chilled iSi Gourmet Whip canister. Charge with 1 or 2 iSi N2O cream chargers. Chill the foam for at least 1 hour.
5. Put the port wine and sugar into a medium saucepan over medium-high heat and bring to a boil. Reduce the heat and boil gently for 10 to 15 minutes, or until the wine is syrupy and reduced to about ¼ cup. Let mixture cool to room temperature.
6. To serve, shake the Gourmet Whip canister vigorously and squirt a small amount of foam onto each plate. Drizzle the foam with port wine reduction.

19

NEW LIFE

*For God so loved the world that He gave His
only begotten Son, that whoever believes in Him
should not perish but have everlasting life.*

JOHN 3:16

As Tru raced into another successful year, I couldn't have been happier.
For the first time in my life, I had a peace and a happiness that went
beyond all explanation. I was learning to put God first in every single
area of my life: my work, my family, and my finances.

For more than a year, Gale and I had been meeting in the parking lot
every morning at 9 a.m. so we could walk into the restaurant together.
At night, we walked out together at 10 p.m. No one knew or even
suspected that we weren't still together. But now that Tru was on track,
we needed to come clean and let our team know about the divorce.
They could handle news like this now. After telling the staff, we would
issue a press release, which would allow us to control the story as best
we could.

We scheduled our quarterly all-staff meeting on a Saturday morning. We had told our employees that the meeting was mandatory and
that we would be making a big announcement. Most were expecting
us to announce either that we were going to have a second baby or that
we were planning to open another restaurant. The staff was buzzing
when Gale and I arrived. We began by talking about menu changes,

scheduling, and other issues related to the business. During our discussion, Rich Melman walked in and stood behind Gale and me. Then I said, "Gale and I have some news, and since the Tru team is like a family to us, we wanted you to be the first to know."

With my arm around Gale and hers around me, I continued, "We have been divorced for the past year. But as you can see, we still get along just fine." The team just looked at each other, confused. Not sure how to react, some of them laughed nervously, turning to me as if to say, *If you're playing a prank, it's not very funny.*

"Look," I said, "this is real. But it would have been very difficult for us to share this news earlier. We had a lot riding on this restaurant, and we wanted to make sure there were no distractions. We didn't want our personal situation to interfere with any one of you doing your job. And tomorrow when you come to work, nothing will change."

Most of the staff still didn't seem to know how to react. A couple of people began to cry softly. I hated that they were hurting. And I understood. Gale and I had always been the dream team: the culinary couple who seemed to have it all. Now the fairy tale didn't seem to be ending so happily.

Over the next couple of weeks, Gale and I continued to do what we'd been doing for the past year—proving that nothing had changed after our announcement. Eventually, some of my staff began encouraging me to start dating again, but I wasn't ready. The idea of exposing my heart like that again terrified me. I shared my concern with Pastor Greg, who I had gotten to know closely over the past year, and he agreed. "The last thing you need right now is to jump into something new, whether it's a new job or a new relationship," he said. "The only thing you need to focus on right now is your relationship with God and the work he has for you to do as a father and a chef."

Pastor Greg and his wife, Grace, had become two of my closest friends and mentors. His advice made a lot of sense to me, so I tried to structure my days around three primary things: God, Gio, and Tru. In addition to spending one-on-one time with God in prayer and Bible reading, I attended the church's men's group and also began volunteering with Feed The Children, Angel Tree, and our church's prison ministry as a way to connect with other people. Pastor Greg kept me accountable and reminded me that I needed to get my relationship with God right before I'd ever be able to get my relationship with anyone else right.

Gale and I had worked out a consistent schedule for Gio. On Sundays, I began my day by attending both the 8:00 a.m. and the 10:00 a.m. church services at Life Changers before meeting up with Gale to bring Gio home with me at 1:00 p.m. We called Sundays "Day with Dad," and Gio got to plan the day. We'd have lunch together and then do something fun; he loved to go fishing or play at the park near our house. We went to church together on Sunday nights and then headed home for bed.

Monday was my day off, but since Gio was enrolled in Montessori school, I usually tried to put in a couple of hours of work while he was gone. Then after school, we'd come back home and just spend the evening together, hanging out, reading books, watching TV, and going to the movies. I spent as much time as I could with him when he was at my house.

Once Gio moved to Gale's for the second half of the week, I could stay as late as I needed to at the restaurant. But surprisingly, I found that God was even changing my perspective on that. In the past, work had been the only thing that mattered, taking precedence over everything else in my life. Now, as much as I valued Tru and still continued to give it my best, my priorities were definitely shifting.

For the first few years after Gale and I split, my world was fairly small—the Word, work, and Gio—but that was just fine by me. I had so much to learn about God's truth, I couldn't seem to get enough of it. When I had first started attending Life Changers, I didn't have any idea how to navigate the Bible. But I picked things up quickly—more quickly than I had ever learned anything in my life. It was as if God was just pouring himself into me, teaching me all of his principles and practices. I was in church every chance I got: marriage seminars, Bible studies, parenting conferences, Old Testament classes—it didn't matter what it was, I showed up. It was an amazing time of growth and understanding for me. I loved the way Pastor Greg uncompromisingly taught the Word of God, as well as how to apply it to my life. I often wondered how he knew just what I was going through, but eventually I realized the Holy Spirit was speaking to me through his words.

Pastor Greg often said to us, "If I ever start to contradict the Word of God in my teaching, you need to leave this church." I loved that. It was so good for me to see a Christian leader willing to be accountable to his people. He was a man just like me, and like me he could easily fall and disappoint me. But God would never disappoint me. As I built trust in God and my pastor, I also began to trust myself. The church was a healing place for me. I hadn't realized just how far I had gone into darkness until God started to shine his light into my life.

Two years after Tru's opening, Eileen called to wish me a happy birthday. During our chat, she mentioned some of the frustrations she was facing right then as a single mom. I knew how tough it was for me and Gale—and we had a pretty good system in place. I couldn't imagine doing it under less than ideal circumstances.

"I am so sorry you have to deal with that, Eileen. I definitely know how hard it is," I said. "Hey, why don't you bring the kids down here for the weekend for my birthday? We'll go see Cirque du Soleil and just have some fun."

The next night the three of them showed up at my door, sleeping bags in tow. Their visit offered me a perfect reason to take a rare day off. We celebrated my birthday in downtown Chicago. Gio got along great with Eileen's sons Sean and Brian, who were a few years older. Eileen and I just enjoyed hanging out and talking about old times back in Rochester.

She also filled me in on the church she was attending with her boys. Eileen had been intrigued when I had told her about Life Changers several months before. She told me then that she thought it would be good for her boys to start attending church, but she had no idea where to look. I checked with Pastor Greg, who gave me a few recommendations to pass along to her. She had picked one and begun attending regularly with Sean and Brian. Now she told me how much she, a lifelong Catholic, was getting from that church's teaching. "It's so amazing that I can apply what the pastor is saying. It makes sense."

Eileen had always been a good, caring person. In fact, I like to joke that she is the only person I know who always puts the grocery cart back. But by the time she visited for my birthday, she had also begun to follow Christ.

After they went back home, I found that I couldn't stop thinking about Eileen. We had always had a great friendship, a great connection. I loved that I didn't have to explain the journey I'd been on because she knew all of it; in fact, she had walked much of it with me.

I decided to reach out to her and see what happened. I picked up the phone and dialed her number.

"I don't know if you feel like this too, but I think we have a connection that's more than just a friendship," I said. "Somewhere deep down inside, I think I have always loved you. I know things are tough for you up there. I want to take you away from all that."

"I don't need you to save me," she said, offended.

"I'm not trying to save you; I just think we should be together and do life together, that's all."

"Well, invite me up for a proper date, and then I'll let you know," she said.

She hadn't completely shot me down. Taking that as a good sign, I invited her to go to Life Changers with me on her next visit. She told me she'd like that.

The next time she came to Chicago, I made plans for us to have dinner at Tru to show her what I really did. Since I'd never brought a woman there before—or even eaten there as a regular guest—the staff was at least as nervous as I was. I presented Eileen with flowers and a card over a great meal, and then we walked down Michigan Avenue to the lakefront and talked about everything: our pasts, our families, our careers, our hopes for the future. It was as if we had been together forever—and in a way, I guess we had been.

When I had been with Gale, I had been so focused on advancing my career that I didn't know how to communicate unless it was about food or cooking or business. This time around, I vowed I would do it right. This time, I would make sure my priorities were straight, and I would not hold back anything I was feeling, even if it meant being awkward and vulnerable.

I completely trusted Eileen with my heart, but more than that, I trusted the Lord. Even if things didn't work out for the two of us, I had everything I needed to survive and to thrive.

On Sunday, I took Eileen with me to church. Eileen's church

consisted of about fifty people, so I had told her, "I have to warn you—Life Changers is a huge, really dynamic church." I was nervous about how she'd react to the sheer size.

The place was packed that morning. As we walked toward the front where I always sat, I could feel my heart racing. *What if she reacts like Gale and thinks I'm crazy? What if she never wants to see me again?*

Throughout the service, I kept stealing glances at Eileen from the corner of my eye, trying to get a read on what she might be thinking. When the service was finally over, I breathed a sigh of relief. At least she was still there, sitting next to me.

"Well," I said, somewhat hesitantly, "what did you think?"

"It was great! I loved it! I love your pastor."

I almost asked her to marry me right then and there. I was so excited to be in a relationship with someone I could connect to on a spiritual level.

After she went back to Michigan, we continued to talk nearly every day. I sent her a Bible, along with other spiritual books and recordings of some of Pastor Greg's sermons. We tried to see each other as often as we could; sometimes I would head up to see her and sometimes she would come to see me. The boys all got along really well, and Gale was happy for us too.

I knew beyond a shadow of a doubt that I was meant to spend the rest of my life with Eileen, and that God was in this. Now my four-bedroom house made sense!

Eileen is beautiful and smart and kind and supportive. She is a good mom, and I knew she'd make a great wife. And above all else, she loved the Lord and didn't care who knew it.

In the fall of 2001, I sent her a letter that said only this: "On Wednesday, September 12, a car will be waiting outside your house to take you on an adventure."

I had booked flights to Las Vegas, and my plan was to propose there. I was so excited, I could hardly keep from calling her and spilling the beans. I asked Pastor Greg and his wife, Grace, to pray about it with me.

On the Tuesday before our trip, Gio was eating his breakfast while I was getting ready for work. Gale was in New York with her dad to accept *Bon Appétit's* Pastry Chef of the Year award, but she would be home later that afternoon. I had told her my plans, and she had agreed to pick up Gio from school so I could meet Eileen in Vegas.

"Daddy, a plane just crashed into a building on TV," Gio called from the kitchen.

"Oh really," I said absently. Gio liked to narrate his cartoons for me, and I figured he was watching the Road Runner or a similar cartoon. But when I popped my head out the bathroom door with shaving cream still on my face, I was surprised to find him watching *The Today Show.*

Hmmm. That's odd, I thought, as NBC replayed the footage of a plane flying right into the Twin Towers of the World Trade Center in New York City. I turned up the volume as the screen flashed back to live coverage of the still-smoking building. Just then, a second plane slammed head-on into the second tower.

Suddenly the severity of this event hit home. This was not an accident—this was an attack.

Recognizing the red, white, and blue United Airlines symbol, Gio cried, "Is that Mommy's plane?"

Gale! My mind quickly raced over her itinerary. I was pretty sure her flight was scheduled for later this morning, but I wasn't certain. Surely, she wasn't on that plane. Gio looked up at me, worry stretching across his face.

"No, no. That's not Mommy's plane," I assured him. "She's not leaving until later this morning. Don't you worry about that. Let's go to school."

I scooped him up, put him in the car, and headed for the Montessori school.

People all over the city were huddled together, talking on cell phones, huddled around car radios and television sets. The reality of the morning's events was starting to sink in. Thankfully, Gio's school was open. I needed to get my head around this. I went back home and started making phone calls. I started with Gale's cell phone, but I only got a busy signal. I called her hotel: busy signal. I called her dad: busy signal.

My own phone rang and I jumped to pick it up.

"Gale?"

It was my managing partner from Tru.

"Hello, Chef. Mayor Daley is shutting down the city. We can't open Tru until he gives us the go-ahead. Stay home; don't come into the city if you can help it."

I asked him if he had heard anything from Gale, but he had not. I hung up the phone, eyes still glued to the television screen. The reporters were now talking about a third plane that had gone down somewhere out in Pennsylvania. The FAA was grounding all air traffic indefinitely.

Then it hit me: Eileen! We were supposed to go to Vegas tomorrow! I quickly dialed her number.

"Rick! I'm so glad to hear your voice. Isn't it horrible?"

"Unbelievable," I said. "We need to pray."

"Oh. I have been."

"I am so sorry, but the trip that's in that envelope I sent you isn't going to be doable now. Can you get a train down here?"

Eileen said she would check but then called back to say that the earliest she could get to Chicago would be Friday or Saturday. I didn't have much choice but to wait.

I picked up Gio from school, and we spent the afternoon together, watching the news, feeding the ducks, playing in the park, and praying. I went through the motions of fixing us his favorite blue box macaroni and cheese for dinner, but I felt like I was walking in a dream. Finally, as the sun was beginning to set outside my apartment, the phone rang. It was Gale. She had been trying to reach me all day. She was going to be stuck in New York for up to a week until she could get a car to drive home.

I hung up the phone and breathed a sigh of relief. Unfortunately, my joy was short lived. Now that I knew Gale was okay, my mind was free to think about other things, like how many people I knew who lived and worked in New York: Alfred Portale, Mario Batali, Bobby Flay.

A good friend of mine, Michael Lomonaco, was the executive chef at Windows on the World, which sat at the top of the World Trade Center. The planes had hit a little before 9:00 a.m. on a Tuesday morning, just as Michael and his staff would have been finishing up

RICK TRAMONTO || 237

breakfast and starting to prep for lunch service. I tried to get ahold of Michael but couldn't even connect with his voice mail. I knew the odds of him surviving were slim to none, but something in me needed to keep trying. I called everyone I could think of who might have some way of knowing his whereabouts.

Finally on Thursday morning, he answered his phone. I couldn't believe it!

"Michael! You're okay!"

"Yeah man, I'm okay."

He sounded really shaken up. I couldn't begin to imagine what he must be going through.

We talked for a while, and he told me that Windows had been booked solid on the morning of September 11. His crew finished serving a breakfast party and then began setting up for lunch. As it turns out, Michael never made it up to the restaurant that morning because he needed to have his reading glasses repaired by the optometrist on the building's first floor. He told me he had been with the eye doctor for about thirty minutes when the first plane struck.

"The doctor's office was on the ground floor of my building, and I was in the chair getting my eyes examined when the first plane hit," Michael told me. "They made us evacuate the lobby areas and stores, but I didn't know what was going on. I watched the building fall, killing everyone on my morning team, as well as all of our customers."

He stopped, a sob catching in his throat.

"I don't know why I am still here," he said. "I should have been in that restaurant."

I knew that Michael was a Christian, and I reminded him that God's ways are not ours.

"He must still have work for you to do," I said. We prayed together, and when we hung up, I promised myself that once things settled down, we would do something at Tru for Michael and his surviving staff. The following year we held a Windows on the World charity fund-raiser for the families of those who died at the restaurant that day, which enabled us to donate a substantial amount of money to the Windows of Hope Family Relief Fund.

On Friday, Gale made it home, and on Saturday, Eileen and I spent much of the day just sitting in my apartment and talking about the magnitude of what had happened, though I don't think any of us could have imagined just how much the events of September 11 would forever change the world for our children.

The next day was beautiful. The sun was shining and the sky was blue. Eileen and I decided to take a walk around the pond outside my apartment building. Like everyone else, we couldn't stop talking about the attacks and wondering what was going to happen next.

We sat down together on one of the park benches, and I pulled the ring out of my pocket. I told her about my elaborate proposal plans and how I had really wanted to do it up big.

"I know you've always said you didn't want to get married again, but I believe that God brought you into my life for a reason," I said. "Now more than ever, I don't want to wait to be with you. I want to marry you. Life is too short, and it can be over in a blink, as we just found out."

Eileen searched my face, as if she was looking to make sure I was really serious. And then without a second's hesitation, she smiled and said yes.

MOCHA PANNA COTTA

My new life apart from Gale led me back to an area of cooking I'd never had to spend much time thinking about before—dessert. I've always had a soft spot for coffee and chocolate. One of my favorite dessert combinations is also coffee and chocolate, which is why I developed this recipe. — *SERVES 6*

> 1¼ c. heavy cream
> 1 c. whole espresso beans (do not crush)
> 6 Tbs. granulated sugar
> 2½ oz. Valrhona Guanaja chocolate or other high-quality bittersweet
>   chocolate, chopped
> 2 sheets gelatin
> 1¼ c. sour cream
> 8 small sheets of parchment paper, each about 2-by-2 inches
> Heavy cream, whipped to soft peaks
> 6 kumquat slices, for garnish

1. In a saucepan, heat the cream, espresso beans, and sugar almost to boiling. Remove mixture from heat and set aside to steep for 5 minutes.

2. Strain cream mixture through a chinois or other fine-mesh sieve into bowl holding the chopped chocolate. Whisk gently to blend and melt the chocolate.

3. Meanwhile, soak the gelatin sheets in cold water for about 2 minutes. Using your hands, lift sheets from the water and squeeze out the excess water. Add to chocolate mixture and stir until dissolved. Whisk in the sour cream until mixture is smooth. Spoon chocolate mixture evenly into 6 eggcups or espresso cups.

4. Lay a sheet of parchment paper on each of 6 plates. Place one eggcup or espresso cup off center on top of each piece of paper, so you can see the paper. Refrigerate for at least 2 hours, or until set, and for up to 3 days.

5. To serve, top each cup of panna cotta with a dollop of whipped cream. Lay a slice of kumquat on top of the whipped cream.

20

TAKING BIG CHANCES

*We know that all things work together for good
to those who love God, to those who are the called
according to His purpose.*

ROMANS 8:28

Through Pastor Greg's teachings, I was learning to center my life on God rather than work. And as a result, I was becoming much more balanced in the way I viewed my career.

Eileen kept me grounded as well. I began inviting her to industry events, such as the James Beard Awards, where I'd been nominated for the Best Chef in the Midwest. I asked Eileen to book a flight to New York for the awards presentation, not even thinking about how much that might stretch her financially. When we met in the lobby before heading to the ceremony, I asked her, "How do I look?"

"You look great," she said.

"I should," I said. "This tux set me back twelve hundred bucks."

"How do you like my dress?" Eileen asked.

"Very nice," I said sincerely.

"Four dollars from the secondhand shop," she said. Suddenly the gulf in our incomes hit me. From then on, I covered her expenses for such events, which made them much more fun.

Not only was I encouraged by our relationship, I was pleased at how well Tru continued to do and that Gale and I had settled into a nice rhythm, both personally and professionally.

At the same time, I began to work with Rich to develop another restaurant concept in the old Papagus location downtown. I had always wanted to do another Italian restaurant, and when Rich asked me to help him with Osteria Via Stato, I was thrilled.

We started with a three-week tour of all the great Italian osterias, eating our way through Rome, Milan, Venice, and Tuscany. We took pictures of everything: the floors and the chairs and the tables and the food and the glassware.

Once we got back to the States, we sat down with our notes and began to craft the concept using huge storyboards. With an opening budget of two million dollars, Osteria Via Stato was much less of a production than Tru had been. This opening was actually a lot of fun, and the osteria was an immediate success.

While Tru was still my primary focus, I did try to spend as much time as I could at both restaurants. At the same time, my publisher had asked me to put together another cookbook, this one on osteria cuisine and my Italian background.

After my trip to Italy, I certainly had enough material to fill another book—more than enough, in fact. Once we got into the writing and began submitting chapters, my publishers jumped all over the material on antipasti. The idea of "little Italian plates" was enough to fill a whole book. Since my *Amuse-Bouche* book was such a huge success, they asked if we could do *Fantastico*, an antipasto cookbook, first and then come back to *Osteria*.

Sure. Why not? My cowriter, Mary, and I had been working on one cookbook after another for the past six years. At this point, why not add another?

Although it was a lot of work, I knew this was all part of the deal. In years past, a famous chef might have one or two restaurants over the course of his or her entire career, and *maybe* a cookbook. But in today's world of celebrity chefs and Food Network superstars, it was all about the food and the brand. And building a brand took time. It meant cookbooks, multiple restaurants, endorsement deals, product lines, and television spots.

After a producer from Oprah ate at Tru, she raved about the restaurant to the talk-show host. Not long after, I was invited to appear on a show where Dr. Michael Roizen (author of *The RealAge Diet* and coauthor with Dr. Mehmet Oz of *YOU: The Owner's Manual*) would explain the best type of diet to help prevent aging. My task was to develop a menu that followed Dr. Roizen's recommendations. I prepared a roasted salmon with lemongrass and spring vegetables, among other dishes. I had a great time, and I remember Oprah joking about how hard it was to get into Tru: "I couldn't even get a reservation—but I bet I'll get one now!" I made a second appearance on *Oprah* to talk about my experience cooking for Princess Diana and Prince Charles following a polo match at Windsor.

Advancing in the culinary world also meant cooking for the stars and their events—like Elton John, Bill Clinton, Bette Midler, Barack Obama, and Nicolas Cage. I was even asked to cook at Oprah's house in Santa Barbara with her chef, Art Smith, for her Legends Ball. The culinary world was becoming a multimedia business, and we knew we had to run fast to keep up.

In the midst of all this, Eileen and I were planning our wedding, to be held in the new house, which had just been completed. We asked the guys at Tru to do the catering, and we limited the guest list to about thirty people. Eileen's parents and my dad flew out, and we set up chairs in the living room. Pastor Greg married us, and we followed up with a simple reception in the backyard.

Of course, nothing involving food is ever truly simple when you're dealing with an Italian chef. Our feast included grilled lobster, BBQ pulled pork, grilled corn, all kinds of salads, lots of side dishes, Italian cookies, cannoli, and, of course, wedding cake.

Blending families is always tough, and it was no different for us. Gio, who was six when Eileen and I married, went from being the only child to the youngest and now shared a room with Brian. Sean, twelve, and Brian, eight, had to adapt to a new home and community. Between Gio's schedule, the restaurants, my traveling, and church, I'm sure they all felt like they had been dropped into the center of a hurricane.

On top of that, Eileen and I had different parenting styles. Looking back, I realize I could be hard on the kids because I was so concerned that I not miss any signs of trouble like my own parents had. Sean, in particular, pushed away as a result. Though I continued to express my interest in the boys' lives, I learned to back off and trust Eileen's instincts about discipline.

Eileen became vice president of Tramonto Cuisine, and I gladly trusted her with the company's finances and scheduling. She was quick to jump in and protect family time when the invitations to culinary events and appearances piled up. Eileen was much better than I was at keeping family and career separate. She made sure I remembered that Sundays were set aside for family dinners and time together.

Not long after we were married, my dad was diagnosed with terminal lung cancer. Although Eileen encouraged me to bring him to Chicago to live with us, I was hesitant. It wasn't that I didn't want him here. But I knew how crazy my life was. If my dad came to live with us, Eileen would end up becoming his primary caregiver. I wasn't sure she was up for that.

I quickly learned never to question Eileen. We set up a space for my dad in our finished basement. Within hours of moving him in, the two of them were cracking jokes and teasing each other, just like they had when we were growing up. My dad trusted her completely.

I was glad that the boys had this opportunity to get to know my dad and hear all of his stories, though it broke my heart to see this once larger-than-life guy deteriorating so quickly.

My dad really wanted to see *The Passion of the Christ*, which was playing in theaters at that time. So one afternoon, I loaded up his oxygen tank and we headed out to catch a local matinee. We were the only people in the entire theater, and when the movie ended, I turned to my dad. Tears were rolling down his cheeks, and I reached out to hug him.

"Dad," I said, "do you get that? Do you get what happened on that cross? I'm not sure I ever understood that when I was a kid, but now I know that Christ died on that cross for me, for my sins. And he died for you, too. If you can accept that sacrifice, his death wipes the slate clean for you. Do you believe that?"

He nodded, unable to speak.

"Do you want to pray with me?" I asked.

He nodded again, and together we bowed.

"Dear God," he prayed, "I don't have much time left. I know I've made some mistakes in my life—some pretty big mistakes—and for that I am so sorry. Please forgive me. Thank you for sending your Son to die on the cross for my sins. I believe in you and I give you my life, whatever time I have left."

We opened our eyes and looked at each other. My father was beaming.

Two weeks later, he passed away. But for the first time in my life, a loved one's death was bearable. I knew where he was, and I knew I would see him again. I thanked God for giving me the opportunity to spend those final days with him and for the assurance that he had become a born-again Christian.

After I went back to Rochester to bury my father, opportunities continued to pour in for me career-wise. One afternoon, I got a phone call from a development group associated with building a Starwood hotel.

"Hi, Chef Tramonto. We are building a $150 million hotel in your neck of the woods," the developer said. "We've been following you and Gale ever since your years at Trio. We love what you did at Brasserie T, and we love what you're doing now at Tru. We're big fans of your cookbooks and Gale's cooking show. We think a Tramonto brand would be a perfect fit with what we are trying to do with Starwood up in the Westin on the North Shore. Over the next three years, we will be putting up a total of four hotels, three in the suburbs and one in the city. We would like you to come up with a series of restaurant concepts we can link to our hotels, not only in Chicagoland but eventually in other major metropolitan cities."

Now this sounds interesting, I said to myself. "What exactly are you looking for?" I asked. "What type of restaurants?"

"That would be up to you. This is your area of expertise, not ours. We're looking for a cross section of offerings: fine dining, Italian, steakhouses, sushi—whatever. We've got the funding, but you have the knowledge and the talent. Together, we should be able to do something off the charts. What do you think?"

Gale and I agreed that the opportunity sounded almost too good to be true, but we agreed to at least set up a meeting with them and give their proposal some thought. This was bigger than anything I had ever been a part of. Talk about playing in the big leagues! Once we realized how serious they were, I immediately went to Rich to set up a meeting.

Gale and I really felt like we owed Rich and Lettuce a lot. I didn't want to ruffle any feathers with the Lettuce partners, but at the same time I felt really drawn to this new opportunity. It was just too lucrative and too interesting to pass up, so we thought we'd give it a shot with Rich's blessing.

"Things are going so well for Gale and me," I said. "We love working with Lettuce and we couldn't be happier with the way things are going at Tru. But I feel like I have to at least consider this offer. What would you do if you were in my shoes?"

"Ricky, this is a great opportunity for you guys," Rich said. "Financially, I don't think you can afford to pass it up."

Because of the way our agreement had been written, we would stay on as founding partners at Tru, but at the end of the day, we would have to give up our connection to Lettuce. This meant losing my salary and benefits, as well as my partnership with Osteria Via Stato and Nacional 27, other Lettuce restaurants in which I had partnerships.

This was it. I was finally going to get the chance to create a brand and develop concepts—my favorite part of the job. I would have a management company to back me up as culinary director of the company, and once we got these initial concepts off the ground locally, we would take our brand to additional key locations, including Las Vegas, South Beach, New York.

I met with some top-notch attorneys who helped me put some pretty solid safety nets in place so my creative content would be well protected. Our corporation with the developers would be Cenitare— "to dine often" in Latin—but we would also maintain our own identities and individual projects—in my case, Tramonto Cuisine and Tru, along with my multiple books and television appearances. Even though we would be developing prototypes for Cenitare, my ideas would still belong to Tramonto Cuisine. That way, if I ever left, I could bring these concepts to another development group or hotel.

After all the years of scraping and struggling, the top rung was finally in sight. I hated the thought of having to start in the suburbs;

I knew from Trio and Brasserie T that a city needed to be able to support a celebrity chef restaurant with walk-in traffic and tourism and big hotels, and I told them what I thought. But these guys said they had done their homework and studied the demographics. They were building a $150 million, five-hundred bedroom hotel, so I figured they must know what they were doing.

Gale and I had faced some tough challenges in our careers, but this one definitely topped the list. We needed to come up with four entirely different concepts—ideas that would eventually be replicated in hotels around the country. Then we needed to develop those concepts into viable businesses and get them off the ground in less than a year. It had taken us more than a year to develop just one Lettuce restaurant; now we were trying to do four at once. The mission was more than a little daunting; it was nearly impossible.

We started by determining exactly what we wanted each of the concepts to be. Given the insanity of the schedule, we decided to stick with what we knew best: Italian, steak, seafood, and pastry. We would start with two concepts, Gale's Coffee Bar and Osteria di Tramonto. This would allow us to offer breakfast, lunch, dinner, and room service from day one—365 days a year. Once we got those two ideas up and running, we would open the dinner-only Tramonto's Steak & Seafood restaurant and the RT Sushi Bar Lounge thirty days later. These four restaurants would provide travelers and neighborhood residents a cross section of cuisine in the hotel, which the advance media coverage described as a Las Vegas-style hotel on the North Shore with a celebrity chef offering multiple food outlets in one location.

We flew to Atlanta to meet with our longtime designer and architect, Bill Johnson, and after a week's worth of meetings, we had a plan. Moving at 100 miles per hour from the start, we knew we needed to build our corporation first and bring in key people right away. We put together a public relations team and came up with a logo and marketing plan. Then we hired an accountant, a director of operations, and executive chefs who would hire their own teams for each of the four concepts.

We met with each of the teams one day a week, all day, to work on the menus, write the staffing manuals, and talk about dining room setup. But when it comes to building a restaurant, there is only so much that can be done on paper. Eventually, we needed to move out of the office and into the kitchen. Unfortunately, the kitchens were still under construction.

Knowing that we couldn't afford to lose even a single day, we started making calls, finally getting permission to use a dungeon-like kitchen at the Ambassador East Hotel, one of the developer's other properties downtown. Now the teams began the real work of cooking through the breakfast menu, then the lunch menu, and finally the dinner menu. I worked with the Osteria guys and Gale worked with the pastry team, trying to condense the process as best we could along the way.

In the meantime, we met with vendors, kitchen designers, and food suppliers, trying to put together a solid team we could count on to get us the amount of product we would need as often as we would need it. I knew from experience that usually when you're under that kind of pressure and timeline the thing that suffers the most is the budget. We have a saying in the industry: When you do a restaurant, you can do it good, you can do it fast, or you can do it cheap. You might be able to do two out of the three, but you'll never get all three. For this project, we knew we could do it good and we hoped we could do it fast. But we probably weren't going to be able to do it cheap. Because of the quick turnaround the developers demanded, we were unable to find many vendors willing to provide bids without charging significant premiums.

The developers knew the real money was going to be made on the hotel, but they couldn't have a hotel without food service. They counted on us to bring something different to their hotel, and they expected our reputation to bring in diners from surrounding neighborhoods as well. Unlike a restaurant where you can start slow and ramp up your service a little at a time, working with a five-hundred-bedroom hotel on top of us was a whole different ball game.

From day one, we were slammed from open to close. At first, we even had to turn a lot of the locals away just so we would be able to serve the hotel guests. We were living, breathing, sleeping this place, working 24-7.

After more than a year of running nonstop, we finally managed to get all four concepts open, an amazing feat in and of itself. Even though our restaurants were all physically connected, they were spread out over 20,000 square feet. The space was so vast that we had to use walkie-talkies to communicate with and locate one another.

Due to the longevity of Tru and its amazingly competent and experienced staff, I only needed to check in there once every two weeks. Running back and forth between the two environments was fatiguing. I was looking forward to the day when these new concepts could run as well as Tru—though I knew that could take up to three years, as it had at Tru.

I was so focused on getting things going with Cenitare that I was rarely at home. And when I was, I was pretty much always thinking about work. But Eileen had a great way of reminding me what was important. We always went to church as a family, and she made sure that every week I spent time with Gio, Brian, and Sean. Bedtime was special for all of us. We always prayed together and talked about the day before turning in for the night.

In the summer of 2008, we'd been open for roughly two years and were finally starting to hit our stride. We were planning to open a second Osteria in Rosemont later that year, with a steakhouse in Schaumburg the following year. Then we would do a whole new concept downtown in the Pump Room the year after that.

I knew I hadn't been spending enough time with Eileen and the kids, but we were working on that. Now that we had finally gotten things going at the Starwood, I hoped to slow down a little and start focusing on my family.

The only thing that worried me just a little was the management company itself. They didn't seem to be staying on top of things as well as they had in the beginning. Executive meetings lately had been so focused on where we could cut costs, I was afraid the Rosemont location might end up suffering. No one was pointing any fingers, but they were definitely looking for ways we could bring in more revenue.

Though I didn't know all the details, it was obvious our developers were having some cash flow problems. My vendors were complaining about not getting paid and things were falling behind. We were often asked to do more with less, and I had already had to lay off some of my support staff. I had been able to make do, but I knew fewer staff would affect the quality of our service.

Even so, I figured we'd be fine. The cranes were already in the air in Rosemont and the steel girders in place. I had already begun to hire people for this next step in the process.

Little did I know we were about to go under.

ASPARAGUS RISOTTO WITH TRUFFLE OIL

Be sure to buy high-quality Italian rice for the risotto—you'll notice a difference in the final texture and taste. In a good risotto, the grains will remain a little chewy. Another secret? To give it a light and airy texture, fold whipped cream into the risotto at the very end. I learned this trick from my great friend Anton Mosimann, with whom I staged in London many years ago. — *SERVES 4*

½ lb. asparagus, ends removed
2 Tbs. salt
Ice and ice water for ice bath
4 Tbs. olive oil
1 clove garlic, chopped
1 medium onion, diced
1½ c. Arborio or Carnaroli rice
Reserved asparagus cooking water or chicken broth
4 Tbs. butter
¾ c. grated Parmigiano-Reggiano
1 Tbs. mint, chopped
1 Tbs. flat-leaf parsley, chopped
⅛ c. heavy cream, whipped until stiff peaks form
1 Tbs. truffle oil
Freshly cracked black pepper

1. Bring 4 quarts of water to a boil.
2. While water is coming to a boil, set up an ice bath by filling a large bowl with cold water and ice.
3. Add asparagus and 2 Tbs. salt to boiling water, blanching asparagus for one minute.
4. Place the asparagus in ice bath. Keep the asparagus cooking water for later use.
5. Place a 14-inch sauté pan over medium heat and add the olive oil, garlic, and onion. Cook over medium heat until the onion is translucent, not browned.
6. Add the rice and cook, stirring constantly, until the rice turns opaque, about 2 minutes.
7. Add the asparagus cooking water (or chicken stock) until it covers the rice. Turn the heat up to high, stirring constantly, and cook the rice for 15 to 20 minutes. While cooking the rice, continue adding more warm asparagus water or chicken stock, one ladle at a time, to maintain the liquid level above the rice.
8. Drain asparagus and chop it into 1-inch pieces.
9. Add asparagus to rice; cook mixture until rice is soft but still al dente.
10. Add butter, grated cheese, mint, and parsley. Remove the pan from heat and mix well. Fold in whipped cream and stir until mixture is smooth. Drizzle the risotto with truffle oil and season with black pepper. Serve immediately.

21

STARTING OVER...AGAIN

The LORD is my shepherd; I shall not want. . . .
Surely goodness and mercy shall follow me all the days of
my life; and I will dwell in the house of the LORD forever.

PSALM 23:1, 6

One Thursday morning in October 2008, I was sitting in one of the large booths at the steakhouse. As usual, I was juggling several tasks at once—putting together menus for a party that night, finalizing schedules, and answering staffers' questions. Details of our scheduled openings in Schaumburg and Rosemont were also running through my mind. In the background, I heard the droning of a CNN reporter who was covering another bank failure—just the latest story in the financial meltdown that had begun a few weeks before with the government's seizure of Fannie Mae and Freddie Mac and the collapse of Lehman Brothers.

I was totally absorbed in my work when an e-mail from one of the owners of the development company popped up on my BlackBerry. With everything else going on, I didn't pay much attention to it at first. And then I read the subject line: Urgent.

Good morning, Rick. We regret to inform you that we are no longer able to continue paying your salary or keeping Cenitare afloat. . . . Cenitare will be declaring bankruptcy later this week

*due to the financial tsunami that has hit us so hard. Today is
your last day. Good luck in your future endeavors.*

*We will be closing the restaurants over a period of months.
Please have your attorney contact us for further details. Thanks.*

I blinked and then I read it again. Yep, it was still there. I walked
into the dining room at the Osteria and showed the phone to my
manager.

"Am I reading this right?"

He leaned over and began to read the e-mail aloud.

"Whoa," he said. "Talk about the ultimate punch in the gut. What
does this mean?"

I shook my head. "I'm pretty sure it's not good."

I forwarded the e-mail to Eileen and then drove home to call my
lawyer. After doing a little digging, she finally got some answers. The
financial tsunami that had flooded the entire country had finally
reached Cenitare and its parent development company.

"Apparently, they are completely out of money," she said. "They
were spread too thin when the economy crashed. All construction has
been halted in Rosemont, Schaumburg, and the Pump Room. The
only way to keep the existing restaurants open is to close Cenitare, and
even then they may have to close Osteria di Tramonto and possibly the
hotel at the end of the year. They want to renegotiate the terms and
do a licensing deal so they can honor all the parties they've booked
through the holidays while they figure out their next move."

I soon learned that after January 1 the Osteria would shut down,
and the management of the steakhouse and RT Sushi Bar & Lounge
would be handled by Westin. I had not seen this coming at all. I would
have expected them to slow it down, not shut it down. I would never
have guessed they would do it this way.

I supposed it was really just the art of war: every man for himself.
These guys had much bigger problems than I did. I was just another
check mark on someone's to-do list: shut down the Osteria, file bank-
ruptcy, close Cenitare.

My attorney explained that since I still had a separate licensing and
branding contract, I did have some recourse, but she also reminded

me that I would have to stand in line behind everyone else they owed money to. Because the economy was now so bad, it was a long line.

Over the next couple of months, I really had to work hard not to spiral into depression. I had been a good steward of my money during the past several years and was debt free so I wasn't concerned about my family's financial situation, but I couldn't believe I would have to start over yet again. I was also concerned about the well-being of my ninety-person Osteria staff. I couldn't imagine how they would take it when they learned right before Christmas that they had been let go.

It took me a while to really digest what had happened. Looking back, I could see how much we had going against us: a suburban location, a crash opening schedule, multiple concepts, and inadequate funding. As I began to put the pieces together, I realized we had probably been hemorrhaging money right from the start. The collapse of the financial markets was like cutting off a limb of an already bleeding patient.

Every day, I fielded phone calls and e-mails from vendors, staff members, even reporters, all wanting to know what had happened. I spent hours pacing the floor and replaying in my mind the chain of events that had led to our demise. The day they finally closed the doors at Osteria di Tramonto had to be one of the most painful days of my life.

Why, God? I asked. *Why, after all this time, all these years, why are you sending me back to square one?*

Since I had met the Lord, I had tried so hard to live my life in a way that was pleasing to him. Was this how he was repaying me?

I had no idea what my next step needed to be. I really needed a job, but I was also exhausted and burned out. As much as I wanted to fix things, there was only so much I could do. I was bummed that I had just turned down several television opportunities, including Food Network appearances, some PBS work, and even participating in the first season of *Top Chef Masters* because I was so stressed out at the hotel.

Finally one night, Eileen encouraged me to just rest.

"You need a break," she said. "You need to be still and spend time with your family and wait on the Lord. Let God be God."

This was a whole new concept for me. I had been working since I was fifteen years old. I didn't know how to rest.

"I've never *not* had a job since I was fifteen," I argued. "I don't know if I can do this."

"You *do* have a job," she said, not even bothering to hide the frustration in her voice. "You just don't have a place to run to for fourteen hours a day. Look at your event calendar. You've got things scheduled all the way out into next year. On top of that, you've got three boys who need you, and you're always in demand for consulting and endorsement deals."

I knew she was right. Before, I had been juggling two or three or four jobs at once. Now, I would just be doing my job out of my house. In addition to numerous charity events and cooking engagements, I was also working on a new cookbook, my seventh. Though it was based on the recipes I'd developed for Tramonto's Steak & Seafood, we were talking about reworking it into a book focused on home cooking and grilling out with family and friends, adding sections on appetizers, salads, and sandwiches. With its focus on entertaining at home, the photography for *Steak with Friends* could be shot in my backyard and out of my kitchen. That wasn't my only book project, however: I had been thinking about writing my life story for years and had just signed with Tyndale House Publishers to write that book. Suddenly I knew that my memoir would end with a twist I hadn't seen coming.

For the first time in my life, I was extremely uncomfortable. I was such a creature of habit, and now my whole routine was turned upside down. It was as if God had stepped in and stripped away everything that made me *me*. I wasn't sure I even knew who I was without my career. Did I even exist?

The catch-22 of success is that the more successful you are, the fewer opportunities you have. I could certainly start over and do something different—be an executive chef at a hotel or restaurant, but I'd already done that. I wondered if I should think about going to Bible school or maybe even open a Wendy's Old Fashioned Hamburgers franchise of my own. I really had no choice but to do exactly what Eileen suggested: sit back and wait on God's timing.

In the coming months, I really struggled to quell my inner feelings of worthlessness and incompetency.

One afternoon, I was especially tense and frustrated that things weren't moving as quickly as I wanted them to. I had talked to all kinds of people—from major hotels to independent operators—about opportunities in Cleveland, New York, San Francisco, Napa Valley, Miami, and New Orleans. But nothing was really resonating.

I went into my office and closed the door, thinking that some time in the Word might soothe my soul. As I sat there at my desk with my Bible open in front of me, I felt a strange prompting to turn on the television.

No, I'm not going to turn on the TV. I'm in here to read my Bible and get a word from the Lord.

Nudge, nudge, nudge. *Turn on the TV.*

No matter how hard I tried to concentrate on the words in front of me, I couldn't stop thinking about that silly television. Finally I gave in and turned it on.

As the screen flashed to life, I realized it was one of my favorite Bible teachers, Bishop T. D. Jakes.

You've got to let go and let God take control, he was saying. You've got to get out of the familiar, out of your comfort zone. It's time to be like Peter and get out of the boat if you really want to go deeper.

Okay, he had my attention. Peter had always been one of my favorite Bible characters. Uneducated and a troublemaker, he was the kind of guy you'd never expect to be a disciple. Pretty much like me.

I thought about our last night at the Osteria. I had done so much in this industry by that time; I had been at the top of my game. It was definitely my comfort zone.

Once you step out of that boat, Jakes continued, your stable environment suddenly becomes very unstable. Your first instinct is to try to normalize yourself. You want to go back into environments that are familiar. But that's not the answer.

I thought about all the times in my life when my environment had been the most unstable. My first instinct had always been to work. For me, a true workaholic, work had become my god—even after I had become a Christian. In fact, I still struggle with this tendency.

Jakes pointed out that in the church environment, we think of backsliding as falling into sin, but sometimes backsliding is falling back into places that God has already called us out of. I felt as if Jakes was speaking directly to me.

He went on. That was the spirit that drove Peter back to fishing when everything else in his life had gone crazy, Jakes said. There was nothing wrong with fishing—it wasn't a sin. But for Peter, fishing was the one thing that he used to fill the void that only God could fill.

I thought about this. There was nothing inherently wrong with my profession. God wanted me to provide for my family. What made it wrong for me was the fact that I had used cooking to do what only God should do: direct me and define me.

Jakes's message was sinking in. He noted that Peter was already a very effective fisherman when God called him, with great natural instincts when it came to finding the fish. But what did Jesus say to Peter? "Follow me, and I will make you fishers of men." It all made sense to me. God wants to use us right where we are, in a place that we are familiar with, but he also wants to take us places we've never been before. That's where getting out of the boat comes in.

By now, the tears were streaming down my cheeks, and some of the truths that had shaped me over the past several years rushed through my mind:

God is not mad at me; he's mad *about* me.
I must decrease; he must increase.
I was lost but now I am found.

God did have a vision and a goal for my life, but he wasn't asking me to follow my career. He wanted me to follow him.

There was still a great difference between who I was and who God wanted me to be. And he had given me this gift—protecting me my whole life for this very moment. All those years, all that reckless living, all those near misses, my life had been spared for just this time. Yes, it was scary standing here outside this boat. I had no idea what the future would hold or how I was going to make a living or what my next steps should be.

But I knew in my heart of hearts that God had a firm hold on my life—and always had. For the first time in my life, I had the chance to rely on *him* to tell me what I was supposed to do next.

And then I knew: I am not my work. Being a celebrity chef is not what defines me. My identity is not in my career, but in Christ I am a child of God first and foremost.

And I was ready to step out of the boat.

ROAST CHICKEN WITH GARLIC ROASTED POTATOES

Even though I'm not able to do a lot of cooking at home, when I do have some downtime, I like to make this recipe for my family. By the way, I believe you can tell the measure of a good cook based on his or her simple roast chicken. — *SERVES 6*

Roasting chicken (5 to 6 lb.)
Kosher salt and freshly ground black pepper
1 large bunch fresh thyme (set 6 sprigs aside)
1 lemon, halved
1 head garlic, cut in half
3 Tbs. butter, melted
1 large yellow onion, sliced
4 carrots, diced into large pieces
2 stalks celery, diced into large pieces
1 bulb of fennel, tops removed and cut into wedges
1 bay leaf
Olive oil

1. Preheat the oven to 425°F.
2. Remove chicken giblets. Rinse chicken inside and out. Pat the outside dry. Liberally salt and pepper inside of chicken.
3. Stuff the chicken cavity with the bunch of thyme, lemon halves, and garlic.
4. Brush the outside of the chicken with the butter. Sprinkle outside with salt and pepper. Tie the chicken legs together with kitchen string and tuck the wing tips under the body of the chicken.
5. Place the onion slices, carrots, celery, and fennel into a roasting pan. Toss vegetables with salt, pepper, the reserved 6 sprigs of thyme, bay leaf, and olive oil. Spread vegetables around the bottom of the roasting pan and place the chicken on top.
6. Roast the chicken for 1½ hours, or until the juices run clear when you cut between a leg and thigh. Place chicken and vegetables on a platter. Cover with aluminum foil for about 20 minutes to rest.
7. Slice chicken; serve with the vegetables.

Garlic Roasted Potatoes

3 lb. Yukon Gold potatoes, peeled and quartered
¼ c. extra-virgin olive oil
Kosher salt and freshly ground black pepper, to taste
2 Tbs. minced garlic (6 cloves)
2 Tbs. minced fresh parsley

1. Preheat oven to 400°F.
2. Place potatoes in a bowl with the olive oil, salt, pepper, and garlic; toss until the potatoes are well coated.
3. Transfer the potatoes to a sheet pan and spread them out into single layer. Roast the potatoes in the oven for 30 to 45 minutes or until they are browned and crisp. Flip the potatoes twice with a spatula during cooking in order to ensure even browning.
4. Remove the potatoes from the oven, toss with parsley, season to taste, and serve hot.

EPILOGUE

He who is of a merry heart has a continual feast.

PROVERBS 15:15

For the first time in thirty years I didn't have an official, full-time job. But it wasn't like I was bored. With a calendar that had been booked a year in advance, I knew I would be spending the next twelve months wrapping up my schedule, working events, and writing two books.

And even though I still had no idea of my next step, there was certainly no shortage of opportunities. From the Cleveland Clinic to a hotel chain in San Francisco, it seemed like every time I turned around, another new option was up for consideration. I decided to fully explore every idea that came along and take my time before jumping into anything.

I really wanted to be in the right city, the right church, the right job—both for me and for my family. My career was hard on Eileen and the boys; I knew that. Whatever came next needed to be the right thing for all of us. On every fact-finding trip, I asked God, *Is this where you want me? If not, please make it clear and close the door (but while you are at it, could you please open a window so I don't get too discouraged?).*

Never a man of patience, I didn't want to remain in limbo forever.

Although we weren't really hurting financially, the worsening economy did worry me. And more than that, I just wanted to feel settled. But for whatever reason, God always seemed to be saying, *It's not time yet, Rick. Wait on me.*

Finally after months of flying from one coast to the other to talk about career possibilities, I had to face the truth: an entire year had passed since my last day at Cenitare, and I was no closer to having the answers than when I had started. It had been easy enough to trust in God's provision and guidance when I first started. But back then, I didn't think I would need to trust for *this* long.

Over the coming months, I thought a lot about T. D. Jakes's message on Peter stepping out of the boat. And I started noticing other "storm stories" in the Bible. I found comfort in reading about the experiences of people like me who thought they'd been following God, only to have their lives yanked off course.

In the book of Luke, for example, I read about a violent storm that terrified Jesus' disciples. Just a few minutes before the winds started raging, he had told them, "Let's cross to the other side of the lake" (Luke 8:22, NLT).

As the disciples set sail, Jesus lay down for a nap. And then, unexpectedly, a violent storm settled over the lake. Everyone on board—except Jesus—panicked. Considering that several of the men had been professional fishermen, I can only imagine how the boat must have been tossing and quaking. As the boat began filling with water, the men woke their Master. First Jesus rebuked the wind and the waves, and the water was smooth as glass once again. Then he turned to his disciples. "Where is your faith?" Jesus asked.

Just a few minutes before, Jesus had told the disciples to cross the lake. They had willingly obeyed him, yet as soon as the ride became bumpy, they were terrified, seemingly persuaded that Jesus wouldn't get them to shore after all.

How I could relate to the disciples' situation! Over the past several years, my life had been filled with storm stories too—times when I presumed I was following God, only to be blindsided by a devastating loss or disappointment. *Why does God make his followers go through the storms?* I kept asking myself. I found no ready answer. Now I had to remind myself daily to rest in God and listen for his voice. I can't say I was very good at it.

When New Orleans Chef John Folse called to invite me down for his latest book launch, I was grateful for the distraction. John's a true Cajun, having grown up in the bayou. Since meeting years ago, we always tried to get together whenever he was in Chicago or I was in New Orleans.

Desperately wanting to help in some way after Hurricane Katrina hit, I had called John Folse and flown down to New Orleans, where we spent two weeks serving meals and praying with the emergency responders in the city's Ninth Ward.

There's nothing like a crisis to cement a friendship, and that was certainly true for me and John. Our strong Christian faith and shared interest in humanitarian work kept us connected even after I had returned home from New Orleans in the fall of 2005.

But now John wanted to talk about more than just his latest cookbook. Apparently, a large hotel group in New Orleans was asking him to open some restaurants in the downtown area to help revitalize the city. Though he was definitely interested, he didn't want to do it alone. Would I ever consider a move to the Big Easy?

Moving to New Orleans had never been on my short list, but if I'd learned nothing else over the past year, I had learned to always walk through an open door. I flew down and spent the week just hanging out and touring possible restaurant locations with John. We went to a Saints game, did John's television show, and then went to the book release the next day. As we drove up to Barnes & Noble in Baton Rouge, I was amazed to see hundreds of people lined up on the sidewalk outside the store. This guy was rocking.

The next day we toured John's food manufacturing facility where he produced custom-manufactured foods for the retail and food service industries. I had been there and seen a version of his plant post-Katrina, but growing demands had pushed him to expand even more, and as we toured the 68,000-square-foot facility, I couldn't help but shake my head at John's success. In addition to this plant, Chef John Folse & Company also encompassed a publishing division, a catering and events management division, a culinary school, a pastry division, and a production company. Clearly, my friend John was doing quite well.

Even so, New Orleans was a long way from Chicago. As much as I admired what he was doing, I wasn't sure about packing up the family and starting over in Louisiana. I was particularly concerned for Gio. His mother and I had worked so hard to ensure he spent lots of time with each of us. Even though I knew my son and I had forged a close bond over the years, I realized that we'd have to adjust yet again if Gale and I were close to a thousand miles apart.

Before I headed back to Chicago, John wanted me to meet one of his favorite people: Sister Dulce Maria of the Mercedarian Sisters of the Blessed Sacrament. Sister Dulce welcomed us with a hug and led us to the garden where we talked about John's work in New Orleans and her ministry among the people of the bayou.

Then she asked me a little about my life and my history. I found myself sharing everything, from my childhood all the way up through my recent career setback.

"I just don't know what God wants me to do now," I said. "I know he has a ministry for me, but where? It's been more than a year; I just wish he would tell me."

Surprisingly, I felt at home with Sister Dulce's world. I had to chuckle. I had come so far from my days at Sacred Heart; how ironic that I would now be sitting with a Catholic nun talking about my search for God's direction.

"So, Sister, what do you think about this whole idea that John has about me coming to work here in New Orleans? Are we crazy?"

I wasn't really expecting an answer, but Sister Dulce grabbed my hand and looked me square in the eye.

"My son, what are you afraid of?"

I was so taken aback, tears immediately sprang to my eyes. As much as I tried, I couldn't stop them.

What was wrong with me? Why was I crying like this?

"Do you believe in Poppa?" Sister Dulce asked.

Poppa? I looked at her quizzically.

"Poppa—Father God."

"Yes!" I said. "I definitely believe in Poppa."

"Do you believe in salvation?"

"Of course."

"Then what are you so worried about? Do you know the story of Mary and Martha? You are being just like Martha. Don't you think he could move you here and set you up? He raised Jesus Christ from the dead! Don't you think God's big enough to help you? Don't you get it? This is all Poppa's problem. Your job is to sit at his feet and believe he will work out all the details."

As I looked into her eyes, it was as if a weight had been lifted off of me. Of course! Why had it taken me so long to see it? The demise of Cenitare had certainly felt like an end, but now I realized that it was God's way of putting me on a new path in a new city.

And I thought again of how frightened the disciples were during the raging storm, while Jesus slept peacefully beside them. After weathering more storms than I cared to remember, I finally saw that I didn't need to be fearful—God was indeed fulfilling his promise to get me to my destination, the same guarantee he makes to anyone who lives by faith in him. He doesn't want us to quit. He wants us to lean on him and draw on the same faith that led us to set out on our journey. And when at last we reach shore, we are to encourage others who are still navigating the choppy waters.

Yes, the storms in my life have been painful, but they've all been designed to get me to reach out for God. He has always been eager to satisfy my inner hunger, but in a sense, he had to get me out of the kitchen first. Nothing I'd tried on my own—a drug-fueled lifestyle, professional acclaim, even a healthy blended family—ultimately satisfied.

At last I realized why that was: what I'd been longing for was God, the one who had been right beside me all along.

JONAH CRAB CAKES WITH SPICY TARTAR SAUCE

One of the highlights of the past few years has been spending lots of time in New Orleans and the Gulf region, participating in special events designed to promote Louisiana's seafood industry. One of my favorite seafood is blue crab. There are many great ways to use this crab—here's one of them. — *SERVES 6*

2 c. Jonah or other high-quality cooked crabmeat, picked over to remove any shells. Keep as whole as possible.
⅓ c. fresh bread crumbs
½ c. aioli (recipe follows)
¼ c. finely diced red onion
2 Tbs. finely diced red bell pepper
2 Tbs. finely diced yellow bell pepper
2 Tbs. chopped fresh tarragon
2 Tbs. chopped flat-leaf parsley
About ¼ c. clarified butter (recipe on next page)
Spicy tartar sauce (recipe below)
½ c. herb oil (make ahead; recipe on next page)

1. Mix together the crabmeat, bread crumbs, aioli, red onion, bell peppers, tarragon, and parsley in a small bowl.
2. Place a 16-inch-long piece of plastic wrap on a work surface, with the long side facing you. Spread out the crab along the edge of the wrap nearest you, leaving a two-inch border at each end. Roll the plastic wrap over the crab mixture to make a log about one inch in diameter. Hold the ends of the plastic wrap and roll it along the work surface to tighten the roll. Prick a few holes in the plastic wrap with a small pin to release any trapped air. Freeze the roll for at least three hours.
3. Without unwrapping it, slice the frozen log into 12 one-inch-wide pieces. Remove the plastic wrap.
4. Heat 2 Tbs. clarified butter in a large nonstick sauté pan over medium heat. (You may need to cook the crab cakes in two batches or use two pans.) Cook the crab cakes for about five minutes without turning until they are golden brown on the bottom. Turn and cook the crab cakes for about four minutes longer or until they are golden brown on both sides. Add more butter as needed to prevent sticking.
5. Drain the crab cakes on paper towels.
6. To serve, arrange the crab cakes on a serving plate or platter, spooning a little of the spicy tartar sauce on top of each.

Spicy Tartar Sauce (makes about 1 cup)
1 c. aioli (recipe follows)
½ shallot, peeled and minced
1 tsp. chopped fresh chives
1 tsp. finely chopped fresh tarragon
1 tsp. paprika
¼ tsp. cayenne pepper
Kosher salt and freshly ground black pepper

1. Mix together aioli, shallot, chives, tarragon, paprika, and cayenne pepper. Season to taste with salt and pepper.
2. Cover and refrigerate the sauce until ready to serve. The tartar sauce will keep for up to 3 days.

Aioli (makes about 1½ cups)
4 cloves garlic, chopped
4½ Tbs. fresh lemon juice
6 large egg yolks
1½ c. olive oil
Kosher salt and freshly ground black pepper

1. Put the garlic, lemon juice, and egg yolks in the bowl of a food processor fitted with a metal blade. Process until smooth.
2. With the motor running, slowly add the oil and process until the mixture is emulsified. Season to taste with salt and pepper.
3. Transfer the aioli to a small glass or ceramic bowl. Use aioli immediately or cover it with plastic wrap and refrigerate for up to 2 days.

Clarified butter (makes about ½ cup)
½ c. unsalted butter

1. Place butter in small saucepan over low heat. Butter should slowly simmer for about 8 minutes so water evaporates and milk solids collect on bottom of pan.
2. Skim any foam that collects on top of butter. Carefully pour clear liquid through fine-mesh sieve into glass measuring cup. White milk solids should remain in pan until they can be discarded.
3. Cool butter completely before covering and refrigerating. Clarified butter can be kept for up to one week.

Herb oil
2½ c. canola oil
¾ bunch fresh flat-leaf parsley, leaves only
3 oz. fresh chives
3 oz. fresh tarragon
3 oz. fresh chervil
½ tsp. lemon zest
2 Tbs. kosher salt

1. Heat 4 Tbs. oil in large sauté pan over high heat.
2. When oil is hot, add parsley, chives, tarragon, chervil, and lemon zest. Sauté about 2 minutes, or until herbs wilt. After seasoning with salt, let cool.
3. Transfer herbs to blender. With the motor running, slowly add the rest of the canola oil and blend for 2 to 3 minutes.
4. Transfer to a glass container and cover. Allow to steep in refrigerator overnight.
5. Strain through a fine-mesh sieve into small container. Cover and refrigerate for up to 2 days.

AUTHOR'S NOTE

On August 25, 2010, John Folse and I officially announced the formation of a new restaurant development company, Home on the Range, LLC. Our first project is Restaurant R'evolution, a two-hundred-seat establishment in the French Quarter's Royal Sonesta Hotel.

The press conference was held at the historic Cabildo building in Jackson Square, where the transfer of the Louisiana Purchase to the United States was made in 1803. After a speech by New Orleans mayor Mitch Landrieu, John talked about our plan to combine his expertise in Creole cooking with my ability to adapt and present classic dishes in new formats, and I told the crowd of my love for the city and people of New Orleans. Following the announcement, eighty guests and members of the press boarded limousine buses and drove to the Royal Sonesta, where we were greeted by Louisiana and Dixieland bands. It was quite the party.

I now commute back and forth between Chicago and New Orleans, but we have already begun putting down roots in our new hometown.

Restaurant R'evolution is scheduled to open in 2011.

ABOUT THE AUTHORS

Rick Tramonto served as executive chef/partner for ten years at the world-renowned four-star restaurant Tru in Chicago. He has received a bevy of awards and honors including the James Beard Foundation Award for Best Chef Midwest, Relais & Châteaux Relais Gourmand, Robert Mondavi Award for Culinary Excellence, *StarChefs* Rising Star Award, and *Food & Wine* magazine's Top 10 Best New Chefs. He started his culinary career in 1977 at Wendy's Old Fashioned Hamburgers in Rochester, New York, and has gone on to work with master chefs around the world. An accomplished cookbook author with seven titles to his credit, Tramonto has also appeared on shows such as *Oprah*, *Today*, and *Iron Chef America*, as a judge on *Top Chef*, and as a contestant on *Top Chef Masters*. He is currently executive chef and partner of Home on the Range, a restaurant development company based in New Orleans, with executive chef John Folse; their projects include Restaurant R'evolution located in New Orleans' French Quarter and Seafood R'evolution located in Jackson, Mississippi. Tramonto is also president and culinary director of Tramonto Cuisine Inc. He is active in his church and supports a number of charities, including Feed the Children and Angel Tree. He also speaks to groups around the country about his journey. Tramonto and his wife, Eileen, have three sons.

A twenty-five-year veteran of the publishing industry, **Lisa Jackson** has worked with many top-selling authors over the years. Formerly the associate publisher of nonfiction at Tyndale House Publishers, she is currently on staff at Alive Literary Agency in Colorado Springs. Passionate about books, words, and helping writers find their voices, Lisa lives in Colorado.

Online Discussion *guide*

TAKE *your* TYNDALE READING EXPERIENCE *to the* NEXT LEVEL

A FREE discussion guide for this book is available at bookclubhub.net, perfect for sparking conversations in your book group or for digging deeper into the text on your own.

www.bookclubhub.net

You'll also find free discussion guides for other Tyndale books, e-newsletters, e-mail devotionals, virtual book tours, and more!